Other Writings by Cliff Seruntine

Llewellyn's 2016 Herbal Almanac (contributor)

Seasons of the Sacred Earth (Llewellyn, 2013)

Llewellyn's 2005, 2009, and 2012 Witches' Calendar (contributor)

An Ogham Wood (Avalonia Esoterica Press, 2011)

The Lore of the Bard (Llewellyn, 2003)

The Faerie Queens (Avalonia, 2013) (contributor)

Faerie Craft: Weaving Connections with the Enchanted Realm
(Llewellyn, 2012) (contributor)

D1600414

THE
WILDWOOD
WAY

About the Author

Cliff Seruntine is a psychotherapist in private practice and an ardent practitioner of deep ecology—actively engaging with the natural world in ways that promote spiritual growth and a greener Earth. Inspired by the lifeways of ancient peoples who lived close to the land and by the insights of anthropology and experimental archeology, Cliff and his wife, Daphne, have immersed themselves in traditional living in order to understand "from the inside" the sacredness of Nature and the power of its enchantment.

Cliff, Daphne, and their two daughters reside on an old Scots farmstead deep in a misty wooded hollow of the Nova Scotia highlands, ancestral Canadian home of the Gaels. There they maintain organic gardens, raise dairy goats, and keep alive old skills such as horse driving, woodscraft, and cheesemaking. They also teach classes on how to live green while living well. In his free time, Cliff may often be found wandering with his horse, Aval, among the deep green places of the wildwood.

CLIFF SERUNTINE

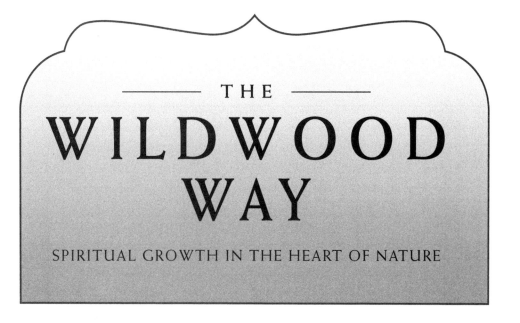

THE
WILDWOOD WAY

SPIRITUAL GROWTH IN THE HEART OF NATURE

Llewellyn Publications
Woodbury, Minnesota

FIRST EDITION
First Printing, 2015

Book design by Bob Gaul
Cover design by Kevin R. Brown
Cover illustration by Meraylah Allwood
Additional cover images: iStockphoto.com/4686039/©Diane Labombarbe,
    iStockphoto.com/44626350/©mashuk,
    iStockphoto.com/25329133/©KsushaArt
Interior photos and maps by Arielle, Cliff, Daphne, and Natalia Seruntine except:
    Mushroom rings on page 112 © Aisling Ryan
    Faerie House on page 264 © Sara Valentim
    An Alembic on page 297 © Demmarest Haney
    Big Bad Wolf on page 305 © Rachel Lauren
    Boletes and Leccinums on page 315, Black Bear Climbing Tree on page 327
        and Lord of the Meadow on page 421 © Tammie Lee
    Bald Eagle on page 385 © Brooke Oland
Interior art: iStockphoto.com/4686039/©Diane Labombarbe,
    iStockphoto.com/44626350/©mashuk, iStockphoto.com/25329133/©KsushaArt
Editing by Ed Day

Llewellyn Publications is a registered trademark of Llewellyn Worldwide Ltd.

Library of Congress Cataloging-in-Publication Data
Seruntine, Cliff, 1968–
    The wildwood way: spiritual growth in the heart of nature/Cliff Seruntine.—First Edition.
        pages cm
    Includes bibliographical references.
    ISBN 978-0-7387-4032-4
    1. Nature—Miscellanea. 2. Nature—Religious aspects. 3. Nature worship. 4. Occultism.
    5. Spiritual life. I. Title.
    BF1623.N35S47 2015
    917.16—dc23
                                2015027002

Llewellyn Publications
A Division of Llewellyn Worldwide Ltd.
2143 Wooddale Drive
Woodbury, MN 55125-2989
www.llewellyn.com
Printed in the United States of America

To Daphne: We've lived more than half our lives together, shared good times and countless adventures in far-flung places, weathered hard winters, and rejoiced hand-in-hand come spring. The green world may be my heart, but you are the other half of my soul. And to my incredible daughters, Arielle the Ever Reliable and Natalia the Little Warrior: you are like the rising sun and the pole star. So very different one from the other, yet bright and true and always certain.

And to my friends and readers, thank you for your support of our work at the Hollow, for your supportive emails and high praise of my books, and for your zeal to make a wiser, kinder path for Earth and all her children. Standing fast, we can create that greener, kinder tomorrow, for ourselves and for generations long away.

Walk we shall the moonlight path,
Stalk clever fireflies in far glades,
Slake our thirst in secret brooks,
Rake the sands of inland lakes,
Canter dells where old woods stand,
Banter tales of the fair and fey.
Come let us wander the Wildwood Way.
—Cliff Seruntine

The best magic words are those which
come to one when one is alone out
among the mountains. These are always
the most powerful in their effects.
The power of solitude is great
and beyond understanding.
—Knud Rasmussen
Intellectual Culture of the
Iglulik Eskimos, 1929

Contents

Whispering Lake

Marsh Maze

Rusalka Bridge

Chanters Slope

Old Rock Wall

Elderberry Ditch

Low Meadow

From ancient stone walls of centuries-gone farmsteads to glades and glens that are the haunts of wild animals and wights, the highlands around our Nova Scotia homestead always seem to offer another marvel down the next hidden woodland path. My daughter Arielle has drawn a simple map reflecting the country a few miles around us.

Long before we came to Nova Scotia's highlands, we dwelt at a remote cabin deep in the Alaskan bush. Situated in a cove at the edge of a vast lake, we had no roads, no power, and wanted for nothing. Nature saw to all our needs. My daughter, Arielle, drew this simple map of our long-ago remote home.

Introduction

And the aged trees whose great drooping crowns loomed
    high above our heads, standing omniscient in the wisdom of
    the ages, seemed to brood and to whisper, and look down upon
    our useless vigil, in a mighty and compassionate comprehension.
And they stood about us in a serried dark array, as though
    to shield us and this spot from further spoliation by the
    civilization that could be at once so benignant and so ruthless.

—Grey Owl
Pilgrims of the Wild

I grew up poor. Poor like few in the modern West grasp anymore. Poor where you felt fortunate to have food in the pantry. Poor where having clothes that weren't worn to threads was a treat. Poor where things other kids took for granted—like a hamburger while out with their friends or a buck to catch the dollar movie—most of the time these just weren't even in my life equation.

But paradoxically I had no real sense of how deep was our poverty. My Acadian grandparents had a tiny farm and grew bushels of fruit and vegetables all year in the fertile soil of the Louisiana bayou country's near eternal summer. We always had figs and pears, mulberries and plums off the tree. We had corn and watermelons, pecans and persimmons, potatoes and yams from the field. My grandmother kept chickens and we always had fresh eggs.

I did my part to help out the family, and as there was nothing in the way of paying work thereabouts for a young boy, I learned to hunt and fish and so contributed to the larder. With my friends Matthieu and Gaston, we romped the backwaters. Matthieu's family preferred frog legs and his father taught us to always carry a large machete so that we could hack back brush and make sure our next step didn't land on a venomous snake. The black moccasins with their bright pink mouths were exceedingly deadly and were one of the few snakes in the world that would go out of its way to strike you, and Matthieu and his father taught me the habit that persists with me to this day of constantly sweeping my eyes over the land in front and around me, close and far, watching for snakes and other perils as I travel on foot across wild country. It is a habit that has saved my life more than once over the years. And they taught me how to swiftly kill a frog and even some snakes that could yield good meat.

Gaston's family had more traditional tastes—at least among Cajuns—and they preferred the enormous squirrels that haunted the oak and hickory forests as well as the catfish and garfish of the bayous. With them I learned to take those squirrels at a hundred yards with a .22 rifle and how to use crawfish to bait the big bayou cats and gars. We took little gear with us when we ventured into the swamps to camp, and by the skills we developed, we ate very well.

My mother and grandmother knew their bits of woods lore, too. They taught me how to identify the wild pecan and persimmon trees, the passionfruit vines and wild onions, and other useful foliage. I learned that when identifying wild edible plants, you didn't have to know all the poisonous look-alikes; you just had to learn the plant you were after so well that anything different stood out as wrong as naturally as water flowing up a hill. And so I came to be able to spot many wild edibles with unconscious ease.

My mother took me to the murky streams, so dark with mud you could not see the bottom even if they were only two inches deep, and taught me how to catch fat crawfish one by one by dangling a string in the water with a piece of rancid meat tied to an end then bringing it up so slowly the crawfish didn't realize it was being extricated. And she taught me how to whip together an improvised net from a pyramid of twigs and make a crawfish trap and catch them even faster.

And when times got really hard, I learned from an old woodsman whose real name I never even knew that robins, thick as bees in the hedges, tasted like duck and a half-dozen added up to enough meat to make a good gumbo for the family.

But my grandfather was a different kind of man. Quiet and surly, he was nevertheless gentle spirited. He didn't speak much, and when he spoke his words dripped Cajun-lilted French, but he had lessons to impart. He taught me how to plant a thousand feet of potato rows in an hour and how to get corn seed in the ground in such a way as to ensure every space held a viable stalk. He taught me how to cut wood properly with an axe and how to shape it with little other than a knife so that I could build anything I ever might need. He taught me how to sharpen any piece of metal like a razor, and then taught me how pointless it is to make tools oversharp. But some of his lessons I thought were impractical. He taught me, for example, that while it is natural for a man to hunt to feed himself and his family—just as he would sometimes kill a chicken or pig for the pot—a good man would take the utmost care to ensure the kill was clean and quick. And if the quarry were only injured and escaped, a good man would take all day if need be to find and finish it to minimize its suffering. In those days we were poor, and I figured that while there was truth to his words, I could not let such scruples get in the way of getting food. I learned to hunt ruthlessly, efficiently, vanishing into the land like a sniper, supporting my rifle on cushioned platforms to remove the slightest hand tremor, compensating for wind and terrain. I could take game that never knew I was there, or that it was being hunted. I could wing a rabbit from as far away as I could see it. Bullets, even .22 bullets, cost a whole dollar for a box of fifty, and that was brutally expensive at our level of poverty, so I did not waste a second shot if the animal was only injured. Despite my grandfather's lessons, I walked over to the animal and finished it off with a rock, and if it squirmed and suffered in the time it took me to get there, so be it. We had to eat.

But then came the summer day I saw the fox.

My closest friend was Gaston. His family was as poor as mine, and he lived in a tiny, battered farmhouse about three miles away. The fastest way to get there was to hike up a seldom-used back road and where it turned right I would continue straight, leaving the road and striking out across woods and scattered meadows, some occasionally used for cattle, most long since gone feral.

While summer days in this part of the world were typically baking hot with stifling humidity, that day was splendid. There was a mild breeze. Marshmallow clouds drifted in lines across a cerulean welkin. I had a small huntsman's knife on my belt and my trusty bolt action .22 slung across my back, as I nearly always did when going through backcountry. One never knew when one might stumble across a rabbit or squirrel, and out of season or not, it would be meat to help the family. I didn't think much about seasons in those days. The world of civilized rules was too far away, and poverty was a rule all its own.

I had passed through a copse of massive pecan trees where the air was cool and still and a quiet stream wove smoothly between the massive black trunks. The ground around it was sandy and semi-bare, for due to the depth of the forest shadows little foliage could grow. I loved such places. They seemed to harbor old secrets, and they certainly held peace. My life wasn't always idyllic or peaceful. I didn't have much of a father and though my mom and dad had long ago separated, when they did see one another they fought like cats and dogs never dreamed. Any escape was welcomed. But I honestly didn't spend a lot of time thinking about it. My world was the farm, its soil, and these wild green places. I thought perhaps I would come back here soon with a tent and sleeping bag and camp a while. I could stay a long time, living on the pecans and hickory nuts, the passion fruit in the meadows and the crawfish and little catfish that would surely be in the stream.

I left the copse and trekked across a broad green meadow surrounded by thick old woods. Grasses and sedges rose knee-high and undulated like waves in the very slight breeze. It was beautiful and butterflies of various hues flitted here and there in the sunlight, and cicadas, the locust that lives seventeen years underground then emerges for a brief, vibrant summer, chirruped among the trees. My eyes swept the ground for rattle-snakes and moccasins, though I wasn't worried. Watching for them was just habit at this point; I scanned the land constantly without even think-ing about it.

I passed through another copse of hickory and oak and then found myself tracing my way through another meadow. It had been cultivated the past couple years but was now left to lie fallow and recover. Wild legumes grew and tall grasses yielding small heads of wild grain. I let a hand drift over the soft tops as I meandered. A half mile ahead was yet another wooded hedge, and there I would find a trail where I'd turn right and hike the last half mile to Gaston's dilapidated home. I was on the north side of a gentle slope that descended toward the vast bayou lands that lay east, and all around the terrain grew wilder and more re-mote: woodlands surrounding meadows, some wild, some occasionally used for cattle. There was no one to be seen in any direction, no house on the horizon. It was alone and lonely, and that was just how I liked it most times. Remote places such as this ... they felt magical, though I hardly understood the idea of magic in those days.

But movement downslope caught my eye and I glanced that direc-tion. Perhaps an eighth of a mile away, at the base of the slope, there was a field of waist-high grass of deepest green. In the breeze the grass was like rippling waves of malachite. The field was sequestered by hedges of tall oaks and hickory on all sides save that facing me, and it was fed by a little stream that ran along its far edge. Countless daisies and black-eyed Susans and dandelions grew among the grasses and thousands upon thousands of huge buttery and blue butterflies fluttered among them. And among it all was a single red fox. The creature darted to and fro, leaping among the blossoms, jumping at the butterflies. At first I thought it was trying to eat them, but as I stood there, stone still, and observed, I realized it wasn't snapping its jaws. It just ran from hither to thither, jumping up at a blue butterfly, next a butter one, then darted off after another, loping in high, haphazard bounds among the innumerable blossoms.

It was playing, I realized. It was a beautiful morning in the heart of a perfect summer day, and the little red fox was simply leaping among flowers and butterflies for the sheer wondrous joy of it. It was playing. Like any child might have done.

The wonder of it struck me. I had never gone out of my way to be cruel to animals, but I grew up on a farm where animals were food first. They gave eggs and milk. Some were slaughtered for meat. A life of deep poverty had rendered me hardened and practical in regard to that fact, and it had been reinforced by what I had learned in school science classes. Scientists claimed they did not know if animals had emotional lives or really dreamed. I had been raised Catholic, and the priest had taught us that animals aren't really aware because they don't have souls. Both the science and the religion I knew in my youth—I was perhaps twelve then—had led me to believe the sentience of animals was mere illusion. They were more like little automatons, alive but not aware in their minds. Not really. Not like humans. Animals were here to make the world work and to feed us.

But now there was this little fox, weaving and leaping in a meadow of green-beyond-green, among countless bright-hued butterflies on a perfect summer's day. It wasn't after food. It wasn't after shelter. What it did, it did for joy's own sake—there could be no doubt. And would an automaton with no soul do such a thing? Would an insentient being desire to play? All that activity would burn calories and, among wild creatures that must strive for every morsel of food, energy was hard won and precious. Wild creatures must hide, for there is always some other creature that would prey upon them if opportunity arose. If this little fox were merely an automaton with no real emotional life, no appreciation of beauty, no dreams, no joy... then why was it risking no cover and burning energy to play in a meadow of flowers and butterflies?

And it was there in that moment I began to question all I thought I knew of the natural world, all that priests and science alike had taught me. It was, so many years ago, a transformational moment for me. I was barely more than a child, but it was like I woke up inside. I had loved the natural world before, but as I realized its creatures were so deep, so profound, so full of life and spirit and joy, it was like Nature took on color and marvel, depth and mystery, and I knew all of a sudden that that little fox down there was my brother or sister in all of life's wonders and perils. And if the fox, then perhaps all the creatures that shared this world were likewise. Even the slow green spirits of trees were my kith and kin, and the realization was so profound it brought laughter to my lips and tears to my eyes. That moment, I think, was the first time I ever touched the deep magic at the heart of the wild in a truly spiritual way. It was a gift of the Great Spirit. And though I did not know it at the time, because of that fox, my life would be changed forever.

At the age of seventeen I fought my way out of that well of poverty and earned my way into college. I had won a number of awards in arts and science, had topped some key measures of intellectual aptitude, and many persons suspected I had a bright career ahead of me in academia. But by the age of nineteen, I felt I needed more than the cold hard knowledge of mere science, or the dogma of religion. To learn, to really learn, I needed to go back into the green world. Deep, this time, far deep into the wild. That was where I had seen the fox and experienced a truth clear and perfect beyond the scope of the rational mind. I left university, sold all I had, bought a few essentials, and set off for the wilds of the Mojave, later the Adirondacks, and later still the Canadian North and Alaska, where I hoped to discover the insights of a wilderness so pure it barely knew the hand of Man.

I would have a long and sometimes harrowing journey ahead…

◆ ◆ ◆

It was almost another decade til that moment I believe I truly gained a shamanic perspective into the ways of Nature, and it was preceded by many years of hands-on learning to live well in the wilds—skills I am convinced are as essential now as they ever were both for the land and our own spiritual well-being. Yet becoming a shaman was not a thing I had intended, but as in the old tales of aboriginal folk, it happened regardless of my whim, when a brush with death unmade and remade me. For many shamans, this occurs in a meditative state called the initiatory spirit journey. For me, it was a very real experience. I remember that day, clear as if it were etched upon glass. It was a day of mortal peril and raw fight, hard lessons and deep insights.

At the time, I was a grad student living in Anchorage. I divided my time between university and my beloved bush life at a remote cabin on a chain of interior lakes, far deep among plains of tundra and rolling hills of taiga forest. It was such a wilderness a man might walk months without encountering a soul. Such a wilderness that herds of caribou roamed free. Such a wilderness that wolf packs sang by night and great grizzlies owned the forest copses. And for many years, it had been home to me, my Canadian wife, Daphne, and our two daughters. We had bought and moved to the cabin in my mid-twenties. And there we sought to live good and simple lives in harmony with the land.

Two good friends, Seamus and Janet, had wanted to come up and visit the cabin and get a taste of the wilderness. They were from Anchorage but as urbane as any dwellers of a modern city. Having no more than rudimentary bushcraft skills, they wanted to come see how we lived, learn about the land, and experience this magic of wild places I had told them about so often. So we brought them up for a spell, and early one morning Daphne and Janet cooked up a fine breakfast of fresh-caught lake trout. I had an eighteen-foot flat-bottom boat that was my primary means of transportation in that roadless wilderness. With a draft of only a couple inches, it could go most anywhere the chain of lakes or its tributaries led. After breakfast, Seamus and I brought a daypack out to the boat and a little prefiltered water (beaver are abundant and water had to be filtered or boiled to guard against giardia). I made sure the fuel tank had a full six gallons, and Seamus, Janet, and I set out. It was very early, though I cannot say in truth that it was the crack of dawn or first light or any of the other expressions ordinarily used to express time. In the summer of the far north, the sun moved around the sky twenty-one hours per day, and concepts such as sunrise, sunset, and even east and west, had little meaning much of the year.

Over the next several hours we motored north. We lived at the southernmost lake but several huge lakes were connected to it, one after the other, and all the lakes were fed by a small river and innumerable streams. The plan was to take them all the way to the river and a few miles up it, a journey in the relatively slow boat—designed more to ferry supplies to the cabin than for speed—of a good five hours because we'd have to carefully work our way through the connecting passages and around numerous shallows. But the day was fine, clear and cloudless, and even warm. It had all the promise of a lovely trip with lots of prospects for observing wildlife.

And so we progressed north. I pointed out ptarmigan and spruce grouse whenever we were near the shores. We spotted huge Alaska moose (the largest subspecies on Earth) and espied groups of caribou like dots on the far off high tundra. I took them through sidelong waterways and little, connected lakelets and showed them immense growths of lilies and vast, colorful patches of fireweed. I stopped and showed them a beautiful glen of huge, old cottonwoods and birches where the trees had been scarred by an enormous bear sharpening its foreclaws...at eight feet height! And not far from there was an abandoned camp where I sometimes put in to sleep when out fishing or hunting.

Eventually, we made it all the way to the mouth of the river and got a couple miles up it, but there had been little rain and the water became shallow all too quickly. While the boat itself had a draft with its light load of only two inches, the motor required a foot to operate. I didn't want to risk damaging the propeller on rocks. Without it, getting home would be an arduous hike of days through difficult, dangerous country, where grizzlies visited the lake often, and often we would have to detour over long stretches of tundra. Walking on tundra is a lot like walking on a trampoline. It's springy and can easily trip up your footing with hidden stones and roots. And it grows in flats, with something like tiny crevasses between—a mere foot deep but frequent and oft hidden—and it was all too easy to get one's foot caught and trip with a painful, if not injurious outcome. Indeed, the very word *tundra* is Eskimo for "ankle breaker." So we paused for an early lunch in the boat, and I lifted the motor and let us drift downriver back to the lake.

Upon reaching that northernmost lake, which was narrow and shallow, as if here the river had simply decided to swell up and out a hundred yards in either direction, we started motoring south again, in no particular hurry. We were surrounded by gorgeous foothills of tundra on all sides, and we watched avidly for more sightings of caribou herds, hoping to catch a glimpse of gray wolves. But whereas on our way north the air had been nearly dead calm, a slight breeze now kicked up out of the south...more or less. It was a shifty wind, neither here nor there, and it troubled the lake. I took that as an unwelcomed sign. South winds caused the worst weather this time of year, bringing warm air into conflict with cold, leading to fierce and sudden storms. Yet the sky remained cloudless: there was no usual sign of foul weather brooding. Still, I throttled the motor to maximum, making turns for ten knots—not fuel efficient but the boat's best speed. If weather was coming, I hoped to beat it back to the cabin. Meanwhile, my friends, oblivious to the ways of Earth and Sky, chattered idly about the sights and reveled in the mild sense of speed over the water.

Then we reached the narrow passage between the northernmost lake and the next. The next lake was very long and much larger, a couple miles broad and a dozen north to south. To get to it, we had to pass through a narrow, sandy, winding channel. Several times I had to get out and push the boat along because the bottom became too shallow to use the motor. We finally reached the channel's end where the depth dropped, and we motored out into the next lake. And without the shelter of the channel, we found the breeze was much stiffer. Here it could be called a wind, blowing fifteen knots, and now a steady south by southwest. But that was manageable, so I hugged the shoreline and we carried on.

What I did not realize was that what I thought was shoreline was actually a long, narrow island that presented a false shore and created a windbreak. Wind by itself is not the real enemy to a boat—it is the waves which build up massive energy if the wind can move them far enough to gain height.

Halfway down the lake, at its widest point, the island suddenly quit, revealing true shoreline about a mile beyond. And suddenly, without the island's shielding effect, the wind's power and the waves hit us full force, as if a switch had been flipped. The strength of the storm was massive and here on suddenly open water I realized the wind was actually blowing maybe forty knots. My little flat-bottomed boat was not cut out for this. Not by a long shot!

Immediately, I thought to turn us around, and a second later the first full-force wave hit us. It picked up the boat like a toy, passed under us and suddenly we dropped five feet back down to the water, hitting it with a slam. Fortunately, we had been heading straight into that wave, otherwise it would have overturned us right then and there. Seamus and

Janet, sitting on the middle bench in front of me, thought it was great fun and hooted as if riding a roller coaster. They did not realize our peril. Seamus could not swim. Janet could, but was small and I wasn't sure how fit she was. They had life preservers but the water was icy. I was fit, and the shore was less than a hundred feet away, but such water only needs a couple minutes to set in hypothermia. Then numb limbs won't move and you sink and drown, and even if you do manage to make it out, hypothermia is still likely to kill you without prompt access to warm insulation—and we would be soaked if we capsized.

I glanced back to the slowly receding island's point, still less than a hundred feet behind us, and decided to risk turning around, but just then we were hit by the next wave. It rolled under us, dropping us hard into the wave's wake as did the last. And instantly came the next wave. They were only seconds apart. I could try to turn the boat in the trough between the waves, but I didn't think it could turn fast enough. If a wave caught us not directly facing it, I was certain it would flip us. There was no choice. I had to drive the boat straight into the weather. I had to make sure we hit each wave exactly straight on and wrestle the motor into position as we plunged down its backside to ensure we were lined up to start climbing the next one. And all the while I had to keep Seamus and Janet calm and utterly motionless, for if they panicked or moved, the shifting weight would certainly overturn us. And, with the far shore miles beyond and a powerful wind beating into us, I knew we were in for an exceedingly dangerous crossing of at least an hour.

I shouted over the wind. "Hang on, folks, and don't move. I need to keep the boat steady. This will be a lot of fun so just enjoy the ride. Just like riding rapids!" I hooted as we went over the next wave, and I hated myself for the deception. But I needed them to think everything was fine. If they panicked, if I couldn't focus everything I had on managing the wild water, we were dead, and I knew it. As we pressed deeper into the vast, tumultuous lake, it became evermore certain that if we were to survive, I had to focus all my being on a single goal: the far shore. And the wind and water were going to try to kill us with every foot of the journey.

As we pulled ever farther from the sheltering island, the waves had more room to build in the wind. A wave of water possesses force exponential to its size. Thus, a two-foot wave has double the power of a one foot wave and a four foot wave's power is doubled again. Here, where the lake was more open, the waves were as much as ten feet high and sometimes one would manage to merge with another, creating incredible power. Those waves would ram into the bow of our little boat so steep and hard that the stern would threaten to slip backward into the green water, which would have pitched us vertically. But each time, at the last second, the faithful little boat would rise to the challenge and top the crest, teeter there a moment, and the outboard motor—suddenly out of water as the front came down and the rear lifted—would scream in protest of the open air. Then the boat would plunge down the other side of the wave like a sled on a steep, snowy hillside. I had to time letting off the motor then throttling forward just right so that we did not lose forward momentum, or it would have been impossible to steer the boat and that would have been quite literally the death of us. As the lake became ever more confused in the maelstrom, I began to fear three waves might coalesce and slam into us, creating a mountain of super-powered water. Sailors call this the Three Sisters Effect—a super wave of titanic power we could not possibly survive.

To make matters worse, boats want to turn broadside to resistance, be it wave or wind, and each time we skidded down the backside of a wave, the engine tried hard to jolt us one direction or another. It took all my strength to hold the motor on course. After only minutes, my arm was growing numb from the exertion.

As we pressed deeper into the enormous lake, the waves developed foamy crests, and as they slammed into the bow the foam tore off and sprayed over Seamus and Janet. Seamus was a bit on the windward side and took the brunt of it. Sitting behind them at the helm, I was almost entirely shielded by their bodies, though the spray-foam hit with such force it sounded like the roar of a waterfall. At first Seamus thought it was all good fun and hooped and hollered, and even Janet screamed joyfully. I realized they thought I was just toying with the water! But it was not long before the inevitable happened. Seamus became soaked and the cool wind was sucking the heat from his bones. A wet person can lose heat seventy times faster than a dry person and by the time we were halfway across, Seamus was becoming pale. He called back to me, "Hey, you got a blanket in the pack?"

I couldn't allow him to move; any little shift in balance at this time would throw the boat off enough for a wave to inundate us. I yelled back, "No, but it's no big deal. Just stay seated and we'll build a fire on the other side." And just then I realized, they were catching all the water. Janet was wet and Seamus was soaked while I was nearly bone dry. There was nothing I could do to help them just then, but it was a good thing for all of us. If the spray had wet me, the cold would have stolen my strength and I couldn't have maintained steerage.

All around the wind screamed, and it was like the cry of banshees; elementals of the air crying a dirge of death. *Come and join us in this watery place!* The aboriginals I had met in my wilderness wanderings had told me many tales of the land's wild spirits. In some villages where they still spoke the old tongue of Yupik, they called them Inuqun. In other villages where English predominated, they just called them Shorties. There were all kinds, some benevolent, some not so much, and most indifferent. I could sense a gathering of otherworldly presences as we pressed across. Under my breath, I said, "Lady Brighid and Lord of the Forest, if ever you were going to listen to me, now is the time. I need strength and luck like I've never had." And we pressed on. There was nothing else we could do.

Forty-five minutes later, Seamus was looking bad. Dark-haired with a tan complexion, he had become pallid and he was shaking. His words were slurring. Hypothermia will draw the strength and coordination right out of you, and fearing he might lose his grip and slip into the water, I called up to Janet to hold on to him. I don't know if she even heard me over the roaring-splashing-crashing-churning waves and the screaming of the engine. But ahead I could at last see through the foam and spray: the far shore. I knew from previous treks this way there was a tiny island there, not a whole acre in size, but it was solid rock and at its highest point were two tiny cabins, each no bigger than a garden shed. It would do.

The last few moments of the journey were the worst. Rocky outcrops and the twists of the far shore played havoc with wind and water and rogue waves occasionally caught us from the side, though fortunately they did not have half so much power as the southerly waves. And then we reached the lee of the little island and, as the waves diminished, I steered us around the south side of it into a little sheltered area. I ran the boat aground on a grassy bank. I jumped off, grabbed a rope that was tied to the bough, slipped the other end around a stout spruce and secured it with a locked Siberian hitch, and went back to retrieve my friends.

A few minutes later I had gotten them to the cabins. No one was there, and in my experience there never had been. But both were secured with heavy padlocks and stoutly barred windows to keep out bears and the improbable looter. I had nothing on me to pick a lock, but no matter. In the circumstances, I'd have kicked a door down if I'd had to. But when I tried one of the cabin's padlocks, it gave and pulled open. I thanked my lucky stars; I had to deal with Seamus promptly. Inside, out of the wild wind and the rain just now starting, there was a bed, a small wood stove, and a few basic supplies: a box of the large round crackers Alaskans call pilot bread and a small, half-used jar of peanut butter. Again, it would do. I told Seamus and Janet to get out of their wet clothes and get in the bed, get covered up and stay there until Seamus stopped shivering. Janet asked me to build a fire.

I said, "No fire. I wouldn't appreciate it if someone built a fire in my cabin." But that wasn't entirely true. Not many bush folk would begrudge persons in our circumstances the use of their cabin and a little firewood. What I was worried about was Seamus. He was trembling hard and his words were slurred. The hypothermia was not too serious yet, but it was heading that way. If you warm up a person who is hypothermic too quickly, the shock can make things worse. It can kill. But I didn't share this because I didn't want to scare her. I softened my tone. "Just strip out of the wet clothes, all of them, and lie down with him til he stops shivering. I'll see if I can find us some food. If we're stuck here a while, I'll get a fire going." She nodded and I stepped out of the cabin to give them some privacy to undress. It was raining hard now, but I had on a good coat and out of the wind I'd been able to don a good hat, so I wasn't worried about getting wet. Nearby, there was a small toolshed. It was open and I found an axe, shovel, and a few other simple tools. We had only a couple sandwiches left in the daypack.

I had a rifle with me and knew if it came to it, I could take the boat the hundred yards to the far shore, staying in the shelter of the islet, and shoot a couple snowshoe hares or porcupines to roast, but we weren't that hungry yet. I decided it'd be better to be hungry and warm for now. If the storm persisted til tomorrow morning, I'd hunt down some food for us. So I would let them have the sandwiches and I'd make do with some of the pilot bread and peanut butter, and some wild blueberries and rose hips I could see growing on the east side of the island. If worse came to worse, I could always kick in the door to the other little cabin where I had seen, through the window, a cooking wood stove, cabinets, and various boxes of dried foodstuffs.

And it was then the tension melted away. We were, at last, safe.

So, in the wind and rain I tramped downhill to the little open area on the eastern side of the island and began picking rose hips. The Alaskan variety are crisp, tart and sweet—much like apples, but with a lot of seeds. I ate a couple handfuls and pocketed another, along with some birch twigs to make us some tea later. Something hot to drink would brighten everyone's spirits.

When I thought I had enough for the tea, I meant to go back to the cabin, but a mere hundred yards away was the mainland, and there grew a thick grove of tall cottonwoods and white spruces right down to the bank. Something about that wood caught my attention, held my gaze, pricked my mind's eye. The wind howled over the hill and the rose hip bushes soughed in the gusts. They seemed to whisper in myriad voices. From the north side of the tiny island I could hear the muted roar of crashing waves like bellowing demons deprived of their prize. And then I thought I saw a shadow move in those woods, something big. I froze and watched and then I was sure—something was there. A moose? A wolf? I took a step forward to try to see more clearly, but could not make it out. Had it been my imagination? I was exhausted in body and spirit, worn down from the cold wind and worry for my friends, though the elation of relief had taken the edge off. But I felt there was something yet to happen here. Something was in that wood . . . waiting . . .

I looked skyward and asked the Lady Brighid and the Horned Man what it was. But only the storm raged in all its glorious and frightful might. And the trees howled with the wind. And the rose hip bushes swayed and whispered incomprehensible secrets. And the day darkened with thickening clouds. My rifle had a powerful scope and I shouldered it to peer into the forest shadows better, and it was in the failing light that I saw the sign: a line of gashes across a stout spruce at the edge of the water on the far bank, the pale hue of the wood contrasting starkly with dark bark.

Bear had been there. A grizzly, and not long ago, from the looks of it. I lowered the rifle and studied the grove. Had the movement over there I sensed been the bear? It seemed that all my life, at the most pivotal moments of spirit and deepest meaning, some wild creature had played a pivotal role.

"Show me," I whispered. The words tumbled into the tempest. But something came and changed me then. Maybe that bear shadow in the forest. I could not say, but what I knew in that moment was that there in the untamed cradle of the wilderness I underwent a rite of passage and entered someplace between the world of spirit and the world of reality. This is the place the shaman walks. And its beating heart is the wilderness, that enchanted place where truths are birthed and keep their own company. There, tossed upon a tiny islet on a furious subarctic lake, surrounded by whistling winds and raging waters and stark, beshadowed forest, my only respite the tiny cabin at my back, I suddenly knew with a clarity that is impossible to put into words the spirit of the wild had changed me, and there was no going back. And I knew, as well, I was okay with it. And holding that in a secret place in my heart, and never speaking of it til now, I went back to the cabin and contrived a meal for my friends as they shook off the cold.

The next day came clear and calm, and not long after full light, I wrote a note for the owner of the cabin explaining we had been washed up on the island, left my contact info, and asked the owner to send me a bill. Then we set out again, plying calm waters all the way back to my cabin well down the next lake lying south. When we arrived back home, Daphne, like a prescient nurturer, somehow knew to prepare for us and had laid a spread: a fine, hot breakfast of powdered eggs, lake trout, and potato pancakes. It tasted like the best food in history, and I ate my fill, chased it with a mug of hot tea, and excused myself from the cabin to go out and walk the rocky shore. Everything seemed different now, as different as that long ago day I met a fox who changed my life, and I had a lot to think about.

At that point I had lived almost my whole life in wild places. I had always loved them for their great beauty and bounty, though I knew they could be dangerous and I had learned from a young age never to take Nature lightly. Nature was not a foe but I had known persons who had died unnecessarily because they failed to respect Nature at the wrong moment. And I realized I had failed to do so yesterday. It had nearly cost me and my friends our lives. But we had overcome the peril and something else had come out of the journey. Something entirely unexpected. In the lashing wind and pounding waves I had found an iron-hard focus. The waves slamming into the bow had become the pounding of drums. The wind's howling became the notes of wild flutes. The hissing foam became the lashing of contrary spirits eager to tear me apart. Crossing the lake, I had undergone the initiatory shaman's journey where the self is unmade and remade. I didn't even know what a shaman was at the time, but I knew I had changed. My relationship to the land had changed. My relationship with its spirits had changed. The fox I saw all those years ago had awakened me to a deeper world. Crossing that lake, I had found a way in. And as I walked that windswept island, Bear had come to me. Bear who would eventually become my spirit guide. And that was how I first came to truly *know* what I call the Wildwood Way.

This book is about coming to that knowing. It will teach you something of the denizens of the natural world, and something of its spirits, its myth and its enchantment. But *The Wildwood Way*, more than anything else, is a red fox on a sunny day, and a storm-tossed feral lake. If I have written this book well, you will see it is the teacher you don't expect, and understand at a soul-deep level its intent is to help you become part of Nature's balance by opening your mind to her subtle truths.

In a 2013 interview regarding my last book, *Seasons of the Sacred Earth*, I was asked why I felt it was important for any pursuant of spiritual truth to understand Nature. I wrote, "What I find is that the more I know of the natural world, the more aware I become of the marvelousness of it all. That so many pieces of such a puzzle could fit together so perfectly, that each could in and of itself outsparkle the shiniest gemstone—it is a true wonder. And as each part of Nature's picture is filled through my studies of natural lore, it is like watching another tree grow. Eventually the trees form a forest—and within that forest is enchantment."

It is my hope that as you venture through the pages of this tome, you will gain a deeper understanding of Nature's spirit and magic through these stories. They, like faerie tales, have powerful truth at their heart, truth that cannot rightly be conveyed as simple facts to be taught to the rational mind. The best way to come to the fullness of these truths is to enter their tale, become part of them. And so in these pages you will read tales of woodland creatures, of bear and deer and towering maples and mysterious brooks. And there are other stories of my family's lives with Nature's creatures and spirits. All the stories are true, based on things I have seen or been part of, though I have changed a few names to protect the privacy of the persons I mention.

Of course, there are a lot of forests in the world, and each one's character is a little different. Neither I nor anyone else can claim to know them all, and I want to tell this grand story well, so I will tell the stories of the woods I know best—those of the Canadian Maritimes. Such woods are none too different in flora or fauna from most of the woodlands of North America, Europe, and any other temperate to sub-boreal region, so most readers will have a sense of the creatures I will write about. Throughout, I will diverge and bring up woodlands of the far north and the far south—other wilds I have been privileged to come to know intimately. Ultimately, my desire is that the reader come to a real and deep sense of wild Nature, from its earthly denizens to its hidden spirits and elusive green magic! They are all well and truly intertwined.

The Wildwood Way is divided into four Seasons and begins when the green world begins its slumber at the onset of winter. In this way the reader can join the turning of the land and experience the glory of its emergence from cold into a new spiral of life. Each Season is divided into three Journeys identified by month, and in that Journey the reader will be taken on a trek through a true story into the wonders of Nature. The goal is to help the reader see it like a naturalist, a beautiful symphony of life, and like a shaman, a wondrous amalgamation of many spirits. And following each

Journey are four essays that teach the magical-spiritual lore of the forest as well as impart the skills required to venture into it with confidence. These essays are:

- *Wild Life*—essays on the creatures of wild places and their relationships;

- *Enchanted Forest*—myths of Nature;

- *Wood Witchery*—magical and spiritual thoughts and practices to get to know the natural world;

- *Woods Lore*—wisdom and skills of bushcraft.

So, let us go on a journey together where the hills roll gently, and the brooks chuckle merrily, and the trees whisper secrets when the wind tumbles down the brae. Let us learn together the skills that allow us to enter the forest well, to know its creatures, to converse with its spirits. Let us drink from little springs and discover what to eat and where to shelter, so that we might know the deep dark wood as a friend. But mostly let us enter the wildwood softly, with dreaming eyes, as you would a faerie tale, for it has more to teach than we can know...

WINTER

The Long Sleep
of the Land

DECEMBER'S JOURNEY

Inuqun Places

The wild spirits are fey and largely indifferent to Man, but that is not to say they are unfriendly. They are elementals of Nature, personifications of the essence of winter ... And if animals or persons are hurt by the forces of the cold, it is not as if the winter elementals meant it, it simply is, for it is a fact that the time of ice must come.

—Cliff Seruntine
Seasons of the Sacred Earth

In the Maritimes the first snow is quiet and soft. It falls into the welcoming embrace of Earth lighter than the tumble of autumn leaves. It seems such a small thing, this first snow. Such a little whisper of the coming winter. It lies over the land like a sugary dusting, accentuating any remaining greenery, bringing out the piercing red of winter berries and late unharvested apples. If one were unwary, the deceptive gentleness of it could set you off your guard. But to a woodsman, the first snow is the most alarming of all: a reminder set in unmistakable white that winter is only a stone's throw away and the time to finish preparing for it is now. Anything left undone must be finished now. At our semi-remote homestead, Twa Corbies Hollow, this means we must complete harvesting the potatoes, leeks, and Jerusalem artichokes still in the ground. I tend to those. And for Daphne, she sets off into the forest to gather feral grapes before it is hard to cover ground. Between us, we work day and night to keep a fire going in the smokehouse so any venison, pork, and cheeses can finish receiving a preserving baste of smoke. Most importantly of all, as much firewood as can be managed must be split and stored beneath the covered deck. For the first snow, soft and silent, will likely pass quickly with the next sunny day, but it is a sure sign that Old Man Winter has awakened, and his icy wights will soon claim dominion over the land.

These apples, late on the tree, stood out dramatically against the first snow, beauty marking a warning: prepare for the long sleep of the land.

It was a sunny day after just such a snow that I was outdoors, wandering east of the homestead in the forest we call the Old Wood, a vast expanse of old maple and spruce. The thin snow was already fading from the ground in the open areas. But among the forest shadows, it lingered, a fresh thin carpet of white and a perfect medium for the tracks of wildlife. I had been tracking deer to get a sense of their numbers and territories and followed a network of trails to the foot of the great forest. There were thirty yards or so of scrub and clustering trees, then suddenly a vast wild realm of towering trunks and woven branches that stretched on for miles. I followed the spoor deeper into the woodland, going down, down, down the long stretch of hill into a little valley. I smelled the change in the land before I saw it … a certain living, fresh, green fragrance, far different from the autumnal, icy scent everywhere else. And then I crossed a slight rise like a fold in the slope and saw below me a place like something out of a faerie tale, with gold shafts of noon sun spearing through high boughs and landing upon an emerald greenery, with summery blossoms and the chirruping of insects and the songs of small birds. I was halted and dazzled by the sight of it. How could it be? What enchantment lay over this wood to hold a little piece of summer against so strong a coming winter?

And then I became aware of the gurgling-chuckling melody of running water. I had hiked this way before, just a bit to the south, and knew no stream cut through here. But my ears weren't deceiving me; water flowed deeper in the little valley. I continued downward, rounding trees and pushing through foliage preternaturally lush so far into December when everywhere else the land had long since lost its colors and passed into sleep.

I pushed on til I found at last the flowing water, and then I understood the source of the magic. A vigorous spring emerged from the hillside not fifty yards to my right. And the water was warm. Cool to the touch but much warmer than the air. It spread through the deep porous soil at the bottom of the tiny valley which was sheltered by its steep sides and towering trees. They served to hold the spring's slight warmth like a blanket, and so created this vernal redoubt in the heart of a wintry land. Some might say, *Well, now you know the explanation, so it's no longer magic.* But natural magic often has explanations. Its marvel is in the wonder of the way it all comes together. Of one thing I was entirely certain: this was a sacred place. A place worth sitting and contemplating a while.

So I took a seat upon a convenient log, reveling in the warmth of the sunbeams and the music of the sparkling brook, soaking in the sight of green grasses and colorful blossoms which simply should not be, and the sweet music of birdsong, eerie to hear so far into winter. It was a sweet last gift of the Green Man himself before descending into his long dreaming.

As I sat there, it came to mind that I seemed to have often stumbled upon enchantment in winter. Was it an especially potent time for magical things? It is the time the Green Man sleeps … who knows what might rise out of his strange sylvan dreams. So my thoughts wandered back to the warm American Deep South where I grew up in the bayou country, where December was little more than a time the grass browned and farmers planted winter crops that would grow quite fine, for it rarely dipped below freezing. I laughed to consider how it used to feel so cold if the temperature dipped to 50 F that my mother would insist I wear a heavy parka. Now, after so long in the north woods, I wouldn't consider 50 F anything more than sweater weather. I recalled one wondrous December morning when I was a child and the wind blew in hard out of the east all night. Miles away there was a half-wild region of lowland where some fields were used to grow rice and corn, depending whether the ground was above or below water level. There must have been some kind of silkworm in one of the crops because that morning when I went outside, I discovered long strands of silk had been carried by the wind and were now slipping out of the sky, falling thick as snow. The silken threads, some many feet long, drifted to the ground like downy feathers, great fine strands of it. My sister and I ran about the meadow catching the strands which were so delicate they felt like nothing in our hands, broke effortlessly, and collapsed on themselves as if melting. I tasted one and found it had a mild, simple sweetness to it, like flower nectar. It was a very strange wonder, indeed.

Yet most of my December memories were from places far different from the gentle winters of the Deep South. For about half my life, I lived in the wilds of the far north—the Yukon Territory and Alaska. There, winter was another thing entirely: severe and bitter, a dangerous thing one must at all times live with wisely. Autumn was brief so far north. It began in late August and ended with September. By mid-October, deep snow had settled upon the land, bringing with it endless nights with as much as twenty hours of darkness, and intense cold such as few people ever know, weeks and weeks of -40 F and worse, so cold a cup of hot tea would develop a coat of ice in minutes. So cold it hurt to breathe. So cold that firewood stored outside would burn slow, as it needed time in the wood stove to warm up. And it was upon one such subarctic December my mind settled, upon one of the uncanniest experiences the wildwood has ever given me in my life.

◆ ◆ ◆

Daphne and I lived at a remote cabin deep in the bush. The cabin was snug, a mere sixteen-by-twenty-foot structure with a large loft. The lower level was just big enough to provide a living area that was a combination living-dining room, and the back section was the food storage and a tiny kitchen. We cooked a lot on the wood stove, too, which was in the living area. Upstairs, the loft was divided into two wee bedrooms and the side walls were sectioned off for storage. It was compact but we were committed to living green lives and knew the difference between wants and needs, so we found the cabin adequate and comfortable. Beside it, I had built a storage shed/workshop nearly the size of the cabin to hold the tools that were essential parts of life in the bush, as well as provide space for additional food storage, brewing, and some of the traditional crafts that were part of daily life, like drying berries and mushrooms.

Our land was situated in a sheltered cove beside a massive inland lake. It was a lovely place of expansive tundra, vast taiga forests, and breathtaking mountains. Long ago, the tundra flats had been the site of heavy glaciation, which left thousands and thousands of broad depressions in the land. Since the melting of the last ice age, those depressions had filled to form a vast network of lakes. Indeed, there were more lakes than land and traveling by foot in these parts often meant navigating narrow isthmuses a mere few dozen meters wide that wove between expanses of clear, icy waters. The lakes provided abundant, enormous trout and burbot, so often we ate fish. The isthmuses were fertile and heavily wooded, and often we foraged among them for berries, greens, and mushrooms. In places, the land widened out to form large wooded tracts that I scoured for dead and diseased trees to harvest for firewood. The problem was it was hard to harvest those trees until the lakes froze and I could drag them with my snowmobile, so we could never collect much firewood until the winter freeze-up. Oh, we could have cut live trees closer to home, but we were committed to sustainability, and it felt like a great crime to cut live, healthy trees. The short growing season of Alaska restricted trees to extremely slow growth. A tree even a man's arm thick might be fifty years old. So I couldn't bring myself to fell healthy trees, especially knowing how long it would take the land to rejuvenate. So we waited for the freeze-up, then I harvested only naturally fallen logs, standing dead trees (snags), and ailing trees—things the land could spare. But waiting til winter to stock up firewood made getting it an ongoing process that happened all through the winter.

Our remote Alaska cabin was small and simple, and entirely self-sufficient.

So mid-December had come, and it was time for another firewood run. The week before I had been ice fishing for burbot at the mouth of the creek that ran into our cove and had espied several tall, ailing birches and a couple nice white spruce snags. None of the trees were especially large, but between them they could fill the cargo sled with another couple weeks worth of wood. So Daphne made me a fine breakfast of powdered eggs and pickled bacon, and after a couple cups of hot tea and a little leisure reading, I hitched up the cargo sled to the back of our Skidoo and set out. The Skidoo was a Tundra model, austere and built not for speed or fun but more practical uses, like towing. It was slow but powerful and reliable, and I drove it over the frozen brook a mile through the woods til I reached the first of the dead standing trees. I came to a stop and shut it off. It was at least -30 F and the sun was low in the south.

The sun never rises in the far north in winter. It winds a circular course around the southern horizon. It never goes very high, so the light always has a "dawnish" quality. Today was an overcast day, and though the cloud cover made of the sky a weak glowing slate, I was happy for the clouds. In the far north, clouds warm the land like a blanket settling over it. By tomorrow, we might enjoy temperatures closer to -10 F, and while to southerners (the rest of the world), that might sound terribly cold, in these parts it was cause to celebrate.

I was in the heart of a vast stretch of boreal forest. The trees here were primarily varieties of birch and spruce with the odd, majestic cottonwood thrown in. This region of the brook was marvellous, for it was sheltered and things grew here that did not normally grow in the interior of Alaska, most remarkable of which were little ice frogs—tiny creatures the size of diminutive tree frogs that had the unique ability to freeze solid during the winter only to thaw and revive in spring. A natural antifreeze in their bodies allowed their cells to survive freezing, but how they revived was a mystery. I had spoken with biologists about the presence of the frogs in this glen and they had said, "Those frogs don't live in that glen. It's too far north." I'd tell them, "Well, I've seen them. I've caught them. I've held them in my hand." They would say, "No, you didn't."

After I turned off the Skidoo, I stood, stretched, then looked around. The deep silence of a boreal winter wood is amazing. It is an absolute silence punctuated by an absolute stillness. On a windless day such as this, there is no sound at all, no movement save the silent, slow passage of clouds far overhead. And on such days, I hated to move. It felt as if any motion, any sound—even the soft crunching of snow underfoot—was a violation of the natural order.

"Oh well," I murmured to no one but myself, "might as well get it done." I stood up, intending to retrieve the chainsaw from the cargo sled where it was stowed safely in its case. It was then I heard a bizarre cry. I had lived in the wilds of this north country many years, knew all its creatures, but I could not place the cry. It was neither wolf nor bear nor the womanly scream of a cougar, but it had the immense bellowing quality of some kind of enormous animal. And then I heard the snapping and gunshot cracks of a large tree collapsing. It was distant, though. How far was uncertain. This land was wound with hills and the tall trees and the landscape had a way of turning sound around and sending it echoing every which way. But I guessed it might have been half a mile, maybe a mile, off. Sound could carry a long way on a still day like this.

I stood there, semi-alarmed, pondering what to do. Had a grizzly awoken in mid-winter for one reason or another? It didn't sound like a griz. Yet if it was, I knew I needed to be especially cautious. Winter grizzlies can be cantankerous and hungry. I always carried a .44 magnum revolver in the bush, and I took some comfort knowing I had it, but I also knew good and well a .44 is a small weapon to face off a determined grizzly. I had been charged by grizzlies in the past, and once had even been hunted by one for over a week. But the odds of such an event occurring again were small, and the odds of whatever creature made that noise even being a grizzly were smaller still. I finally concluded that maybe a tree had toppled under the weight of winter ice and perhaps injured a moose, and that maybe what I heard was some sort of fear or pain vocalization I'd never encountered before. But the more I thought about it, the more it didn't add up. I was doubtful a moose could make such an unearthly noise? A black bear, perhaps? They sometimes den up for winter in the hollows of large trees. But no... black bears did not make such sounds either.

But several minutes passed and there was no more sound of it. Had it been an injured creature and continued to cry out, I'd have gone into the woods to look for it, if nothing else to give it a mercy shot to end the pain. But in the quiet, I'd never find it. There literally was no telling what direction a distant sound came from among these hills. There was nothing to do but resume my task.

I went to the cargo sled and retrieved the chainsaw from its case and walked over to the snag which had once been a proud tree growing right beside the brook. I was contemplating how to fell it and realized I could make the cut so it fell right out across the brook, which would greatly simplify the task of reducing the trunk to six-foot logs and loading them into the sled. I had just grasped the chainsaw's pull cord and was about to fire it up when I heard the strange cry again. This time it was a bellowing roar, high and deep notes blended. And this time there were more sounds of trees breaking, brush snapping. And it was much closer than before. Whatever it was, it was close enough now I could tell it was headed roughly in my direction. I glanced back at the Skidoo, a stone's throw away, and contemplated jumping on it. If it did turn out to be a winter grizzly, I could take off on the Skidoo and the sound of the gunning motor would probably turn it away. But then it bellowed again, and it was like nothing I'd ever heard in the world, a great echoing bellowing cry like horn blasts and thunder, and it was much closer still. How had it moved so fast? One thing I now knew, it was barreling in my direction and there wasn't even time to get on the Skidoo. I did the only thing I could. I drew the revolver and dropped to a knee, unsure what to expect, hoping it wasn't some injured—or worse, rabid—grizzly rampaging toward me. From experience and what the old sourdoughs had taught me, I knew even six rounds from a .44 magnum were unlikely to stop an enraged grizzly. I had once been driving up to Fairbanks and came across a moose that had been hit by a car. Both its front legs had been broken, and I realized the only humane thing to do was end its pain. It took ten well-placed shots at point-blank range. Big northern animals are tough, and a .44 is a mere light backup in the deep subarctic bush, something mainly used to fire off a warning shot in hopes of turning an aggressive animal around.

The brook wound between a low slope and was about forty feet across with thick wooded growth on either side. About seventy-five yards off, I saw young birches and alders being knocked aside as something began to barrel down the slope. But I could not see what it was because of the thick underbrush. Whatever it was, it must have been huge! A grizzly could move shrubbery like that. A moose could, too. Maybe a muskox. *Were there muskox here?* I knew there were herds thirty miles north, but in this land of lakes and isthmuses I had never seen spoor of them. Whatever it was, I was going to have to deal with it. I hoped it was a griz. If I held my ground, an aggressive griz was likely to turn and go elsewhere, unwilling to challenge another predator. On the other hand, herbivores didn't think like that. An injured or terrified moose or muskox would be completely unpredictable, and even harder to stop than a grizzly.

Moments after I dropped to my knee and assumed a shooting position, the brush beside the stream bank exploded outward, just as if some huge charging creature had burst out onto the brook. Bits of twig, branch, and woody detritus burst across the frozen surface and there came again that eerie cry. And so close, I felt its bellow in my bones, and I knew that whatever this thing was, it was utterly alien to any creature of the north I had ever known or thought to know. I held my ground. There was nothing else to do but hold my ground, fight if I had to. I determined to let it pass unless it turned straight at me. If so, I would empty the revolver into it and make to get behind the cargo sled and hope to have time to reload.

But there was nothing there. Which is not to say there wasn't anything there. I could hear it moving across the snow like some enormous lumbering thing, so huge it had knocked small trees aside like matchsticks, but there was just nothing to be seen. The sky might have been slate, but the air was clear and it was far from dark. There was no fog. No precipitation. And though I could sense it a mere seventy-five yards away, there was just nothing to see. As if whatever it was, was invisible to the naked eye.

Then it turned downstream and began to lumber away. I could only tell because I could hear the movement, like some great crashing/stepping/sliding over the snow.

A lot of thoughts went through my head in the next instant. *What in hell was it? Why couldn't I see it? What was it doing?* But one settled like a hot brand at the center of my thoughts: it was going upstream in the direction of my cabin just a mile away, where Daphne and our daughters were. Abandoning the chainsaw and wood, even the cargo sled, I slipped the .44 back into the shoulder holster, pulled the rod that detached the sled from the snowmobile and dropped it, then jumped on the Skidoo and yanked the pull cord. Nothing. I pulled again and again. Still nothing. The machine some-times flooded right after it was turned off, especially when it was towing a load. It was rarely a problem because by the time I had the sled loaded, it was cleared and ready to start again, but I had barely been here five minutes and I knew from experience it could be twenty more til it would start again.

"Goddammit!" I blasted and leapt off the machine, turned in the di-rection the thing had gone and went running down the brook, doing my best to stay on the track the Skidoo's tread had pressed into the snow so I could move faster. When I reached the place where the thing had burst out of the woods, I paused and looked around. There had to be tracks. If I could just see a track, I'd know instantly what it was. But there wasn't a track to be seen, and that was ... well ... it was impossible. The snow was dense and one or two feet deep. A large animal would have made enor-mous tracks—no doubt about it!

I heard it cry out again, eerie, echoing. It didn't belong here. I mean, I was starting to feel it didn't belong on Earth. I took after it again, running at first for all I was worth, but soon realizing I had to pace myself. I kept sinking into the snow and it was hard, hard going. If I utterly exhausted myself, I wouldn't have much fight left in me when I caught up to it.

As I jogged, I became filled with doubts. Doubts like had I imagined the whole thing? Was I losing my mind? How could there be no tracks? I stopped several times, glanced behind me. I sure as hell was making tracks. What could be as big as a grizzly or larger and make no tracks? Even a vole leaves tracks in the snow.

The brook went a couple hundred yards straight, then wound sharply through a thick patch of old cottonwoods, and as I ran around the first turn I heard a crashing sound ahead that told me it must be getting off the brook. I felt some relief, as it might be veering away from my cabin. But I was more determined than ever to at least see the thing and try to understand what was going on. I reached a place where there could be no doubt it had left the brook. There was a new hole in the streamside thicket of willows and alders big enough a truck could have made it. And there were sure no trucks in this roadless wilderness. And nearby was a small cabin. I had never seen anyone at it before, but it seemed there were visitors this time, for three people were standing out in front of it. Two men, middle height, nondescript, and a woman: small, blonde. I gave them no more thought than that as I cut through the woods in front of their cabin, still in pursuit. But the three were looking stunned and confused and the woman waved for me to stop.

I did.

She called, "What was that?"

I shook my head. "I didn't see it. Did you?"

"It ran right past our cabin. We heard it. It knocked some things over." She pointed to a couple weathered sawhorses and an ancient barbecue. "But we couldn't see anything."

I could see the path it had made through the forest, plain as day. "You folks all right?" I asked.

She nodded. The men just sort of wandered about, looking around the grounds in front of the cabin as if trying to make sense of what they had just witnessed.

I drew the revolver from the shoulder holster under my coat. Such a holster was the safest way to carry a sidearm in the bush, keeping the weapon away from brush that could catch the trigger and keeping the gun close to the body so it stayed warm. Really cold weather can sometimes prevent a gun from firing. I started running again, confident I'd catch up to it shortly, for I knew where it was heading. This place was another isthmus between two lakes, and two hundred yards off it dead-ended at a moderate-sized lake. The thing was heading that way and it might stop at the land's edge, or if it continued across the lake, I might finally get to see it because it would be out in the full open. I took off, following the trail of destruction it had wreaked in the woodland like a great big sign screaming: *This way!* I checked frequently for any kind of track, or at least claw marks in the trees it had wrecked. But apart from leaving a path of broken bramble and tree trunks ripped of bark, it left no other sign. It was like it had floated over the ground, but I had heard it lumbering when it first broke out onto the brook. And again I thought: *What in hell is it!*

The tall trees ended at a foot trail. I knew it well. We hiked it during freeze-up and thaw when the only way to get to the road many miles away was to go on foot. Beyond the trail was a patch of blueberry and the thing had clearly gone right through it. Some of the taller shrubs had been broken and tattered. And just beyond was the lake. Running, holding the firearm in front of me and pointed down so as to be as safe as possible, I hurried across the path and shrubs. Here, I would either catch up with it, or if it had run across the lake I would at least get to see it. I had no desire to use the firearm; it was merely a last resort should the creature prove to be aggressive. One shot to try to scare it off, if need be, and five to stop it, if it came down to it. I ran all the way to the bank, right on top of the detritus that marked its trail plain as day, but at the bank of the lake, the trail ended. It just ... stopped. No tracks heading over the ice or to either side. I scanned all around the open lake and along the bank. But there just weren't any more signs to follow.

And there were no more of those eerie, bellowing cries. The forest went suddenly quiet as a subarctic winter again.

Then I heard something rushing at me from behind, almost on top of me, breaking through the low winter shrubs of blueberries. I spun around, lifting the revolver, and saw the woman from the cabin running up to me. I lowered the gun promptly. She came to a stop an arm's length away. "I wanted ..." she panted. "I wanted to make sure you were all right."

I nodded. I had no idea who she was, but I had to admire her spirit. She was risking her life to check on me, a total stranger.

"Where are the men you were with?" I asked, looking behind her. Surely they hadn't let her go running through this country alone with that thing about.

"They went back in the cabin," she said.

Figures. I nodded again. "Thanks for checking. I'm fine." I turned back to face the lake. "It's gone. Just gone."

What more was there to say.

Much later that afternoon, I returned to my cabin with a full load of firewood in the cargo sled. I ate dinner in silence, and Daphne knew that something was off, but she was patient. We'd already been together a long time, and she knew when I needed to think things through. And indeed something was deep on my mind. What had I encountered this most strange December day?

We had a warm fire. We had caribou stew for dinner. The girls were safe and warm. I should have been content. But I had questions such that I was fit to burst. Haunting questions about haunting things.

◆ ◆ ◆

Years before that day, I met Clear Wind, one of many of the aboriginal people I came to know and love in my sojourn in the far north. Clear Wind was a spiritual-naturalist. In some key ways he set the pattern of my own life. He lived by himself in a cabin in southern Alaska he had built of local logs and stone. The cabin was circular like a roundhouse, with a good iron wood stove to one side for cooking and warmth, and a stone hearth at the center for the beauty of it. Clear Wind was a true Haida shaman. I knew this because he would never use the word *shaman* to describe himself. He simply lived his path; he didn't need a certificate to certify it, nor did he hawk his skills, nor did he ever brag of it. He simply was what he was—a man who lived in the wild with Nature and her spirits. He was a shaman to me even before I had any real notion what it meant to be a shaman, before I myself first thought to venture onto that path. Clear Wind was a shaman in the way I was a bushman—it wasn't something he did, it was just who he was. Daphne and I first met him as we settled into our own place in the wild when he came through the woods one morning to greet us and brought us some traditional foods by way of a welcoming gift. And he and I became friends that day.

He told me tales of things you might think were ridiculous unless you lived in the wilds and knew how things went among the land and its peculiar folk. He told of how, not more than a decade before, two rival families had spent a whole day shooting at each other over some offence so small neither could remember what had started the feud, and how the next weekend they were all sharing moonshine at their mutual still. He taught me how to tell old moose tracks from new. He taught me how to be aware of the spirit of a forest, whether it is healthy and whole. I remember one summer day we were walking through the woodlands and he paused and looked at the trees and said, "This forest is sick."

I looked at the trees but could see nothing wrong with them. They were strong, tall trees left from a partial woodcutting some ten years before. "How do you mean?" I asked.

Clear Wind just repeated, "The forest is sick."

It was a long time before I realized what he meant was their brother and sister trees were gone, and now the remaining trees were sick for them in their spirits. It was longer still til I came to understand deeply how trees could be lonely and heartsick. And it was longer yet til I learned how his people truly spoke, for they said as much by what went unsaid. Some things are best communicated by the words left out, and how else can a man say to another that the forest is sick and express the deep soul-grief of trees who miss their kith and kin than to add no more?

And it was Clear Wind who first taught me of the northern beings that walk between the worlds and sometimes venture into ours. Later, I spoke with many Yupik and Inupiat who taught me more. They do not speak of these things lightly to outsiders, for those who don't know their ways will not understand. But they know...

They call them many things because while the northern aboriginals have few languages usage varies village to village. But the term that most sticks in my mind is the first I ever heard of the northern spirit people: *Inuqun* (In*ook*oon, pronounce the OO like in "book"). The Inuqun are various Nature spirits. Some are stout and short and might be likened to the dwarfs of Norse myth. Some are small but grow large and fierce as they approach, like British legends of spriggans. Some are eerie and carry a false head that they might tear off to spook those who see them. Some are diminutive and elfin and play pranks from the forest shadows. Tales of the Inuqun are told by the grandfathers and grandmothers of aboriginal children to keep them from wandering far from home: beware wandering far from the village lest Arnasagpuch, the Old Lady, get you. They are told as living memories by the parent who saw a "shorty" scampering under the floor of the cabin. These are the faerie beings of the north, and they bear much resemblance to the legends out of old Europe, and they come in many forms, some friendly, some indifferent, and some nothing short of feral and dire. Not quite spirit or flesh, they are the beings that dwell in that narrow-vast nexus between the worlds of the living, the dead and the gods. They never walk the path of souls (the Aurora Borealis), nor come quite fully into the here and now. They are the shadows between light and dark.

All my life I had heard tales of magical creatures. In the bayous where I grew up, folk had taught me to be wary of the swamp lights, known in the British Isles as willowisps, who are the little prankish beings Cajuns call *feux follets* (pronounced, foo foe*lae, though this is not quite accurate because there is no English equivalent of the French vowel sound "eu;" the term means the *foolish fires*). My grandmother had taught me to beware of the *palengois* (pal*en*gwah, also not exactly phonetic because there are no nasal "N"s in English), a swamp being that is some amalgamation of bayou mud and detritus and perhaps demonic spirit. Out west, in the Mojave Desert, the Hopi had taught me of the spirits that come in the form of animals. And I had seen things before, strange watery things in the bayous, shadows in the western canyons, things that go bump in the night. But always…always I had wanted to see beyond mere hints. I wanted to experience what it was like when the Otherworld perchance happened upon the here and now. And, given all I had learned from persons like Clear Wind and Grande-Mère Constant (my grandmother), and other folk who still knew the traditional lore of old, I was certain—certain beyond a doubt—that I had come very close to a very powerful being not of this world that cold, gray Alaska day. I perhaps should have been frightened by the experience, but I wasn't. I was thrilled. I had touched upon something of which most people only dream, and some spend their entire lives searching for. I had been close to the Otherworld for a moment. I was delighted. It was one of the deepest magical experiences I've ever had.

◆ ◆ ◆

So, back in the present of my current life in the backwoods of Nova Scotia, I sat in shifting sunbeams swimming over the forest duff as the barest breeze swayed the naked boughs above to and fro. All around me was summer, and quite literally a mere strong man's stone's throw up the hillside was a waiting winter. Many seasons met in this place. This tiny valley of summer—it was magic. It, I knew, was one of those places between where enchantment was a true possibility. A place where the Inuqun might dwell, though the local aboriginal folk—the Mi'kmaq (Mee*mah)—call them the *megumoowesoo*. And so I would come back one day and journey in spirit in this place and make an offering of a bit of bread and cheese and ale to make my peace with them, and spend the night pondering deep truths by the light of a campfire.

But in this moment, I would only sit here and revel in the haunting beauty of this place. The deer trail could wait, for the spring's streamlet babbled and sparkled and seemed to offer secrets in a language just beyond kenning. Maybe if I listened long enough, I might catch a word or two…

I closed my eyes and let myself drift into sleep. Whatever might dwell in this place, great or small, perhaps if it should happen by, we might meet this time on different terms. Here in this beautiful, gentle place, perhaps we could make our acquaintance as brothers and see what wisdom we might share.

No fear or antipathy between us. No chases. Just two denizens of a wildwood, lost in its beauty and wonder. Time would tell ... To meet the Inuqun as friends; it is a good dream.

Wild Life

The Friendliest of Trees

The birch is a friendly tree, for every part of it is good. Like all trees, it purifies air and water by its very existence. It dwells in boreal and temperate forests where its roots form little-understood networks with countless subterranean mycelia and microorganisms. They share nutrients and defend the root system, and the tree shares sugar that it makes from sunlight and water. Above ground, the birch is a fast-growing tree, an early colonizer of burned areas and woodcuts. It grows quickly, helping to heal damaged forests while providing shelter for animals as small as finches and as great as black bears. Generally a short-lived tree, the birch falls and makes fast-decaying logs that go on to feed innumerable insects and fungi and renew the cycle of woodland life.

Daphne stands beside one of the oldest, largest birches in Maritime Canada.
The tree is protected by a good friend who owns the surrounding lands.

For humans, birches have innumerable traditional uses, as well. The flexible bark of an old birch was used by eastern aboriginals to fashion canoes essential to their hunting, and some whole families wandered continuously in their canoes like gypsies. The bark was also used to fashion vessels for drinking and even cooking by dropping in hot stones. More commonly, thin, bone-dry strips are used today by bushcrafters as tinder to start campfires.

The wood of the birch is hard and white. It makes a fine tone wood for musical instruments. Fiddles constructed of birch possess a lovely, bright sound. It is a useful wood for making tipi and tent posts and stakes. When the shelter is taken down, the birch stakes can be left since the untreated wood will quickly compost if left to the elements.

Living and dead birch wood becomes host to numerous fungi, many of which are beneficial. Birch wood is best known for hosting the useful birch conk, birch bracket, and the black fungus called chaga, which tastes much like black tea but without the bitterness. All these fungi are purported to have potent healing qualities when drunk as a tea or tincture. They are also useful in starting campfires as, when dry, they readily catch a spark. Birch conk is known as artist conk because if one etches it, the etching turns dark. A skilled person can render creations on it that resemble scrimshaw. I have also seen fallen birch logs hosting toothed jelly fungus and witch's butter, both of which are useful edible fungi. (If the reader wishes to delve into the world of mushrooming, by all means do so. But explaining how to properly identify most mushrooms for the table is beyond the scope of this book. I recommend Michael Kuo's excellent, introductory though quite thorough work: *100 Edible Mushrooms.*)

Many years ago my younger daughter, Natalia, found this enormous birch conk. It was about eighteen inches across, and dry; it keeps as well as wood. Her first simple attempt at "birch conk scrimshaw" was made merely by etching it with a sharpened stick. No ink is required.

Just like maples, birches can also be tapped, and they make a spritely syrup with a light minty flavor. The sap has only about half the sugar as maple, so you'll have to boil down eighty gallons to obtain a single gallon of birch syrup. Or the sap can be drunk straight. It is a truly delightful beverage and is pure from the tree. No filtering or processing is required beyond setting up a tap and bucket to gather it (covered later in *Gone Mapling*).

If out in the bush one fine autumn day when the leaves are falling from the birch, or anytime from winter through spring before new leaves have reasserted themselves, you may wish to sample the delightful beverage called birch tea. It is easily made by picking a handful of the tender tips of new twigs. You want the small, flexible twigs at the end of the branches. Using a stone, grind the twigs just enough to abrade them, which will help them steep. Make a fire and fill your pot with the twigs. Add water equal to the height of the twigs and bring

the water to a boil. Take it off the fire and let it steep til it's at your preferred temperature and pour. Add sugar or honey if you wish; I prefer
mine straight. It has a lovely, light flavor of wintergreen and is a favorite
warming beverage of the northern woodsman.

Enchanted Forest

The Wood Lady

One of the most beautiful legends of fey beings and northern woods I have encountered, the tale of the Wood Lady comes out of medieval eastern Europe. The Wood Lady is a faerie being tightly bound to the sylvan world, and seems—especially in this tale—associated with birch forests. The legend has elements common to many faerie tales, i.e., the heroine is a charming but poor girl who is befriended by a wildwood wight. The wight is ultimately misunderstood and cruelly criticized by others for its eerie ways. Sensitive to this criticism, the wight departs but not before—in its benevolence—leaving a parting gift for its friend, though the gift is partially wasted due to the ignorance of the heroine. There are so many deep truths in this faerie tale: of irrational fear, of bigotry, of kindness, of hope. It is a wonder it is not more broadly known. I hope the reader enjoys it as much as I do.

◆ ◆ ◆

Once upon a time there was a little girl named Betty. Her mother was a widow and very poor, and owned only a tumble-down house and two goats. Nevertheless, Betty was always cheerful. From spring to autumn she pastured the goats in the birch wood. Every morning when she left home, her mother gave her a little basket in which were a slice of bread and a spindle. "My child," she said, "work hard today and fill the spindle before you return."

And, as Betty had no distaff, she wound the flax around her head, took the basket, and, with a skip and a jump, led her goats to the birch wood. There she sat under a tree and drew fibers of the flax from her head with her left hand, and let down the spindle with her right, so that it just hummed over the ground. And all the while she sang merrily, and the goats nibbled the green grass.

When the sun showed that it was midday she put aside her work, called her goats, and, after giving them each a morsel of bread, bounded into the wood to look for strawberries. When she came back she ate her fruit and bread, and, folding her hands, danced and sang. The goats, enjoying themselves among the green grass, thought, "What a merry shepherdess we have!" After her dance, she spun again. And at evening she drove her goats home, and her mother never had to scold her for bringing the spindle back empty.

One lovely spring day, just as Betty sprang up to dance, suddenly —where she came, there she came!—a beautiful maiden stood before her. She wore a white dress as thin as gossamer, golden hair flowed to her waist, and on her head was a garland of wood flowers. Betty was struck dumb with astonishment.

The maiden smiled at her, and said in a very sweet voice, "Betty, are you fond of dancing?"

When the maiden spoke so prettily, Betty's terror quitted her, and she answered, "Oh! I should like to dance all day!"

"Come, then, let us dance together. I will teach you," said the maiden. And she took Betty by the waist and began to dance with her.

As they circled, such delicious music sounded over their heads that Betty's heart skipped within her. The musicians sat on branches of the birches. They were clad in black, ash-coloured, and variegated coats. They were choice musicians who had come together at the call of the beautiful maiden: nightingales, larks, linnets, goldfinches, thrushes, blackbirds, and a very skillful mockingbird. Betty's cheeks flamed, her eyes glittered, she forgot her task and her goats. She could only gaze at her partner, who whirled her around with the most charming movements, and so lightly that the grass did not bend beneath her delicate weight.

They danced from noon til eve, and Betty's feet were neither weary nor sore. Then the beautiful maiden stopped, the music ceased, and as she came, so she went, and she vanished as if the Earth had swallowed her.

Betty looked about. The sun had set. She clapped her hands to the top of her head, and remembered that her spindle was by no means full. She took the flax and put it with the spindle into her basket, and drove the goats home. That night her mother did not ask to see her work.

Next morning Betty again drove the goats to pasture. All happened as before. Where she came, there she came! And the beautiful maiden seized Betty by the waist, and they danced from noon til eve.

Then Betty saw that the sun was setting and her spindle nearly empty, so she began to cry. But the maiden put her hands to Betty's head, took off the flax, and twined it round the stem of a slender birch, and began to spin. The spindle just swung over the ground. It grew fuller and fuller, and before the sun set behind the wood, all the yarn was spun. Giving the full spindle into Betty's hands, the maiden said, "Reel and grumble not! Reel and grumble not!" And as she came, so she went, and she vanished as if the ground had swallowed her. Betty drove the goats home and gave her mother the full spindle.

Well, the next day all happened as before. Where she came, there she came! And the beautiful maiden seized Betty by the waist, and they danced from noon to eve. Then the maiden handed Betty a covered basket, saying,

"Peep not, but go home! Peep not, but go home!" And as she came, so she went, and she vanished as if the ground had swallowed her.

At first Betty was afraid to peep into the basket, but when she was halfway home, she could not restrain herself. She lifted the cover and peeped, and, oh! how disappointed she was when she saw that the basket was full of birch leaves! She began to cry, and threw out two handfuls of the leaves, and was going to shake them all out of the basket, but she thought to herself, "They'll make good litter for the goats."

When she reached home her mother was waiting for her at the door. "What sort of a spindle did you bring home to me yesterday?" cried she. "After you left this morning I began to reel. I reeled and I reeled, and the spindle remained full. One skein! Two skeins! Three skeins! And the spindle was yet full! 'What evil spirit has spun you?' grumbled I, and at that instant the yarn vanished from the spindle. Tell me the meaning of this."

So Betty confessed how she had danced with the beautiful maiden who had given her the full spindle, and who had said, "Reel and grumble not."

"That was a Wood Fairy!" cried her mother in astonishment. "About noon in the springtime the Wood Ladies dance. Lucky for you that she did not tickle you to death! It's a pity that you did not tell me before, for I might have had a room full of yarn if I had reeled and grumbled not."

Then Betty bethought herself of the basket of leaves. She lifted the cover and peeped in again.

"Look! Look! Mother!" she cried.

Her mother looked and clapped her hands. The birch leaves were turned to gold.

"She told me not to peep until I reached home," said Betty, "but I disobeyed and threw two handfuls of the leaves away.'

"Lucky for you that you did not throw them all away!" exclaimed her mother.

The next morning they both went to the place where Betty had thrown out the leaves, but on the road lay nothing but birch leaves. However, the gold Betty had brought home was enough to make them rich. Her mother bought a fine house and garden. They had many cattle. Betty had handsome clothes, and she did not need to pasture the goats anymore. But though she had everything she desired, nothing gave her so great delight as the dance with the Wood Fairy. She often went to the birch wood hoping to see the beautiful maiden, but she never again set eyes upon her.

—Francis Jenkins Olcott
The Book of Elves & Fairies

Wood Witchery

The Tarbh Feis Rethought

The *tarbh feis* (charv fesh) was an ancient shamanic rite practised by Gaelic sorcerers (call them seers, *tabhaisders*, druids, witches, cunning men, shamans . . . the difference is essentially academic). In this ancient ritual the seer drank the broth and ate the meat of a newly slaughtered bull, then wrapped up in its hide and sought an altered state of consciousness in which to meet its spirit. The accounts of the *tarbh feis* refer to the altered state as sleeping and dreaming, but I think the writers were describing what we might now call a spirit journey. With the meat of the bull within and its hide without, the seer became tuned to the spirit of the beast and was able to meet it as an ancestor spirit. Thereupon, the seer could converse with the spirit, receive a vision from it or follow it into the Otherworld. The spirit of the slain beast became a kind of psychopomp, helping move the seer's spirit into the Otherworld where true knowledge would be revealed.

In the contemporary era there is still a place for the practice, and we see it echoed in many cultures in many ways. As an example, when a shaman collects a natural object of power, such as a bird's feather, it is because it resonates with the beast. Holding it and meditating upon it helps tune the shaman to that animal. But holding a bird's feather forms only a small link. The *tarbh feis* goes much further. The shaman, in eating the meat, drinking the broth, and wearing the skin, virtually immerses the self in the animal's being. Where one goes, so does the other. What one knows, so does the other.

The *tarbh feis* is accessible to the contemporary person, though I would never condone killing a beast solely to conduct the *tarbh feis* as this is greatly disrespectful to the beast and the numinous beings that oversee wildlife. But if one hunts out of need or lives on a farm where livestock are butchered, or knows someone who does, there is the prospect of getting the meat and hide of a recently butchered animal. Using everything the animal has to offer in its passing shows great respect.

The traditional *tarbh feis* required a bull or an ox, but I don't think that is exactly essential. A modern hunter might perform a similar rite with the meat, broth, and hide of deer or elk or even a rabbit. Rabbit, Beaver, and Deer—all game animals—are also great, wise talking creatures in myth. When seeking the guidance of the spirit world, size is of little importance at all. Only tuning the spirit to them is what matters.

To conduct the *tarbh feis*, first study the later sections on spirit journeying and sacred places. (Spirit journeying is covered after September's Journey, and sacred places of many kinds are covered in various essays.) Take some of the meat, broth, and hide of the animal and go to your chosen place. It is traditional that such a place is near flowing water. Perhaps the white noise enhances the meditative state essential to the spirit journey. Perhaps there is power in moving water. Many myths assert this, and for my part I must confess I can feel the power of moving water. It is pure and haunting, promising sweet rest as well as the potential of hidden

A few years back, a hunter took this black bear as a gift for an elderly man, but the man passed away so the hunter gave it to me. After salvaging its meat, I tanned the fur. In the image, it is drying on the rail. It will find many uses, and one will be shamanic practices such as the *tarbh feis*.

mysteries. Water in motion is more a force than a substance and may be a catalyst for the flow of otherworldly energies. So, in an ideal situation, when performing the *tarbh feis* you will go to a natural place beside a brook or little river or perhaps a flowing spring. It will be someplace lonely and sequestered. There drink the broth and eat the meat and then lie down to rest. If the bit of hide you have brought with you is large, wrap up in it. If it is small—like a rabbit's hide—roll it up under your head and use it as a pillow or simply hold it. Lie down and enter the spirit journey or simply let yourself fall asleep and see what dreams may come.

Be warned if you ever speak of what you might find in those dreams. The old Gaelic lore out of which this rite comes to us lays an onus upon those who undertake it to speak only the truth of what they encountered no matter how wonderful or terrible. It was said that to mislead concerning the experience of the *tarbh feis* was to invite death. Perhaps this is because lying about the profound insights of the experience would bring great dishonor to the animal's spirit.

Woods Lore

The Animals Never Knew You Were There

The deeper you immerse yourself in the wildwood, the more you will come to share its perspective. The more you will learn of its enchantment and myriad spirits. The clearer you will perceive the world. It is no wonder that the druids of eld, cunning men, witches, and mystics, have long sought the solitude and revelation of far-cast wild places. And so throughout this book I have sought to guide the reader into those areas of knowledge and skill that will allow you to do so: woodland navigation, wild-food foraging, tracking, herbalism, and more. But if you want to know the mind of the wildwood, you must learn the ways of its denizens. There is no better way to do this than simply observing them. As you do, you will come to understand that they are more than just animals. They are, as the aboriginal folk knew them, "the other tribes," the other children of the Great Spirit who oversees the world, with souls and ways all their own, and a kind of wisdom we modern civilized folk can barely wrap our minds around. Yet if you are to learn from these beings, you must do so on their terms, in their place, and so I will begin our study of woods lore by teaching you how to go about observing wildlife in a gentle way, so their activities are not disturbed by your presence. If you enter the wildwood with care, the creatures who dwell there will hardly know you are there and their secrets will open up to you.

The most important thing is not to betray a human scent. Most animals can detect scent in a way that we humans are utterly unaware of. It cannot even be rightly described. It would be like trying to explain red to a person blind from birth. A typical dog, just as an example, can smell a single teaspoon of sugar dissolved in an Olympic-sized swimming pool. They "see" the world more through their nose than their eyes. Our own noses still have fairly good scent receptors, but the region of the human brain that interprets smell is diminutive. But being aware that scent is a primary sense for most animals, to observe wildlife, it is firstly important to remove your scent. Before heading out to observe wildlife, wash yourself and your clothes with an odor-free soap. There are some expensive, ostensibly scent-killing soaps out there. Use them if you want, but I don't bother. I recommend you just use a good, pure soap with no fragrance added. Afterward, air your clothes outdoors in a natural place. Ideally, hang them from the boughs of a tree so they can pick up the tree's fragrance for a few days.

Even then, as you venture into the backcountry, you must be aware of the wind. Where you plan to observe wildlife, make sure you are downwind. If the wind blows past you before reaching an animal, no matter how much you try to wash off your scent, the animal is likely to detect you. It need detect only a couple molecules of human to know you're there.

If you will watch wildlife near a river or stream, stay downstream of the animal. Moving water tends to drag air along with it. If you are upstream, the air movement will give you away.

Hunters and animal watchers alike often spend considerable amounts of money on camouflage. It's nearly pointless. Animals do not perceive colors or gestalts (distinct objects within a landscape) like we do. Animals are far more oriented to scent and hearing, with a few exceptions such as hawks and eagles, who require keen eyes to hunt from the heights. But even the birds do not see colors and gestalts in the same way as we. The region of the brain that processes what the eye perceives is the occipital lobe, located at the back of the head, and in humans it forms a huge area of the brain. Unlike most animals, we are first and by far vision-oriented, and the occipital lobe allows us to perceive color and gestalts in a way that animals simply cannot. We can detect things even if they are motionless and only very subtly break the pattern of the landscape, though animals—even those with extraordinary eyesight—frequently miss such things. For an animal, vision is often a mere support to more prominent senses. I have sneaked up and petted caribou while wearing a faded khaki coat, and caribou have good eyes. I have sat in trees wearing a blue denim jacket while grouse perched inches from my shoulder cooing and clucking to one another, and they too have good eyes. The color of what you wear matters little, though muted tones are best: greens, blues, browns, and blacks. Learning to blend into the land's wholeness is what matters when watching wildlife.

Of great importance is learning to be still. If you want to observe wildlife unobtrusively, you need to become just another log or stone or tree trunk. This is something of an art that must be practised because our bodies and minds want us to be creatures in motion. You must learn not merely to be still, but to reach deep inside yourself and find the silence of inner being and become that silence. Find it, feel it, be it, and so become the trees in the breeze, the stone on the cool ground. Early work in meditation and later shamanic work taught me this skill, and I honed it in the Alaskan bush. I have been still for so long that songbirds have alighted on my shoulder and once a ruffled grouse walked up to me and began to peck wild seed that had gathered on my boots as I stood in a meadow.

Learn to make use of the land. Animals, with their keen eyes but brains that are less adept at discerning gestalts, are very good at picking out outlines that do not belong but not so good at finding those outlines if they are enveloped by the background. I sometimes choose to vanish from an animal's vision and do so simply by stepping in front of brush. Brush is a complicated and haphazard interweaving of many twigs and leaves, often with things happening in it such as the movement of birds and insects, and usually there are tall grasses and sedges or ferns and bracken growing all about. Merely standing in front of such a tangle, especially if the light is failing, is enough to cause most animals to miss you.

If you need to be more hidden, make use of stones and fallen logs or anything else you can stash yourself behind. It is often enough merely to kneel down in tall grass. Any natural obstacle that can conceal you can work, but it works better if the object is complex, e.g., a log that has brush growing around it and many branches and mushrooms growing out of it. This complicates the visual field and makes it less likely an animal can pick you out.

Go vertical, if you can, by which I mean simply get up in a tree. You needn't go all that high, either. Ten feet is typically plenty. Terrestrial animals, even those much bigger than a human, have low perspectives as they go about on all fours. And large, land-dwelling prey animals are typically watching the ground around them for potential predators. It almost never occurs to them to look up. I have sat in trees with no cover whatsoever and watched deer and black bears casually meander beneath me, entirely oblivious to my presence. If you move, yes, they will see you. The eye is designed to catch movement foremost. But otherwise most animals will never think to look up.

If you want to use a site regularly for wildlife observation, you may wish to make a blind where you can sit comfortably for extended periods. Some companies are selling prefabbed blinds these days. I've seen some high-tech ones that are like large tents that can be set up with little more than a flick of the wrist. They do not impress me. Not only are they inherently fragile and expensive, but animals are keenly aware of what belongs in their environment, and if something new is suddenly added, they will be wary of it for quite some time. Best is a blind made of local materials that naturally fit into the landscape. A blind can be as simple as a frame of slender saplings with leafy branches leaned against it. Or it can be far more complex: a shelter contrived of poles cut from young trees, roofed with canvas with boughs and sedges sewn to it. In chapter ten I discuss a blind I contrived to pursue deer. The blind took advantage of many of the things I have just written about that make gestalts invisible to animals. It was set at the edge of a brushy copse, and any animal that looked that way would have perceived only a complex outline breaking background that would have been darkened by the sharp contrast between bright sky and thick trees. As well, the site had me fifty feet above the area I hunted. Additionally, I scored some of the spruce trunks with my bowie so they bled a little fragrant sap, burying my scent. Taking advantage of all these things, I became virtually invisible to the local wildlife. Even a human, with a biological advantage at picking out gestalts in a complex landscape, would have been hard pressed to spot me.

There are many ways to become invisible in the wild. Learning them is much like learning to play a musical instrument. It is challenging to acquire the skills at first, though one can reach a functional level in fairly short order. But as with an instrument, true mastery will take a great deal of practice over years. You must come to understand the land as well as what you wish to conceal yourself from. Learn the art of vanishing and the mysteries of the woodland denizens will open up to you. And if you follow the path of wisdom, you will love them the more for what you see.

JANUARY'S JOURNEY

A Sliver of Moon

Minnaloushe creeps through the grass alone, important and wise,
And lifts to the changing moon, his changing eyes.

—W. B. Yeats
The Cat and the Moon

Nine days of winter storms had fallen over our mountain and left the Hollow rimed with ice. It made for harsh times. The firewood had to be cut, split and brought in regardless of wild weather. And the livestock of our little homestead had to be shut in the barn. Twa Corbies Hollow is a radically free-range, organic farm and we aim hard to allow the animals access to the outdoors as often as we can, but for their own safety it was not possible during the storms. Even the Belgian horses with their thick fur coats would succumb to cold in the icy rain. And the ice made the meadows a treacherous skating rink where some of the animals would surely have slipped and injured themselves. So, apart from the ducks and geese and chickens—which are seemingly weatherproof—the animals remained shut in the barn throughout the barrage of storms.

But the forest bore the brunt of the weather. It surrounds the cottage and sheltered us from the worst of the winds, but the precipitation was at times snow, at times rain, at times ice. The temperature frequently rose above freezing just long enough for things to melt, then dropped below freezing again. In such conditions ice stuck to every tree and shrub as if glued. Great trees bowed under the strain of thousands of pounds of additional weight. Now and then, while I was out getting firewood in the rare calm moment, I heard the sound of boughs giving way, breaking with sounds like distant gunshots as they crashed to Earth. And here and there ancient trees' roots succumbed to the strain of the ice and, oddly quiet, the trees heeled over. I saw a great one as it toppled. Its branches creaked like the beams of an old timber ship and then the massive, ancient tree slowly fell with a ponderous grace, going ever further over, its roots one by one snapping from the ground, until at last it was on its side. It was sad to see the old one perish, but I made a mental note of its location. Nothing can be wasted at the homestead, and we harvest naturally fallen trees for firewood and timber. It is part of our sustainability strategy: taking only the trees Nature sets aside, leaving the strong and healthy to grow tall in the forest. The old maple would warm the cottage for as much as a month when it came time to cut it up.

But when the season of storms passed, arctic air descended out of the north and temperatures plummeted far below zero. A clear sky cut like cerulean crystal, and a bright gold sun did nothing to bring warmth. In fact, with no cloud cover to trap the land's heat like a blanket, temperatures grew only colder. But after being mostly housebound by the weather over the past two weeks, I could not wait to get outdoors. After so many years living in the subarctic wilderness, I've long since learned how to get by in the cold. So I dressed, donned tough and warm winter boots, and slung my shotgun over my shoulder. Ostensibly, I was going out to look for hares for dinner. Really, I was just happy to be getting into the woods.

I followed my feet down the east path to the Highland Meadow and decided to meander up to the East Glade where I had seen plenty of hares in autumn. As I passed the barn, I could hear the goats bleating. They wanted out, but we knew from experience they would not do well in this intense cold. If we had gone through the trouble of putting them into their meadow, they would shortly have been clambering to get back to their stalls filled with warm bedding of dry hay. But at least the horses were out in the barn corral, nibbling at a hay bale and otherwise impervious to the cold.

I walked on up the path, cut across the Highland Meadow which is often a horse pasture come summer but now was only an ice field, and made my way to a trailhead I had found and reopened last autumn by hacking out some of the underbrush. There was dense snow a foot deep, enough to make hard work of walking, but not enough to justify the extra trouble of snowshoes. But no sooner had I stepped on the trail than I saw a brace of snowshoe hares. Confident their white fur would render them invisible, they were unaware that experienced human eyes can pick out unmoving, camouflaged things quite well. I unslung the shotgun and took one with a single blast. The other bolted and I quickly pumped, lined up the bead and fired off a second shell. That made a brace of hares for dinner. It took another couple minutes to gut them, then I hung them in a tree at the trailhead to pick up on my hike out. The meat of winter hares was very nice and the lovely white pelts would find a use in the many traditional crafts we practice at the homestead. I reloaded the shotgun. Hares were abundant this year, and they made a nice change from our staple chicken and venison. So if a couple more should present themselves, I'd take them, too. My mouth watered at the thought of Daphne's wonderful country cooking. She could do amazing things with wild game. Perhaps I could talk her into making chicken fried hare with Jerusalem artichokes and pickled lamb's quarter weeds on the side later on.

But with hunting suddenly a secondary concern, I shouldered the shotgun and made sure I had easy access to my camera. Due to the cold, I'd have to keep it in an inner pocket where it would be slow to access, so I wasn't sure if I could get a good photo of wild animals, but you never know. But as I left the open lands and entered the wood, I realized the landscape itself was the wonder of the day. Every tree and shrub, every desiccated sedge showing through snow, every miniscule twig—it was all as if set in crystal. Where sedges and low shrubs poked through the snow, it was like stalagmites of quartz stood out of the ground, sparkling diamond-like in the biting cold. The laden trees were bowed, arching over the trail, making a sparkling passage. Overhead, the canopy glittered and refracted the sun and blue sky. And beneath the passage, upon clean, new snow, the light cast through the rime shown pale blue. A mild breeze kept all the branches moving ever so slightly. They clipped and clattered against one another, sounding as they did like glass wind chimes. The effect was beautiful beyond the telling of words.

But even in the depths of winter cold, the denizens of the forest carry on with life. Here and there I espied the tiny tracks of meadow voles and deer mice. When the snow falls over grassy ground, it tends to leave a narrow space over the soil; the grasses, sedges, and numerous shrubs acting like support pillars. This space is kept warm by heat that naturally rises from the ground. The temperature of this microenvironment is always just below freezing, no matter how much colder it is above ground. It is a dark, surreal landscape of semi-frozen ground and snowpack and tunnels where whole primordial dramas of life on a small scale carry on. Voles and mice burrow about, looking for insects and seeds and anything else they can dine on. Moles run their tunnels, seeking earthworms and larvae. And they are hunted by shrews which prowl that subnivean world like little voracious tigers. The activities of that hidden world are evident, however, as the small mammals often emerge to the surface for reasons that are not entirely clear. Do they miss the sun? Are they seeking food? I often see the mouths of their tunnels near dense spruces and observe little sets of tracks beelining for patches of bare ground where they might find seeds, sprouts, and desiccated mushrooms from the previous fall.

This year was a high point in the snowshoe hare population and spoor of their activities was everywhere. Most evident was their nibbling away at the inner bark of young trees and shrubs. Usually the outcome is the tree is merely scarred and responds by growing thicker, tougher bark as a defence come spring. But as the abundant hares get hungrier as winter progresses, they damage and destroy a lot of growth. It is one of the reasons I've taken to hunting them this year: when their numbers are up so high, they go after the cultivated fruit trees near the cottage. If they chew the cambium all the way around the more delicate domestic fruit trees, it will kill them. I'm willing to lose a few veggies from the gardens to hares but it takes five years to even start a fruit tree, and twice that to get it to any meaningful level of productivity. Hares among the groves are simply not allowed, and many that have ventured too close have become dinner.

Still, that is not to say I dislike hares in any way. I love espying them in the brush at the edge of the woods and following their tracks. And they are essential parts of the ecosystem. Food for many creatures from owls to lynxes, hares and their close cousins, rabbits, are an integral part of the food web. They eat foliage and in turn feed other creatures. They are so tied into the food web that the populations of coyotes, foxes, and lynxes are tied directly to the number of rabbits and hares in the environment. Every six or seven years their population cycles. Their numbers go from a low point to a high and then plummet back down. Lynxes, in particular, increase with snowshoe hares and starve back when their numbers decline.

Rimes of ice bowed young willows and alders to form an arch over this trail, and every tree glittered like diamond as its branches chimed like crystal bells in the light breeze.

Spoor of a hare feeding on winter foliage is easy to spot. Here, one has killed a young sapling.

The cause of the rabbit/hare cycle is none too difficult to understand. When their numbers are low, foliage grows and fills the landscape. This provides them a lot of food. Well nourished, both rabbits and hares reproduce rapidly. A rabbit can breed about every thirty days for eight months out of the year, yielding as much as eight young per litter. Hares produce fewer young per year but they probably have higher survival rates since their young can move about, see, and fend for themselves within an hour of birth. As you can imagine, unchecked, their numbers rise exponentially. But they have many predators, and as their numbers grow, so do the numbers of the predators, though the predators' population growth lags about two years behind. Eventually rabbits and hares reach such a population density that they eat the foliage faster than their environment can produce it. They begin to starve out. But for a year or so after they reach this crisis point, their predators' numbers are still on the rise. The rabbits and hares can no longer produce more successful offspring, but the predators still prey on them at the same rate. An exhausted environment and high predation outstrips their ability to survive and their numbers crash. Their predators begin to starve and also decline in number, but since the predators' population cycle lags a year or two behind that of rabbits, they continue to eat the rabbits and hares faster than they can recover, driving the crash to a low. Eventually, though, things balance out. Most of the predators starve out and the rabbits and hares have a moment of low predation. With their numbers low, the land quickly rejuvenates and the rabbits and hares find themselves again in a situation of abundant food and few predators and the whole cycle starts up again.

Rabbits and hares both fascinate me. They are small creatures with no fight in them, yet they are successful and widespread. But they lead hard lives. Everything preys on rabbits and hares—including, admittedly, myself. Their only defence is their attentiveness and speed. Their only survival strategy is to reproduce faster than everything else can eat them.

In Alaska, I often encountered hares while out hiking, and often enough a brace ended up on a spit over a campfire. Here in Nova Scotia, there are snowshoe hares aplenty, but they are fairly elusive, busy mainly at dawn and dusk and even through the night. (Sadly, the ever-continuing encroachment of humans has pushed many diurnal species into nocturnal habits. Not only rabbits and hares, but deer and black bears have shifted their activities to the nighttime hours.) But no matter when they are active, they leave spoor upon the land that tells their tales.

I learned one amazing rabbit tale today after my hike took me far out into the Old Wood. This vast forest is in some places ancient maples and hemlocks, in others high country of young spruce. It is a magical realm of memory where one might find the decayed cabins of long ago settlers, or stumble upon owls dancing with the moon, or perhaps even catch a glimpse of the Green Man while harvesting wild hazelnuts. I've had some powerful shamanic experiences in that forest. There is an old otherworldly power there, benign to all the denizens of Nature.

The homestead extends three-quarters of a mile from the cottage east into the Old Wood, and I hiked all the way to the far end of our land. Much of the way it is a country of rolling hills, wild meadows of raspberry, blueberry; young trees of maple, alder, and chokecherry; and little springs that feed tiny, verdant valleys. Because of the contours of the land, the Old Wood seemed to appear suddenly. Hardwoods predominate and they had long since shed their cloaks of leaves. Wan sunlight sifted down among the naked branches which shifted in the breeze, clattering at times like unquiet bones. But it is rough ground any time of the year, and now with the snow it was slow going. It took about two hours to cover that mere three-quarters of a mile.

On this day I was practising my tracking skills. It is a rare skill these days, but it has allowed me to determine the territories of local wildlife and avoid having my own livestock come in conflict with them. It has also enabled me to be sure of getting venison every autumn when it is time to take the annual deer. But best of all, it has enabled me to track wildlife for the sheer pleasure of understanding them. For the tracker, the land is a page to be read.

As I hiked into that great old forest and the day wore on, I noted tracks of a bobcat, several whitetail deer, numerous squirrels and voles, and many other woodland creatures. Hare tracks were ubiquitous and I generally gave them no more than a passing glance. After several hundred yards, I came to a path that led south. I decided to hike the path and turn back to the cottage in a mile or so because I wanted to split some firewood before full dark.

A couple hundred yards up the path, with tall maples and white spruce looming to either side, I came to a small clearing: perhaps the result of a long-ago firewood cut. Barely fifty feet in diameter, there were willows growing thick around its perimeter, and raspberry canes and wild rose growing toward the center. And a set of very fresh hare tracks, sharp enough to tell me they had been made within the last few hours, emerged from the thick cover of a line of red spruce whose snow-laden boughs hung low to the ground. These tracks were especially large, indicating a mature hare. The tracks were closely spaced, telling me the hare felt secure and was moving idly from willow to willow. It had left marks of its feeding on the willow saplings: bright scars where the outer bark had been bitten away like corn from a cob so the hare could get at the nutritious cambium beneath.

The hare's tracks progressed idly from willow to willow and went ever further from the safe cover at the edge of the dense red spruces. Perhaps it was drawn by the prospect of stretching out in the sun on this cold but clear day. To catch the noontime sunbeams, it would have needed to go to the very center of the tiny clearing. But an open space is a foolish place for a hare to go. Away from cover, it would make an easy target for any nearby coyote, fox, marten, fisher, or any of the many other predators that would happily pounce upon a convenient meal. Who knows what was going through its simple leporidean mind … perhaps it felt confident that after so many storms its predators would be off stalking surer hunting grounds. Perhaps it was certain it would hear the approach of anything in the fresh snow, allowing ample time to escape. Whatever it was thinking, its closely spaced tracks told me the hare was at ease.

And perhaps it had never considered death from above, for right in the center of the little clearing an owl had swept down on the foolhardy hare. The story was etched in the snow: the hare's ambling tracks, a sudden explosion of snow where something had impacted at its right side, leaving two deep bird-claw prints and a pair of wing impressions. Perhaps the hare had shifted to nibble a bit of cane at the last moment. Perhaps it just got lucky. Who knows? Whatever happened, the bird missed the hare by a hair (no pun intended), and a sudden explosion of widely spread tracks tore away from the impact site. It had dashed full bore across the remainder of the clearing to the cover of spruce on the far side. But that wasn't enough distance. I followed its tracks and found it emerged from the spruce thicket back on the trail about twenty-five yards further on, ran up the trail another ten yards, then darted right into the thick cover of willows growing beside a frozen pond. Infused with fear and adrenaline, the startled creature was putting as much distance as possible between itself and the hunting owl. I laughed as I read the tracks like lines in a storybook. Peter Rabbit had been lucky that day. Very lucky. And I imagined that, like Beatrix Potter's character, it had learned in that precarious moment never to take its safety for granted. The wildwood is a beautiful place, but it carries with it a measure of danger, especially if one is by nature food for everything else.

I quit following that most lucky hare's tracks after it skirted the frozen pond. I figured it had endured enough for the day without me following it, too. The owl would have no feast this afternoon and would probably have to endure yet another hungry day. And Peter Rabbit would live to be an older and wiser denizen of the woodland.

It was getting close to dark so I began to hike out of the Old Wood. Rapidly the temperature dropped with the coming night, and soon it was so cold my cheeks burned and I could barely feel my fingers. I withdrew a scarf from the messenger bag I carried over a shoulder and wrapped it around my face, and I let the flaps of my rabbit fur hat fall around my cheeks as well. Able to feel my face again, I poured a cup of tea from my thermos and leaned against a birch to drink. The hot liquid was refreshing in the intensely cold climate. And as I leaned there, I espied a chaga fungus growing from a birch opposite me. This day just kept getting better. Amazing stories in the woodland, and now a find of that rare and wondrous fungus that makes such a lovely, healthful tea. I have not been sick once since I started drinking chaga regularly. Chaga is documented to be rich in antibiotics, antivirals, and anti-carcinogenics, though it is a difficult fungus to find and even more difficult to process into a usable form. It is an art I learned long ago, and it has paid for itself in spades.

I put away the thermos, hacked the chaga from the tree with a hatchet on my belt, and packed it into the messenger bag. It would have to dry for several weeks in order to keep, but a little chaga goes a long way and a large chunk like this would last the four of us half a year. When it was done, I quickly traded my thin work gloves for a heavy pair of extreme subzero gloves. They didn't allow my hands much range of motion but soon, at least, I could feel my fingers again. The light was nearly lost, so I continued on home. I had not taken another dozen paces, though, when I came across another wonder of the winter woodland. At my feet was a large feline track: a lynx.

The lynx, about twice the size of an extremely large house cat with oversized paws that are as good as snowshoes, is an animal that specializes in hunting snowshoe hares. And it too was out seeking a meal after the long hiatus of the storms. Poor Peter Rabbit: he'd already had one harrowingly close call today. But this lynx wasn't a hundred yards from where I'd last sighted his tracks. I hoped luck was still with that unfortunate hare. But the lynx needed to eat, too. It's odd how we humans forget that we too are predators. We almost instinctively side with the prey, yet we are Nature's ultimate apex predator. And unlike humans, at least lynx lived in balance with its environment, and I observed that it was unwise of me to wish the hare luck over the lynx. So I settled for wishing them both lives well lived and pushed on.

I made it to the dirt road that borders the Hollow in another twenty minutes and there turned right, heading west for the cottage. As I topped a hill beyond the ancient hemlocks, Twa Corbies Cottage came into view across the Blueberry Meadow nestled right at the foot of the evergreens of the Elfwood, and a trace of white smoke curled from the chimney. In the twilight, it was a beautiful sight, harbingering a warm hearth and good food, as soon as I split a little wood. A silver moon rode high in the gloaming sky, not nearly enough to add any meaningful light to the journey, but it was comforting nonetheless. Like a lighthouse, I could have navigated by that moon through the dark woodland back to the cottage. And I smiled as I recalled an ancient tale of the Mi'kmaq—Nova Scotia's aboriginal people—a tale of long ago in myth time when the great wildwood covered all the east half of North America. In this tale, Peter Rabbit was not the diminutive hunted denizen we know today but a skilled hunter in his own right, and though traps and snares are often used to make a meal of Peter nowadays, in that time it was Rabbit doing the trapping. And once Rabbit had been so bold as to catch the Man in the Moon.

Ah . . . but that is a myth for another night in the wildwood. Still, I thought as I recovered the brace of hares I'd taken earlier and continued the last few hundred yards to home, nodding to the horses chewing hay contentedly at the foot of the barn, if Rabbit of old can manage a Moon Man, perhaps the hare who escaped an owl today can cope with a lynx in his wood.

Chaga looks like a black scab that grows only on birches. It emerges from the trunk in any number of shapes. Size usually varies from a few ounces to a few pounds, though I've seen chagas of perhaps a hundred pounds deep in the woods high on old trees. In this image, a large chaga is shown together with my hatchet for scale. It probably weighed fifteen pounds and filled my daypack. Hard as wood, it must be cut off with a hatchet or very stout knife. Under the black scab is a bright orange and yellow mass, something like sulphur in appearance. It has a pleasant, wholesome fragrance reminiscent of black tea. The whole fungus is useful in many ways: tea, tincture, medicinal pack, incense, tinder for flint and steel. But never harvest any fungi until you have learned the art and science of identifying and using them.

Wild Life

The Toll of Winter Brooks

In the path of shamanry, I find a sharp and spiritual beauty in winter's ice and cutting cold. But as a naturalist, I am keenly aware of the cost of winter. It is at once sad and yet presents numerous opportunities to find artifacts of the natural world. Often during winter I will wander up and down the brooks of the Hollow. The beauty of winter is far and wide, but it seems to concentrate at waterways. I pass places where the light spray of water passing over stones creates frozen crystal stalactites upon overhanging branches.

But that is the gentler side of winter. I've seen such ice build to the point it bows a great tree over and snaps it in half. A sudden hard freeze can trap sap in a tree and make the trunk fracture, cracking like a gunshot! And sudden cold turns in the weather have a way of snaring creatures, such as this bullfrog I found at the edge of a stream one late-winter's day. It had probably been lodged near the brook, underground and safe against the cold, but was forced out of its refuge by a keenly bitter winter that froze the ground deeper than usual.

A mature bullfrog found at the edge of the brook was forced from its lodge by freezing ground and could not last against the fierce winter conditions.

Some of the things to be found near a brook in winter are quite extraordinary. Year before last, while hiking near the Hollow Brook in the very place I found the bullfrog, I found a rare star-nosed mole. The waters were running hard after a sudden, unexpected January warm period and the brook was a virtual torrent. I found the mole where it had drowned, in a cleft between two stones where the force of the current had wedged it. The star-nosed mole is a creature so strange and peculiar that some people to whom I have described it have accused me of pulling their legs. No larger than a field mouse, it is an adept subterranean hunter, and it also swims brooks and lakesides, feeding on small fish, frogs, crawfish, and most anything else it can manage to catch and subdue. The tentacles around its mouth may make it look like some beast of Chthulhian mythos, but these are in fact highly specialized sensory organs with which it feels its way through its tenebrous domains. Far more sensitive than the most delicate fingers, it searches in the dark underground, or the muddy places in water, feeling with those twenty-two tentacles, and the moment it detects something edible, it snaps it up quick as the blink of an eye. The star-nosed mole is also able to smell underwater by trapping air bubbles in its nose, another feature which—like its strange tentacles—makes it a very unique creature.

Life is competitive for the denizens of the wildwood in winter and every creature must be cautious to survive. In December I noticed that a ruffed grouse hen had taken to living not far from the cottage, just at the edge of the Elfwood. Every morning she would walk to a little copse of spruces and poplars in which is tucked the smokehouse. I'd see her tracks as clear and straight as a manicured path. And there she would pass her days foraging among the assortment of fruiting shrubs and wild apples, cherries, and rowan trees that grow round about it.

But that area of the brook is also home to a couple pine martens and a savvy mink. One day I didn't see Mrs. Grouse's tracks in the snow anymore and knew she had come to an abrupt end. I found the kill site not long after. It is sad, but such is the way of Nature. Life pays for life, and the spiral renews as it brings ends.

Mrs. Grouse would walk alongside the brook to a little copse where she would make her living foraging among the spruces and the desiccated wild fruits and berries.

Winter is hard on all the wild creatures. Like a predator tuned to its environment, it culls away the sick, the old, and the unwary. Yet winter should not be thought of as evil. It is simply a force of Nature. It brings beauty that is sharp as a knife, and at its weary stretch there is always a new spring. The fact of winter is ultimately essential to all life. Animals do not flourish unless their populations are in balance with their environments. Many seeds will not germinate unless they are in a frozen dormancy for months. Winter is merely one of the turns in the continuous process of renewal that is the essence of the living Earth. One need only walk beside a frozen brook in a wild place to see this truth in perpetual motion.

Enchanted Forest

The Star Maiden

I find that in the deepest depths of winter what is most on the mind is green grass, warm sun, and the music of songbirds and flowing brooks. And what better way to turn the mind to such bright thoughts than with the faerie tale of the Star Maiden? This old tale is drawn from the myths of the Ojibway and relates their profound love and respect for the land and all its beings, both earthly and eerie. And living well with all the land's beings causes us to remember Earth is alive and sentient and full of wonder. Winter and summer alike, this is a good truth to bear in the heart.

◆ ◆ ◆

The Ojibways were a great nation whom the fairies loved. Their land was the home of many spirits, and as long as they lived on the shores of the great lakes the woods in that country were full of fairies. Some of them dwelt in the moss at the roots or on the trunks of trees. Others hid beneath the mushrooms and toadstools. Some changed themselves into bright-winged butterflies or tinier insects with shining wings. This they did that they might be near the children they loved and play with them where they could see and be seen.

But there were also evil spirits in the land. These burrowed in the ground, gnawed at the roots of the loveliest flowers and destroyed them. They breathed upon the corn and blighted it. They listened whenever they heard men talking and carried the news to those with whom it would make most mischief. It is because of these wicked fairies that the Indian must be silent in the woods and must not whisper confidences in the camp unless he is sure the spirits are fast asleep under the white blanket of the snow.

The Ojibways looked well after the interests of the good spirits. They shielded the flowers and stepped carefully aside when moss or flower was in their path. They brushed no moss from the trees, and they never snared the sunbeams, for on them thousands of fairies came down from the sky. When the chase was over they sat in the doorways of their wigwams smoking, and as they watched the blue circles drift and fade into the darkness of the evening, they listened to the voices of the fairies and the insects' hum and the thousand tiny noises that night always brings.

One night as they were listening, they saw a bright light shining in the top of the tallest trees. It was a star brighter than all the others, and it seemed very near the earth. When they went close to the tree they found that it was really caught in the topmost branches.

The wise men of the tribe were summoned and for three nights they sat about the council fire, but they came to no conclusion about the beautiful star. At last, one of the young warriors went to them and told them that the truth had come to him in a dream.

While asleep, the west wind had lifted the curtains of his wigwam and the light of the star fell full upon him. Suddenly a beautiful maiden stood at his side. She smiled upon him, and as he gazed speechless she told him that her home was in the star and that in wandering over all the earth she had seen no land so fair as the land of the Ojibways. Its flowers, its sweet-voiced birds, its rivers, its beautiful lakes, the mountains clothed in green, these had charmed her, and she wished to be no more a wanderer. If they would welcome her she would make her home among them, and she asked them to choose a place in which she might dwell.

The council members were greatly pleased; but they could not agree upon what was best to offer the Star Maiden, so they decided to ask her to choose for herself.

She searched first among the flowers of the prairie. There she found the fairies' ring, where the little spirits danced on moonlight nights. "Here," thought she, "I will rest." But as she swung herself backwards and forwards on the stem of a lovely blossom, she heard a terrible noise and fled in great fear. A vast herd of buffaloes came and took possession of the fairies' ring, where they rolled over one another, and bellowed so they could be heard far on the trail. No gentle Star Maiden could choose such a resting-place.

She next sought the mountain rose. It was cool and pleasant, the moss was soft to her dainty feet, and she could talk to the spirits she loved, whose homes were in the stars. But the mountain was steep, and huge rocks hid from her view the nation that she loved.

She was almost in despair, when one day as she looked down from the edge of the wild rose leaf she saw a white flower with a heart of gold shining on the waters of the lake below her. As she looked, a canoe steered by the young warrior who had told her wishes to his people shot past, and his strong, brown hand brushed the edge of the flower.

"That is the home for me," she cried, and half-skipping, half-flying down the side of the mountain, she quickly made her way to the flower and hid herself in its bosom. There she could watch the stars as well as when she looked upward from the cup of the mountain rose; there she could talk to the star spirits, for they bathed in the clear lake; and best of all, there she could watch the people whom she loved, for their canoes were always upon the water.

—Margaret Compton
American Indian Fairy Tales

Wood Witchery

Spirit Ladders—the Art of Incense

Far back in prehistory, early folk noted the smoke of their fires flowed like water, but up ... into the realms of stars and gods. And they noted the fragrances carried by that smoke were more than pleasing, they were deeply moving. Shamans soon came to understand that fragrant smoke could aid them in their work. It was a ladder which their spirits might climb to the Upperworld.

Making fragrant smoke (spirit ladders) is an old art. These days many people buy incense for the purpose, but it is easy to contrive your own from scratch. And it is better to make it yourself if you mean to use such smoke for magical-spiritual purposes. That which your heart envisions and your own hand makes will be uniquely tuned to you.

The first thing you will need is a burnable medium. Charcoal is the typical base. In the old days, charcoal was made by burning hardwood under a nearly suffocating cover of wet green foliage. Starved of oxygen, the heat would reduce the wood to its carbon component. Applying a bit of modern technology, you can make charcoal more easily. You will need a twenty-gallon metal container with a lid. Fill this container with hardwood then put on the lid. Set the lid fully in place, but leave it loose so moisture can escape as the wood is charred.

Now stack firewood around the container and light it. Build it into a good fire and let it burn for two to four hours (how long depends on the quality and quantity of the wood you are charring). Add wood as necessary to maintain the fire but in the last hour you can let it begin to die down. When it's cool, open the inner container and you will find that the wood you placed in there has become charcoal.

Now all you need are dried herbs to create the fragrance. Below I've listed several of my favorite smoke herbs. While I have listed things that grow in many places, nothing grows everywhere so you may have to find your own local favorites, but that's part of the reward of creating spirit ladders for yourself.

The dried berries and leaves of staghorn sumac are easily found in eastern North America and provide good smoke. The berries, when ripe and red, also make a wonderful tart cold summer beverage much like lemonade but with a fruitier flavor (to learn more about sumacade, visit my website at: http://cliffseruntine.wordpress.com/homestead-skills/staghorn-sumac-spice-pink-lemonade). Be aware there are many kinds of sumac, though, and some are toxic. Staghorn sumac, with its unique red berry–covered horns and exceedingly fragile wood and large rowan-like leaves, is easily distinguished.

Pearly everlasting and sweet everlasting are also both common throughout much of the wildwoods and meadows of the east. Dried, they both make good smoke, and sweet everlasting has a sweetish aroma. Knee-high herbs with a distinct silvery hue, both are easily identified with the aid of a field guide.

Mint is another herb that lends itself well to burning as incense. Mint is found everywhere and is uncommon but not rare. I find it most frequently along the banks of streams and ponds. It will usually grow in patches. Never harvest more than 50 percent of a patch so that there is always plenty to grow back next year.

Staghorn sumac is part of our annual harvest. The distinctive staghorns
are tart berry clusters that make a wonderful beverage but can also be
burned on charcoal for incense. In the photo, they are shown with
leaves and berry clusters above the bowl of tomatoes. Above the sumac
in the basket is pearly everlasting, set out for drying. Pearly everlasting
grows knee-high and is easily distinguished by its silvery hue and little
white blossoms that resemble pearls.

Wild rose is a close relative of the domestic rose. Not as large or lavish as a domestic rose, as you can see in this image, it is nevertheless utterly beautiful.

Wild rose and its cousin, apple blossom, lend themselves well to incense. Wild rose in particular can be found in almost any half-wild meadow or hedge in North America. It is not as fragrant as its domestic cousin, but it conveys the subtle, durable strength of the wild in a more primal way.

Unless you live in a perpetually damp climate, drying your herbs is quite simple. The best way is to spread them out on a flat screen stretched out over a frame where they can catch the breeze but are not in direct sun, and leave them to dry for a few days. It rarely takes more than a couple days when the weather is cooperative. Naturally warm, dry, slightly breezy days are best. You don't want to leave them in direct sun because sunlight is very powerful and works quickly at breaking down the volatile essences of herbs. If the weather is less cooperative, you can tie herbs into loose bundles and hang them in airy places around your home. We use both methods depending on the time of year.

My favorite incense, though, requires no charcoal and no blending with other herbs. All by itself it is perfect. It has a fragrance that smells pure and sharp and seems to scour unpleasant smells from the air. This is the chaga fungus that grows only on birches, mentioned earlier. It should not be confused with far more common bracket and conk, which also frequently grow on birches and have other uses.

If you harvest a chaga, let it become semi-dry by leaving it in an airy place of your home for a week or two. This allows it to become corky and brittle. (Fully dry, it will be hard as wood, so work it while it still has some moisture to it.) Then break the chaga up by laying it out on something very durable, like an anvil, and smashing it with a heavy steel mallet. I use an eighteen-inch-long piece of scrap railroad I found at a dump for an anvil. Finger-size is about ideal for this purpose. Then lay out all the pieces for another few weeks to finish drying.

To use, you need only light it. Just touch a match to a corner for a brief moment. Chaga will catch and hold the slightest spark instantly. It wants to smoulder. Once it is smouldering, just put it in your brazier. It will smoke a long time and needs no help from charcoal to stay lit. Be forewarned: it smoulders extremely hot. Set it in a metal brazier that does not rest directly on anything flammable, and be aware the brazier will almost certainly discolor due to the heat.

Chaga is very potent: a little goes a long way. One good-sized chunk weighing a few pounds can make enough pieces to last a whole year. One tiny piece as big as a finger is enough to freshen a modest house.

Many other plants can serve as incense too, such as mugwort, sweet-grass, cedar shavings, alder shavings, and sage. Some smell of pungent, masculine musks, others are delicate, some are spicy, others offer almost ethereal fragrances. To learn to make use of local natural ingredients, I suggest exploring your local plants with the aid of a field guide. Be sure to check if what you are considering using is safe because a few plants give off toxic fumes if burned, e.g., giant cow parsnip.

To prevent herbs catching fire or smouldering too fast, it is best to braid them before throwing them on the charcoal. Or if they are crumbly and break easily, grind them with a mortar and pestle and mix them with a bit of fragrant resin from pine or spruce and perhaps add some mashed raisins and honey, shape into beads and let dry.

To create fragrance, put about a quarter cup of your charcoal in some kind of metal vessel that will serve as a brazier. The brazier will become blackened on the inside by the burning, and the heat might discolor the metal on the outside, so be sure it is a vessel you wish to commit to this purpose. Light the charcoal and let it smoulder. Add a little of the incense and let it smoke on the hot charcoal.

The whole art of incense making probably began with the most primitive shamans throwing herbs right on the dying coals of a fire as they prepared to undertake the spirit journey. They began their journeys by visualizing climbing the ladder formed of incense smoke. The smoke formed the material world connection with the Upperworld realm, and the fragrance of the incense amplified the realness of the experience by increasing sensory awareness of it.

Woods Lore

Finding Your Way with a Compass

Whatever time of the year you head out into the backcountry, it is essential to know how to find your way. Getting lost in truly wild places is frightening, but the greatest danger is from simple exhaustion and exposure. And lost persons often panic and end up burning up their body's precious energy scrambling about without any idea where they are going. One fellow I knew of got lost in the forest and starved for over a day before he was finally rescued by three persons in a search party. The first thing he told his rescuers was the worst thing about the whole ordeal was being so hungry and not knowing when he'd get to eat again. He was so panicked he'd forgotten his backpack was full of food. Getting lost is disconcerting enough to make a man do that.

Yet there is really no reason to ever get lost. There is always a means to find your way if you no how to use what Nature provides. A skilled woodsman can navigate by sun, moon, and star, or by observing natural landmarks such as hilltops, or by the old far north trick of following waterways. These days GPS devices have become popular tools, but I do not trust them. They are complex machines, which means they can fail. No matter how tough you think a GPS is, if you drop it, or there is solar activity, or there is too much cloud cover, or if water somehow gets in the device, it can fail. Or following Murphy's Law, the batteries could simply die at the worst moment.

To this day my favorite means of finding my way in the backcountry, apart from simply being aware of the stationary landmarks such as hilltops as well as the sun and moon relative to my destination, is the old reliable compass. A modern compass is durable. The only moving part is the needle and it is reinforced. The display of a good compass is armored.

There are several ways to use a compass. The best is complex and requires knowing true north versus magnetic north, a knowledge of topographic maps or marine charts, some basic math and triangulation, and a good dozen hours of study to develop a journeyman level of competence. Combine these skills with the knowledge of how to use a sextant and clock and you can find your way anywhere in the world. But for our purposes, we are going to teach you how to use a compass to shoot simple bearings and find your way in the woods without charts and maps. You don't even need to know true north; magnetic north will do fine.

Look at my compass in the following photograph. You will see a magnetic needle that swings 360 degrees. It is painted red and white. The red side is the north half of the needle. The compass needle is surmounted on a rotatable dish with a bearing arrow at the bottom. There is also a hinged lid with a mirror. Each of these components has an application.

Let's say you are entering the deep, dark forest. There are no trails and you want to hike west five miles to get to a friend's cabin on a hill. At the moment, you can see that hilltop but you know once you are in the woods you will no longer be able to see anything but trees and it will be hard to know what direction you are going. What you would do to get there is *shoot a bearing*. Open the lid of your compass and hold out your arm. Look through the sight on the lid and align the compass with your friend's cabin. Holding the compass steady in that direction, rotate the dial which will turn the bearing arrow at the bottom of the dish. Line the bearing arrow up underneath the north half of the compass needle. Your bearing is now shot and set. Now, to get there, just ensure the needle stays over the bearing arrow as you hike.

A handy trick is to look for references on the terrain that you can navigate by so you don't have to constantly watch your compass. If hiking through a forest, I will look a couple hundred yards ahead for an unusual tree, or bright fungus, or fallen log, or any other stationary object that stands out, and I will use that as my course reference. When I reach it, I choose another terrain reference and move to it. After I've traveled about a half a mile (roughly ten minutes' brisk walking), I will check my course against the compass bearing.

This method will move you in the direction you want to go, but you will probably "drift" a bit as you travel, especially in thick country such as a forest where there are few visual references. Drifting happens due to the natural process of moving a little this way and that as one skirts around boulders, thickets, and so on. The farther you travel, the more you'll drift. As a rule of thumb, a hundred yards drift per mile is a good guess for an experienced woodsman. Three or four times that for an inexperienced person. The risk is that due to drift you may overshoot your destination, so it is also a good idea to use a stopwatch as you travel. A person walks briskly at roughly three miles per hour on open, level ground; maybe two miles per hour in the woods; slower in very thick terrain, especially if there is an incline. If you mean to travel five miles by compass without breaks through woods on level ground, figure it will take you 2.5 hours to reach your destination. Use your watch or stopwatch to keep track of travel time. When enough time has gone by, start watching more carefully for any landmarks to indicate you have gone as far as you should.

If you don't see anything helpful, you can walk a simple search pattern by turning 90 degrees left, walking 120 paces for every mile you traveled, then turn 90 degrees right and walk that many paces, then turn 90 degrees right again and walk double those paces, then turn 90 degrees right and walk the normal number of paces again, then right again and go the normal number of paces back to where you began. This will have you walk a large rectangular search pattern covering the ground left and right ahead of you. So if, as in our example, you hiked five miles and thought you missed your destination, you would go left 600 paces, then 90 degrees right 600 paces, then 90 degrees right again and 1,200 paces, then 90 degrees right and 600 more paces, then 90 degrees right again and another 600 paces to return to your starting search point. This rectangular search pattern is easy to navigate with your compass. If that doesn't work, do the same search pattern behind you. Go left 120 paces per mile, but then—instead of turning right—making all lefts. If this still doesn't work, do the whole search pattern again but double or even triple all the distances.

If you still cannot find your destination and feel totally lost, never fear. You may not reach your goal but you can use your compass to safely get back to where you began. Just turn your body til the white (or south) side of the compass needle lies over the red bearing arrow—that gives you a heading opposite the one you just took. Now just follow the opposite bearing back to where you began your trip. As you are already a bit off course, check the compass often as you go to minimize any further drift.

That's the basic method of using a compass in a nutshell. An advanced but none-too-difficult trick is to use the sun to help you on your way. This is simple. It just requires being aware of where the sun lies in relation to your body. If I mean to travel two miles into the forest one morning, I will set my compass. But I will also note where the sun lies in relation to my body—say, off my left shoulder if I'm heading south. As I travel into the woods, I know that as long as the morning sun is still off my left shoulder, I'm going roughly the correct direction. Of course, you can't do that all day or it would literally turn you around as the sun moves across the sky. But for relatively short jaunts of a few miles, it's a useful trick that allows you to pay more attention to wear you are going and spend less time glancing at your compass.

Like all the skills of bushcraft, there is much more to learn and mastery takes practice. If you do decide to get into navigating the backcountry by compass, don't skimp on the compass. A good one is a bit pricey but worth every penny. I made do with a very modest one for decades and it was adequate. But the one in the photo was a strangely timed gift. I had seen it one day and thought how much I would like to have it and a week later someone bought it for me. I never dropped a hint, I swear! There are many good models to choose from, but get one with a transparent bottom that is marked for plotting courses on maps, has a mirror with a sight line inside the cover as well as a gunsight on the cover to help you line up bearings, has a solid lid to armor the compass face, has a jeweled needle post to ensure a well-set, reliable needle, is filled with a fluid that will not freeze, has a good housing that will not leak the fluid, has a dial with no play and good friction so that it reliably holds its bearing, and has every degree clearly marked on the dial. Expect to spend between $60 and $120 for a decent compass.

This is an example of an excellent modern compass. It sits on a transparent base so you can use it to plot bearings on charts. Its top is armored with a cover to protect the compass face. The inside of the cover is fitted with a bright mirror with a sight line, and the top of the cover has a gun-style sight to "shoot bearings." The dish (in which the compass needle sits) rotates so the red bearing arrow can mark your course (explained a little later). You may notice this particular compass has an additional small black needle. It is used to measure slope incline, but is irrelevant to our purposes here.

Through those trees a mile away is a little thicket of wild gooseberry bushes that I want to get to. The forest is tall, dark, and dense, and it will be hard to find my way once I'm in it. So I take a bearing before I get going by holding up my compass in the direction I want to go. Notice the red bearing arrow on the dish bottom below the red and white compass needle. To mark my bearing, I rotate the dial until the red bearing arrow lines up beneath the red side of the compass needle. In the second photo, you can see they are now aligned. Now, as I travel through the woods, I need only ensure they stay aligned in order to hold my course. If I could see the gooseberry bushes from here, I would extend my arm and align the sight at the top of the lid with the bushes, then set the bearing for even greater accuracy. But in navigating woodlands, often its not possible to see the destination and you "best guess" it.

FEBRUARY'S JOURNEY

The Forest of Indifference

> We see environmental knowledge, values, and attitudes,
> together with emotional involvement as making up a
> complex we call "pro-environmental consciousness."
> —Anja Kollmuss & Julian Agyeman
> *Mind the Gap*

This was proving to be an especially severe winter and February came sharp and cold as the preceding months, and we kept the fire hot in the cottage's hearth and dry hay strewn about the floor of the barn. But one day the weather took an unexpected warming turn. In a matter of hours it went from deep subzero to just over freezing, and with the swing moist southern winds blew in off the ocean, meeting cold Canadian air over Nova Scotia—an island but for a small sandy isthmus that connected it to the mainland—and for days the rival cold and warm fronts squeezed humidity out of the air as if the gods wrung a great soggy rag. The atmosphere became saturated with a heavy mist, too thick to be called fog, too light to be called rain. It was a wicked wetness, cold and cloying, that ghosted about, weaving and working its way into all the homestead's outbuildings, so much so that we had to carry many tools inside so they wouldn't rust. The cottage felt damp despite the hearth fire. The barn was technically dry but the animals' bedding became limp with dampness and there was nothing we could do about it. We had to seal their oats in bins to keep it from going mouldy. The chickens hid in their coops, reluctant to scratch for seed and grubs in the dismal muck. As usual, only the waterfowl did not mind. The ducks and geese seemed virtually impervious to wet or cold and they plashed in puddles and even ventured into the little pondlets created by runoff that pooled over the frozen ground. And that was when a confused chicken learned it was not a duck.

You see, we had a hen named Spacer, so-named due to the unusual circumstances of her hatching. The previous autumn several of our ducks had been killed by an otter as they swam in the Firefly Brook. We live in the woods, and now and then such things happen. It is part of Nature's circle and what happens when you allow animals to truly live free-range. But with our little flock suddenly down to just three ducks, we had decided to hatch a few of their eggs, so over a few weeks we gathered all the eggs the ducks laid and when we had about eight and it looked like they were done laying for the season, we put them in the incubator. There was a little too much space between the eggs and they wanted to roll around as the incubator gently rocked from side to side so we put in a single chicken egg to fill the space. Thus, Spacer the Chicken was hatched and dubbed, and she grew up with those ducklings, who adopted her.

When they matured into their feathers, we put them outdoors to live as birds ought, but Spacer never ran off to join the laying hen flock. She went everywhere with the ducks, walking one by one in a line with them, and the ducks accepted her completely. A laying hen is smaller than a duck, less able to fend for itself. But if one of the roosters dared approach her or the geese tried to run her off from waterbird turf, the ducks would surround her and drive off her foes. Those ducks loved Spacer.

But that winter day the ducks got it in mind to do what ducks do and go out in the frigid mist and swim in the icy pondlet gathering in a trough of ground in front of the barn. Meanwhile, sane chickens hung out high and dry in their snug coop. But not Spacer. Spacer insisted she was a duck.

When ducks go trundling about, they always form a little line. As always, Spacer was somewhere in the middle of that line, and they all waddled out the barn door one by one. I happened to be in the barn at that time, doing what I could to try to help the goats keep dry in their stalls, and I saw it all. They marched like soldiers in a row out to the pondlet, a huge puddle some twenty feet long and wide and maybe nine inches deep at the center of the barn corral and each in its turn glided out over the water. One duck. Two ducks. Three ducks. Four ducks. Then it was Spacer's turn, and she took a step into the icy water.

Pu-cawk! I heard her squawk: certainly Chicken for, "Dear gods, that's cold and icky! What's wrong with you birds!"

And Spacer turned that moment and bolted into the hen house and found a perch in a wood-chip-lined laying box high and dry off the ground. And so far as I could tell that was the day Spacer stopped trying to be a duck. I guess she decided life was saner and drier scratching with the chickens.

But apart from the relief of that one amusing moment, it was a very rough period for our little organic farm. Two of our dairy goats had bred early enough to kid in late January, just before the mucky weather started. Goats are very cold hardy and would have been fine, but they don't tolerate wetness well. If you are ever around a flock of goats on a summer day and it starts to rain, listen to them. With all the baying and wailing, you'd swear they were melting like Oz's wicked witch. Even if they have a dry run-in in which to take shelter in their meadow—as ours do—they'll bleat and pine with excruciating urgency until they are tucked away into their stalls. Goats and moisture don't mix, and they know it! The first night that icy rain-mist came, it claimed the two January kids, which we found lying dead in the hay in the morning. Elsewhere in the province, homesteader and farmer friends reported the same. The harsh winter took one friend's beloved family milk cow. Another lost her dear horse. Many people lost sheep and goats. Beekeepers lost as much as half their hives to the weather. Northern animals can stand up to the cold and the wind, but few can last against a wet cold. For that reason, northern-country folk would rather a winter of intense freezing temperatures than a whole season of mild but damp weather.

But after several days the excruciating mist finally faded away and the intense cold returned. We were all delighted. Cold we could manage, and so could the animals. We changed out their damp bedding, gave them extra rations of grain and molasses to kick-start their inner fires, and when all seemed well on the homestead again, I decided to take a break and venture off into the forest. The homestead is a large place and our lands extend almost three-quarters of a mile east and a half mile west, becoming wild instantly once one is beyond the pastures. So I put a thermos of tea and a sandwich in my messenger bag and donned my bowie. It was noon when I stepped outside, and the moment I exited the door I was greeted by the winter sun, bright but cold, riding the sky low in the south as it did this time of year. But the sky was clear and it felt good just to be outside on a dry day.

No matter how hard we tried, several of this year's new goat kids perished due to the unrelenting wet cold of this bizarre winter. We were especially attached to Jane Doe, who loved to hang out with Daphne and Arielle.

I set out and as usual my rambling took me this way and that, never the way I had quite meant to go. I started off intending to hike only our own land but soon came across tracks of deer which I followed out of curiosity and found myself progressing into lands southerly, a patchwork country of feral meadows, windswept heights, and forests that changed from temperate hardwoods to boreal spruce as smoothly and quickly as a cloud shades the sun. Tracks led to more tracks and I came across those of a bobcat that I followed for a while. But bobcats are elusive creatures, and even in snow somehow they find ways to make their spoor vanish. When I came to a field of perhaps fifty acres that had been logged some twenty-five years before, I lost the trail. No mystery how. There were plenty of logs left lying in the field, rejected by the loggers for one reason or another, and the bobcat had jumped onto them and scurried off. Perhaps it walked the logs just because it was easier going than through snow. Perhaps it had actually meant to make its trail disappear. Maybe both. I've tracked mountain lions in Montana and lynx in Alaska, and all I can say is whatever kind of cat you're trailing, it's like trying to follow a ghost.

Cold wears you down and it was bitter today. Arctic air may have warred with southern air for a week, but the arctic had clearly won. The cold was deep and penetrating, and I took a break to have a cup of hot tea from the thermos and a few squares of chocolate for the sugar that keeps the body's hearth fires glowing. But in such cold you cannot break too long, either, or one's metabolism slows down and the chill works deeper into the body. As soon as I had downed the foods, I carried on. Snowshoe hare tracks were everywhere, but I already knew we were only a year or two from the peak side of the hares' population cycle. Ubiquitous hare spoor was to be expected.

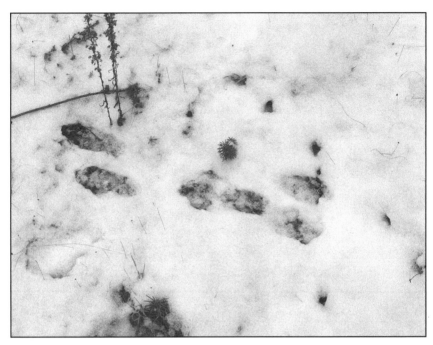

Fresh overlapping hare tracks and numerous older tracks half-vanished in partially melted snow indicate this area is a hub of hare activity.

I hadn't yet seen much in the way of active wildlife on this hike except for birds. Every now and then a redtail hawk flew by, doubtless scanning the old half-regrown clearings for hares and rodents. There were always black-capped finches about, delicately tiny birds that have an amazing resistance to cold and are active at far lower temperatures than the current mere -20 F. Now and then an enormous raven glided by overhead. They are noisy fliers, and I could hear the *whoosh-whoosh-whoosh* of their great wings upon this day of dead calm air. Though less vocal than their cousins, crows, they are always clucking and clicking and trilling to one another in their secret tongue, too. In Alaska I had learned trills to call back ravens and get them to circle, but if I tried the same here, the ravens would only look around curiously, as if thinking, "Strange, that sounds so familiar!" To this day I smile every time I see a raven and wonder at the secret languages of birds, and we will examine it a bit further after October's Journey.

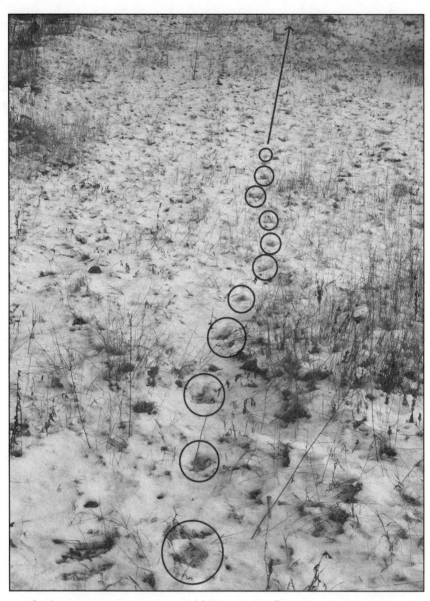

In the snow it is easy to spot and follow tracks. Circled are coyote tracks, probably hunting abundant hares this bitter winter's day. Notice the distinct, business-like way in which this coyote has moved across the land, very much unlike the haphazard zigzagging of domestic dogs, which do not have to concern themselves with conserving energy.

But I meant to hike a long way yet, following my feet toward the high meadows south of the Old Wood where I thought I might have good odds of sighting some of the more elusive wildlife, such as coyote or maybe even a moose. But the going was slow as I kept sinking— even with snowshoes—into the soft snow. Here in this dense second growth young forest, where the ground is close-covered with bramble, thickets and exposed roots, the snow never could really form a dense enough surface to float snowshoes properly. It was hard enough walking through here in summer, but now it was like trying to wade through wet sand. I decided to make my way out to the dirt road about a half mile south and follow it east to a trail on better ground. It took a good half hour to cover that mere half mile, though. I kept tripping as the snow collapsed or my snowshoes caught tangles of hidden brush. But through sheer stubborn determination, I finally made it out to the seldom-used dirt road. Here the snow was windblown and shallow, and I stashed my now unnecessary snowshoes beside a large tree and walked on foot a mile further east til I came to a sudden growth of huge old firs and maples that grew up and down a brae alongside a vigorous little creek that flowed year-round, no matter how cold the weather.

But when I came to the trailhead, I knew immediately something was wrong. The snow here had been packed flat and hard. Occasionally someone might take a snowmobile over this trail, and that tended to leave behind a distinctive track of a single tread between a pair of skis, but this … this looked as if all the snow on the trail had simply been compacted into the earth. A sinking feeling developed in my chest as I realized only one thing could have done this … heavy machinery. Few people opted to live in this rocky high country. Someone pushing heavy machinery back down this trail could only be after one thing … timber.

The first thought that crossed my mind upon the realization was: *Could someone really be foolish enough to cut rare old-growth woods for firewood?* But I've traveled much of the world and been involved in environmentalism most of my life. I recalled fights to save the rainforest of the Alaskan panhandle; loggers with a zealous belief they had a god-given right to cut down that last North American rainforest. I recalled the nightmare that is the Alberta tar sands and local environmental monitors telling me the government had tacitly informed them to ignore environmental violations. I recalled the endless battles of the Sea Shepherd Society to save endangered whales from Japanese poachers and the war on rare wolves in the American west and the stubborn persistence of GMO companies to promote their herbicides despite the demonstrable harm these things wreak upon insect populations, and the vast ecological disregard of industrial scale monocrop farms and ...

Yes. Yes, I knew in an instant that cut like jagged glass. Yes, there are people who would invade rare old-growth forest just for firewood. Yes, just because it was a little more convenient to smash an ancient tree into firewood than to harvest a dozen young, faster-growing trees. Yes, because we have become a species that holds nothing sacred save our own self-interest. And until we once again adopt the balanced wisdom of our ancestors, nothing in the world is safe. Not even we from ourselves.

Heartsick, I made myself pace up the trail, forgetting to even keep an eye out for telltale movement that would mark the wildlife I had been seeking all day. Forgetting to even keep track of time, I hiked until I came across what I dreaded finding: a monstrously huge, clawed logging machine. You see, modern loggers don't get in the woods with chainsaws and axes anymore—those days are long gone. That would require hard work and be too slow. There's quick $$$ to be made! So now they go into the woods with massive machines that look like something out of robot apocalypse movies. With these, they simply bulldoze over the biggest trees. With giant robotic claws these machines grasp the trees and rip them from the Earth, slice off the roots and branches with a couple sweeps of massive grinding blades, and drop them like corpses to be plucked up by equally monstrous super trucks. I found just such a machine in the thick of a beautiful and rare patch of old-growth maples and hemlocks. It had been chewing it down like some hungry demon out of brimstone nightmares.

But it was quiet just now, the machines off, and no one around. The sun was on the horizon and the cold had gone from biting to vicious, with nothing but a building, hungry wind for company. But I just stood there, shocked by the sight of the devastation, unable to wrap my mind around the utter disdain for the ancient, wondrous living thing that is an old forest, a symbiotic super-organism upon which the very life of this world depends. Old and beautiful and wise, it takes centuries for such a forest to come into being. And now humans like parasites were stealing its life in a moment. For firewood!

And as if that realization were not bad enough, there was the simple truth that there was no need. There were sustainable ways to harvest wood. Our own little cottage is wood heated. I cut almost all our own firewood. I do it all the time, summer and winter. But I keep to the young woods where things grow fast, where there are no old, fragile ecologies that could be undone by my intrusion. In particular, I seek out sick trees, or trees growing too close, or trees that have been blown over by winds or died of some blight. Or I could just as well harvest from our coppice woods, cultivated to produce fast-growing trees for all kinds of purposes.

And so the sun sank, night drew on, darkness congealed in pools beneath the boughs of doomed trees. Soon the land fell altogether into blackness, and yet I could only stand there, regarding the destruction in numb shock beneath a spray of cold and silent stars. I could not wrap my mind around this kind of indifferent greed. I felt like . . . I think like what the American aboriginals of the western plains must have felt when they rode out to hunt the buffalo and found instead the new folk—the settlers—had left countless carcasses of the great beasts on the plains, slain and abandoned to lie in their own congealing blood, only their tongues torn away to pay US bounties. We must have shared an utter dismay; a soul-deep inability to understand such vacuous greed. A wonder at the shortsightedness of the persons who would commit such atrocities. No wonder they fought so hard to keep the settlers away from the land they held sacred.

Looking at this needlessly devastated woodland, it suddenly seemed our species had crossed the brink of madness and it was pointless to fight it. And with that darkest thought it was like the hope I tried to hold deep in my heart for a better world slipped away, leaving in its wake only the bitter emptiness of a void. It was a chilling, ugly thing, that void—far, far colder than this midwinter night in the north woods.

I realized my fingers were numb with cold. I had been wearing thin glove liners so my hands could manage the tools of bushcraft, but it was far too cold for just liners now that it was dark. I pawed at my messenger bag with hands like flippers for the heavy gloves stowed in there. I withdrew them fumblingly and pulled them over my hands with my teeth. Rated to a hundred below, my fingers quickly warmed. When I could feel them again, I released a clip that held up the rabbit fur flaps of my hat. The flaps fell to shield my ears, which I realized I could no longer feel. And still I could only stand there, trying to shake myself free of this hateful void.

My eyes were accustomed to the deep darkness, and by starlight I regarded my small messenger bag which held all the gear I needed for a foray of a day or two into the wilds. Often, as well, it might hold a brace of hares or grouse that I had shot for food. A lot of people liked to read my website about how Daphne, the girls, and I lived traditionally by the land, but I knew some of my readers were offended that sometimes we killed and ate wild game. I'd get emails telling me it was heartless, never mind whatever we harvested was an abundant prey species that rarely lives more than a year or two before it is taken by a coyote or a marten or a hawk. It would not matter to them that left unchecked, such animals would overgraze the land, killing off rare plant species and depriving deer and other animals of limited food resources. Nor would it matter that I made sure to take such animals swiftly, ending them in an instant. It would not matter that these animals had lived free and well til their last breath, nor that I did not hunt for sport. I would only hear that it was heartless to take an animal in any circumstance, and this they would write from the warmth of their homes in the comfort of their cities that devour whole landscapes and ecosystems.

I glanced up at the great machines. They were still as stone, cold as the winter sky. Like slumbering demons with giant steel claws, they sat there... waiting for their day of apocalypse. I could be angry with those machines. I could be angry at the loggers who would drive them. But the truth was they wouldn't be here without the rest of us to make it worth their while. Loggers killing forests. Frackers polluting water. Big corporations dredging the life out of the oceans and the remote wilds. We often rant about them. *How dare they do this? How could they do that?* We forget that when we flip the light switch on, coal must be burned in the power plant, coal that must be dug up from some green hill. We lose sight of the fact that when we turn on the heat, oil had to be fracked out of the land to make it possible. When we buy a McBurger for a dollar, it is only because a swath of rainforest was cut down so the meat could be grown as cheaply as possible.

How we choose to live creates ripples.

And the ripples go on and on.

And if we look far enough, we discover every forest falls or not for our own choices.

Such a truth is hard to face. And many will only say it is too big for me and refuse to act on it.

And so in the dark, suddenly foreboding, I knew tomorrow these ancient trees would fall. They would fall for me and for you, and elsewhere in the world so would more like them, again and again. Unique and irreplaceable treasures with souls and voices and immeasurable beauty. Wholly benevolent beings that cleanse Earth and Sky by their very being. And who would notice as we tip Earth ever so slowly into the void to meet our endless wants now and easily, without consideration for a far-off tomorrow, and so we lose our souls and our Earth Mother to a forest of indifference.

The image does not do this ancient birch justice. Like a sentinel of the wood, it has stood here wise and patient for nearly a century. It towers above the surrounding trees, even the great maples. It is broader than a man's shoulders. Innumerable birds and mammals have called it home. Over the span of its life, it has cleaned thousands of tons of water and air. And tomorrow it along with many gigantic maples was doomed to fall, for no other reason than someone determined he could make quick money in the doing. And only indifference lets it happen.

Wild Life

Mushroom Rings

Nature is full of rings. The planet Saturn has rings so lovely it's like a god bestowed them as an engagement gift. And any tree stump bears rings that tell the tale of how long the tree lived and what the weather was like through each year of its life. Now and then we see a ring around the moon, a harbinger of coming wet weather. The symmetry of rings tends to grab our attention and we wonder at the designs of Nature, for the sight of natural rings reminds us that apparently insentient wild forces act with design and create beauty. But the rings mushrooms sometimes form as they grow have perhaps gone furthest in capturing the imagination. Mushroom rings have been part of myth and magic since the most ancient times. And no wonder. One morning, they simply appear in a meadow or deep in the forest following the patterns of inexplicable forces. What else could a mushroom ring be save the creation of some preternatural entity?

Mushroom rings appear in woodlands around trees, in open meadows among wild herbs, and even upon the cut grass of lawns, as shown here. (Photo courtesy of Aisling Ryan.)

Old folklore is replete with would-be explanations for mushroom rings. In Germany, rings were often attributed to witches dancing in circles, especially upon Walpurgis Night. Far off in Austria, folklore had it that faerie rings appeared at places touched and poisoned by dragons. Off in Western Europe, especially through the countries heavily influenced by Celtic tradition (the British Isles, Brittany, and France), mushroom rings were closely associated with faeries, so much in fact that they came to be called elf circles or faerie rings.

Wherever such rings appear, they may be marked by a circle of mushrooms. If mushrooms are not growing at the moment, the ring may show up as pale grass, or very green grass. The folklore of the Celtic lands held that as the elves danced in their wild, racing circles to the music of harps and flutes sweet beyond the kenning of mortal ears, they trod down the grass—hence why it sometimes looked pale and fading. Sometimes Puck (or the Green Man) himself would come and rejuvenate the grass, resulting in a ring that was especially verdant and lush. Some rings grew around trees, and it was thought those trees were the favorites of the elves.

Mushroom rings are the result of subterranean mycelium. When you see a mushroom crop up out of the soil, it is merely the fruit of the fungus' body—the mycelium—which is entirely underground. It all starts when a fungal spore lands someplace where conditions are right and it germinates and the mycelium begins to grow. It grows outward in every direction from that central point. As it grows, only the outer perimeter that is feeding is alive. The mycelium of each previous year dies away, resulting in a ring of live mycelium that every year expands a little further outward.

Mycelium rings that grow in meadows are saprophytic, which is to say the fungus feeds on the dead and decaying matter of grasses and sedges. These saprophytic fungi are beneficial as they break down nutrients gathered by the plants and return them to the soil. However, since mycelium needs a lot of soil-borne nitrogen, it competes with plants for this resource. Able to get the nitrogen more effectively than plants, where the mycelium grows, the grasses and sedges starve, go pale and may die. Thus, a faerie ring is often visible long before and after mushrooms appear, marked by a pale ring of foliage. But some types of faerie ring mycelia restore nutrients quickly to the soil and provide plants with natural growth hormones and antibiotics. This mutually beneficial relationship causes the foliage over the mycelium to become especially tall and verdant, so the mycelium is marked by a ring of vigorous plant growth.

The mycelia that form rings around trees take a somewhat different growth strategy. Rather than feeding saprophytically, they form symbiotic relationships with trees. They provide the tree's roots soil-borne minerals as well as antibiotics essential to fight off pathogens, and in return the tree converts the nutrients to sugars and provides the excess to the mycelium.

However the mycelium feeds, as it grows outward, the ring remains interconnected and is thus a single living organism. When the mycelium has collected enough surplus nutrients and energy, it signals all parts of itself to reproduce. That is when the characteristic mushrooms of the faerie ring emerge, all at once and often overnight. But it is important to remember that the mushrooms are only the fruiting bodies of the subterranean mycelium. They are no more the organism than an apple is the tree.

This symphony of growth is remarkable. Only plants can convert sunlight, nutrients, and water into energy. But they are not so efficient at getting at the nutrients, nor in defending themselves, so fungi help them along in exchange for some surplus sugar. The faerie ring holds a place of remarkable wonder in folklore, but it is also an amazing example of the deep interdependence of life. All living things have their role, their time, and their place, and all depend upon one another.

Enchanted Forest

Rhys at the Fairy Dance

As mushroom rings are so strongly associated with the preternatural, and especially the Good Folk, I thought it only fitting to present an old tale out of ancient Wales that illustrates their magical relation. The story illustrates not only the preference of faeries for merry-making in their rings but is a cautionary tale of approaching the Otherworld unprepared for its mysteries.

◆ ◆ ◆

Rhys and Llewellyn, two farmer's servants, who had been all day carrying lime for their master, were driving in the twilight; their mountain ponies before them, returning home from their work. On reaching a little plain, Rhys called to his companion to stop and listen to the music, saying it was a tune to which he had danced a hundred times, and must go and have a dance now. He bade him go on with the horses, and he would soon overtake him. Llewellyn could hear nothing, and began to remonstrate; but away sprang Rhys, and he called after him in vain. He went home, put up the ponies, ate his supper, and went to bed, thinking that Rhys had only made a pretext for going to the alehouse. But when morning came, and still no sign of Rhys, he told his master what had occurred. Search was then made everywhere, but no Rhys could be found. Suspicion now fell upon Llewellyn of having murdered him, and he was thrown into prison, though there was no evidence against him. A farmer, however, skilled in fairy-matters, having an idea of how things might have been, proposed that himself and some others should accompany Llewellyn to the place where he parted with Rhys. On coming to it, they found it green as the mountain ash. "Hush!" cried Llewellyn, "I hear music, I hear sweet harps." We all listened, says the narrator, for I was one of them, but could hear nothing. "Put your foot on mine, David," said he to me (his own foot was at the time on the outward edge of the fairy-ring). I did so, and so did we all, one after another, and then we heard the sound of many harps, and saw within a circle, about twenty feet across, great numbers of little people, of the size of children of three or four years old, dancing round and round. Among them we saw Rhys, and Llewellyn catching him by the smock-frock, as he came by him, pulled him out of the circle. "Where are the horses? Where are the horses?" cried he. "Horses, indeed!" said Llewellyn. Rhys urged him to go home, and let him finish his dance, in which he averred he had not been engaged more than five minutes. It was by main force they took him from the place. He still asserted he had been only five minutes away, and could give no account of the people he had been with. He became melancholy, took to his bed, and soon after died. "The morning after," says the narrator, "we went to look at the place, and we found the edge of the ring quite red, as if trodden down, and I could see the marks of little heels, about the size of my thumbnail."

—Thomas Keightley
The Fairy Mythology

Wood Witchery

The Enchantment of Faerie Rings

I was a child living in the bayous of Louisiana when I first encountered a faerie ring. I had been hiking through the forest behind our little home, past a place where elderberry trees grew tall and passionfruit vined in every clearing, slowly ambling my way among great black oaks and tall hickories, taking note of the odd wild pecan tree to later come back and harvest. I had it in mind to wander back to a place I knew wild persimmons grew. They were sweet as candy and we were too poor to afford store candy, not to mention the stores were a long haul off in the village. I came to a crawfish stream, with shallow, opaque waters like most of the streams in the bayous, and had tested several vines to find one fit and strong enough to swing across when I saw the faerie ring: a perfect circle of mushrooms growing in a grassy place where the tree cover was thin. I walked all around it, trying to understand the phenomenon. How and why did a bunch of mushrooms manage to grow in a circle in the middle of the forest? It looked like something that had to have been contrived by a person, yet I knew it was exceedingly unlikely that anyone else came back here, much less to sow mushroom spores in a circle. I knew nothing else about these mysterious rings at the time, but I sensed the wonder about them.

I was naturalist-inclined even back then. Believe it or not, by the age of eleven I had actually assembled my own rudimentary lab. My mother had ceded to me a portion of our barn where I had collected a microscope, telescope, beakers, bottles, slides, and test tubes, devised my own Bunsen burner, and amassed quite a collection of feathers, fur, wild seeds, interesting rocks, and anything else a child naturalist who lived in deepest poverty could scrape together. And there in that lab I buried myself in the books I had salvaged from the discards of libraries, trying to discover the secret of the mushroom ring. I learned a lot about how mushrooms grew but nothing really satisfying about how they came to form a circle.

But over the ensuing weeks, now that I knew about them and the telltales to look for, I began watching for them on my rambles. I found them as broad circles of faded or darkened grass in the meadows. I saw their mushrooms appear after the rain, one kind in the open meadows, another kind in the forest. I finally resorted to my ancient Cajun grandmother whose French accent was thick and English was smattered with antique Acadian words. She had grown up in those bayous, had lived in them all her life, and knew their every little nook and secret. When I told her about the rings I had found and asked her what she knew about them, she only looked as solemn as a 4-foot-10 hunched and withered crone can and said, *"N'y marche pas!"* (Don't walk there.) And she would speak no more on the matter. Of course, saying "don't walk there" to an intrepid and especially stubborn boy is as good as daring him to do it, and it only made me more curious as to why I shouldn't.

One day, on a visit to the village to buy and sell produce, I went to the library and looked up faerie rings. I found them referenced in the occult section, and it was among those books that I first began to understand the magical place of not just rings of mushrooms and grass, but apparently all rings in Nature: rings of trees and stones, natural apertures in tree trunks, rings around the moon—in fact, all natural forms of rings were believed to hold magical connotations. But above all, the mushroom rings were seen as focal points of deep enchantment, and I read old myths about how persons who stumbled into them got lost in the realms of the Otherworld. And that notion drew me. What would it be like to see not just another place but another kind of reality? I also knew that those legends warned of dire consequences to the mortal, not least of which was almost certain death upon returning to the here and now, but like most boys I could not think so far down the line. I threw caution to the wind and determined to explore this wonder.

So the night of the next full moon, armed with the tidbits of lore I had acquired in those dusty tomes, I wandered out to the meadow behind my grandfather's farm to a place I knew a faerie ring was then sprouting mushrooms. The grass was illumined by wan, silver moonlight. Owls hooted from the ancient black oaks of the forest all around. Thick cumulus clouds sailed the sky, leaving bare patches of trailing stars. And when I reached the faerie ring and a cloud parted to let the moonlight down, I did the forbidden thing and jumped into the ring. I wanted so much to encounter that hidden realm of ghosts and *feux follets* and *les fées* (faeries) that I was willing to take whatever risk, even if that meant I might be lost for a hundred years and one day find my way back to the mortal world only to turn to dust.

What happened, though, was the black clouds continued to sail overhead, the moonlight continued to illumine the wild land in swathes of silver light, the crickets continued to chirrup and the owls continued to call. I had gone nowhere, though perhaps traveled a bit in the direction of wisdom. For I had learned that while there is much truth in the old lore, experiencing the Otherworld for oneself is rarely so simple as the stories say. Touching upon it takes more than merely jumping into a faerie ring, climbing a beanstalk, or entering an enchanted forest. I knew that a magical realm was real, though. I had witnessed it, and so had my mother and her mother before her. The magical world was out there and I wanted as much as anything to find a way to know it more fully.

For years after I explored the mystery, but it was not until nearly two decades later when I began to study the shamanic path that I felt I really got a good grasp of the link between the faerie ring and the Otherworld. (Bear in mind that I use the term *shamanic* broadly, referring to all the paths and methods that promote a genuine, personal process of interacting with the spiritual and magical side of Nature.) There are power places in the world, pure, natural locations where enchantment flows deep and green. At such places the veil between the worlds grows thin and the land of spirits can mingle with the here and now. Woodland springs, enchanted lakes, stone circles and faerie rings are but a few such places, and at them one is more likely to experience the enchanted, especially if one takes steps to *catalyze* the event.

At our homestead, Twa Corbies Hollow, we take many steps to *catalyze* encounters with the Otherworld. We leave faerie plates (little offerings of bread, cheese, and drink) in the woods. We make sure not to disrupt faerie rings when they appear in the meadows. I enter the woodlands at times with my fiddle and play for the pleasure of the spirits. We respect all life and look after it, taking only what we need and helping it where we may. Along the way, I have collected power objects—things I find in the woodlands that have magical-spiritual meaning to me. Raven feathers, smooth tear-shaped ovals of brook-polished quartz, teeth of coyotes, a perfectly preserved mushroom that a red squirrel set upon a branch and forgot about, and many more. These possess enchantment, and like many shamans I save and ponder them. (The reader should be aware of local regulations regarding saving natural items such as bird feathers. In some places it is prohibited or a permit is required.) Eventually, I give one back to the forest, perhaps tossing it in a brook to float away, or leaving it in a faerie ring. This is after the manner of ancient Celtic offerings. It was long ago noted that the sacrificial items the ancient Celts tossed to bogs and lakes for the spirits were not new things, but old and well used. Archeologists believe they ascribed more value to items much needed and loved than to newly fashioned items that had no other virtue than their worth in coin.

So, if you are fortunate enough to find a faerie ring in a secluded place, think of it as a gift and an opportunity to grow in magical and spiritual wisdom. Show your devotion to the spirits with little offerings. Leave odd little treasures of the natural world. Plant a lovely flowering plant nearby, something the myths indicate is strongly favored by the Good Folk. Marigolds and elderberries are good choices. And take time to just sit and ponder by the place, meditate, and even sleep. Become a companion to the spirits that dwell there. Open yourself to them. Show your willingness to come on their terms as a friend. And in such a way you will cultivate the enchantment of the faerie ring. Later, you might choose such a site as a place of power to undertake the spirit journey (see *Making the Spirit Journey* after Chapter 9), and if you have the knack then your journey will be powerful and deep indeed. But even if you do not follow that path, you will be the better for tending and loving a magical bit of the sacred Earth.

As is the way with natural magic, there is nothing complex to any of this. There are no strange sigils or arcane runes or complex incantations and burning of hard-to-find herbs in gilded braziers. Real magic takes a sincere relationship and an open mind and heart … and maybe a pot to serve as a cauldron to brew a pleasant mug of potion-tea to enjoy as you work. This is simple, earnest, earthy magic, of a kind that dates back deep into primordial ages, to an era when men and women met the land's spirits as friends and allies.

Woods Lore

The Knife—Essential Tool for Trekking into the Wild

The single most important tool for getting by out of doors—apart from decent boots and adequate clothing—is a good knife. A good knife will allow you to get by outdoors for days if need be. With a good knife, you can strike a fire from chert, flint, or quartz; cut wood into tools; flash the sun to signal for help; cut boughs to make a shelter; build traps to get food; or mark shrubs and trees to find your way out of a confusing landscape. You can even use a knife to open tins of food. I have spent much of my life in the wild lands of bayous, deserts and the north woods, and a good knife was the single most valuable tool I ever carried.

If you pop onto the Internet and look up knives for bushcraft, you'll find a lot of recommendations. Many bushcrafters (folks who revive and maintain wilderness living skills) are fond of stout, small- to medium-sized knives. Current favorites are the pudgy, heavy Becker BK2, ten-and-a-half inches long with a tough point and weighing nearly a pound. It is medium-sized and can handle any task. Others favor smaller knives such as the Fallkniven S1 Forest Knife, an extremely expensive, tough, and light knife that is as good for shaping wooden tools as gutting a fish for dinner. And there is an odd push in bushcraft to find the "one tool that will do it all," which seems to be a quest for a knife that can also be an axe, a wedge and a hammer. For my part, I have always favored carrying a large knife and a small axe in the backcountry. Decades of wilderness experience have impressed upon me there is simply not, nor will there ever be, one tool that can do it all. If you anticipate needing firewood or having to build a shelter while in the sticks, there is no better chopper than an axe. It is made of softer steel that handles pounding better than knives, and having all its weight at the end of a shaft allows for far more effective cutting swings. And for slicing, dicing, cutting, and carving, nothing beats a knife with its harder steel and easier handling.

But if you have only one tool on you, make it a large knife because in a pinch it can do a small knife's and an axe's job at least adequately. I learned that lesson decades ago in the dangerous Alaskan wilderness when my friend Skye and I were returning from a caribou hunt and a massive stormed pinned us down for several days. We were nearly out of food, and it was cold and wet. I had forgotten to bring a hatchet, but I was able to use my ever-present bowie to secure firewood and harvest wild forage. And I knew if the storm persisted, I could use it to fashion some traps to get us more food.

A bush knife should be made of true carbon steel as that will strike the best sparks from flint, chert, and quartz. Many modern bushcraft knives, like the Esee 6, are coated to protect them from rusting, but to strike sparks, the metal must be exposed, so either choose an uncoated knife or remove part of the coat. The solution to rusting is to keep the steel oiled with a natural, nontoxic oil. When I go into the sticks, I always carry an old 35mm film canister with a couple cotton swabs drenched in mineral oil. At the end of every day (or after any period of heavy use where it's gotten wet), I just wipe the knife down with one of those swabs. Even good vegetable or olive oil works for this purpose.

A bushcraft knife should be kept sharp. But there is a tendency these days—with less and less truly wilderness-savvy people in the world—to want to make knives atom-splitting sharp. This is not only unnecessary but dangerous. The safest knife, contrary to the old wives' tale, is not the sharpest. Years of looking after traditional homestead tools like axes and scythes, and farrier tools which must be ungodly sharp, has taught me how to put a razor edge on anything if I want, but I do not go to such lengths with bushcraft knives. If you even lightly brush yourself with such an edge, it can cut, and even a shallow cut in the sticks makes you that much less functional and that much more inclined to infection. (Besides, a major cause of fatal accidents in the bush is bleeding out following a knife-related injury.) And you will likely have to touch your edge if you are using the knife to harvest wild forage or clean game, make delicate carving cuts on wood, or cook and eat. Plus, an extremely sharp edge is also fragile. Such an edge is thin and fine, prone to dulling quickly, denting and chipping. Better is what the old timers called "knife sharp." This is a good cutting edge that will handily slice meat or vegetables and carve with ease but would not easily shave the hair from your arm. Such an edge is strong and will last.

A good way to tell if a bushcraft knife is appropriately sharp is to try to slice paper with it. If you can merely push the blade edgewise and it cuts the paper (called a push cut), it is too sharp. If it slices the paper easily if you draw the knife toward you as you push, as in a sawing motion (called a saw cut), then it is knife sharp.

Sharpening a knife properly is a skill in itself, and one that often takes people years to master. Many never manage to become more than marginal at it. It is so tricky that over the years countless companies have come out with innumerable gizmos to simplify the job. I've tried a number of them and never cared for any, though I find the little $10 modern carbide and ceramic sharpeners to be one of the more serviceable options. These tools are usually about a couple inches long and have a set of tiny carbide surfaces set in a V, and another set of ceramic surfaces. You lightly but firmly press the knife first into the carbides and saw back and forth about eight times. Then you do the same on the ceramic side. That will quickly give you a blade with a modestly good "knife sharp" edge.

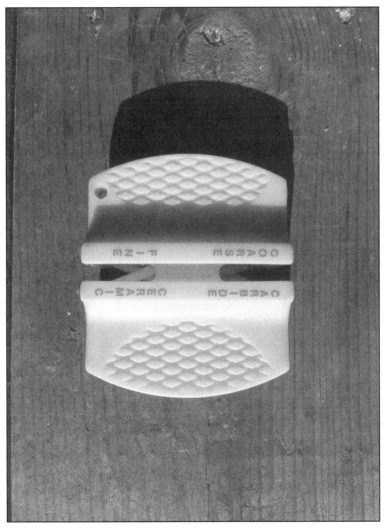

A typical carbide sharpener. One side has tiny, effective carbide rods set in a V that will sharpen an edge with a few firm strokes. The other side has ceramic rods that will strop and finish the edge.

The downside of carbide sharpeners is they are so hard they strip metal from the edge too quickly, and if you use them much they will rapidly wear down your blade.

But the best way to sharpen any knife that I know is also very ancient. All you need is a pair of Japanese water stones of roughly 1,000 and 4,000 grit. Often these stones are sold bonded together, the low grit on one side, the high grit on the other. (The dark side is the lower grit.) Unless you do a heck of a lot of sharpening, the stones are going to last you a lifetime, so get the largest you can afford. Big stones have big sharpening surfaces and make for better work. They run around $70 for a stone about 9 × 3 × 2 inches. I also advise getting a tiny Japanese 1,000 water stone about 2 × ¾ × ½ inches to keep in your pack as a field sharpener. It costs only a couple dollars. I am very fond of the very affordable King Water Stones.

A typical Japanese water stone, the dark side of this medium-sized stone is 1,000 grit, excellent for bringing blades to "knife sharpness," and the other side is 4,000 grit, for finishing an edge to a keen effectiveness. Using just this one combination water stone, a skilled person can render a knife razor-sharp.

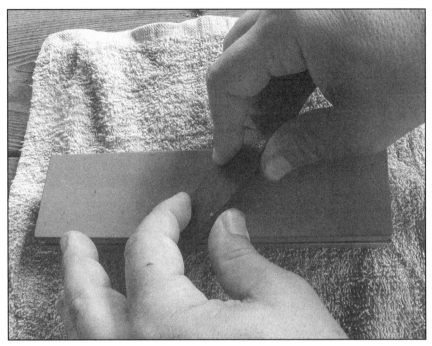

When using a water stone, rotate the blade to an angle to get the maximum amount of edge on the stone at a time, and use your index fingers or thumbs at the spine (depending on which side of the blade you are sharpening) to hold the angle consistent. Press the edge down onto the stone with light but firm pressure. It is a good idea to put the water stone on a rag to hold it in place as wet stones are prone to slipping on smooth surfaces.

Before using, immerse the stones in water for about 30 minutes. They must be saturated to be effective. Ensure they stay wet as you work with them. If you have to pause for more than a couple minutes, re-wet them before continuing by running them a moment under a tap.

Start with the 1,000 grit stone (the darker stone). Hold the knife as illustrated in the photo above, using your fingers or thumbs (depending on which side of the blade you are sharpening) to steady the blade at an angle of about 25 degrees. Don't worry about being super precise with the angle, just eyeball the angle and do your best to keep the cutting edge evenly on the stone. Keeping your fingers or thumbs between the knife's spine and the stone will keep the angle consistent. You should be able to feel when the edge makes full contact with the stone's face. Hold the knife at an angle as shown in the photo to get as much of the edge as possible on the stone for consistency. Slide the blade forward and back along the whole length of the stone about ten times, applying no more than moderate pressure. A slurry will build up on the stone as you work. When you are done with one side of the edge, rinse the slurry off the knife and stone with running water. Sharpen one whole side of the edge, then flip the knife over and do the other side. Then change to the 4,000 grit stone and repeat the process in just the same way.

As you sharpen on the higher grit stone, you will see dark streaks appear on its surface. This is the abraded steel wearing off the edge. It means you are doing the right thing. Sharpen one side, then rinse the stone, rubbing it with your finger til the dark discoloration is gone. Then do the other side and, as before, rinse and rub the stone til it's pale again. The abraded steel must be rinsed and rubbed away or the fine stone will lose its sharpening properties.

If you use a fine stone greater than 4,000 grit, you will not be able to just rub the dark staining away. You'll have to use a small, special stone called a nagura stone to scour the fine-grit stone. To do this, just lightly but firmly press the nagura stone to the fine-grit sharpening stone and rub back and forth, rinsing frequently. Soon the surface of the stone will clear up and its sharpening properties will be restored. However, before you start rinsing away that slurry, you may wish to rub your knife's entire blade with it. Just get the slurry onto the blade and firmly rub it over the metal with your fingers, being careful of the now very sharp edge. A couple minutes of this rubbing will polish the blade, which some persons feel will improve its function by reducing friction. Others, including myself, let the stains that will collect on the steel build up over time. They form a dull patina which helps protect carbon steel from rusting.

Japanese water stones wear down with use so I flip mine end to end each time I finish sharpening a knife so I am always working from a fresh side. This promotes even wear. Even so, eventually they will develop uneven wear and will need to be re-flattened. You can buy a special truing stone to level them. Just set the truing stone on a table, soak the water stone, then rub it on the truing stone til the surface is again level. You can also fashion a truing stone by simply gluing some sandpaper of about 300 or 400 grit to a level surface like a glass pane, or even by just using the flat side of a cinder block.

A final bit of VERY IMPORTANT advice: be sure to remove ALL OIL from your knife before sharpening it on a water stone. Oil will ruin a water stone.

If you would like further information on how to use Japanese water stones, visit my website at http://www.cliffseruntine.wordpress.com and look under the section: Homestead Skills.

When buying a knife, get quality that doesn't break the bank. Some bushcrafters will spend many hundreds of dollars on a knife and tell you it's because if you're in the middle of nowhere and your life depends on your knife, you need the best. But the real truth is bushcraft has become something of a hipster fad lately, and many bushcrafters nowadays buy expensive knives just to look cool. A real woodsman wouldn't say, "Oh goodness, my knife is broken. I'm a goner." A real woodsman would just break a rock and use the jagged edge to cut whatever needed cutting. That's what a knife is, after all, a cutting tool, and like all the tools of bushcraft, it can be improvised. But the simple fact is there are many decent knives of modest expense that are incredibly tough. The first bushcraft knife I ever had was my grandfather's KA-BAR from WWII. That knife was over forty years old when he gave it to me and still solid. It lasted me many years of hard use til I lost it one day in the Alaskan wilds. Fortunately, such a knife is only $50. The second bushcraft knife I owned was a large puukko that I recently passed down to my daughter when she was ready for a good one of her own. It cost $120 and I expect she'll have it til she loses it or passes it down to her kids. Now I have a good fifteen-inch Cold Steel Trail Master bowie. I bought it on sale for $118, though they sell more commonly for around $180. Unless I manage to lose it or give it to my other daughter, it will probably last the rest of my life. You can get a good knife for between $50 and $150. Spend any less and you're probably getting junk; any more and you're likely going to be afraid to use it, in which case it will be useless to you.

When knife shopping, a few things to bear in mind are:

- Get good-quality carbon steel; O1, 1075, 1085, 1095 and D2 are my favorites. If you live in an area of high heat and humidity, a proven stainless steel like AUS-8 might work better for you.

- The point of a knife is the part that most commonly breaks, so get one with a stout point. I am partial to well-made clip points.

- Ensure the hilt is comfortable and tough.

- Bigger (within reason) is usually better. A knife between eleven and fifteen inches overall length with a $\frac{3}{16}$- to $\frac{1}{3}$-inch spine and flat grind blade will weigh approximately ten ounces to a pound and be sufficient to almost any task.

- If you live in an area that is not so wild or you are small, a small- to medium-sized knife may be just fine for your needs.

You now have the information essential to choosing and maintaining a good knife for the backcountry. If you decide to wander down the bushcraft way, there are many other skills you should know, but a knife is the single most valuable tool to have on you. Learn the skills to use it well and it will take care of you. For further information on bushcrafting, I highly recommend *Essential Bushcraft* by Ray Mears.

SPRING

The Renewal
of the Wood

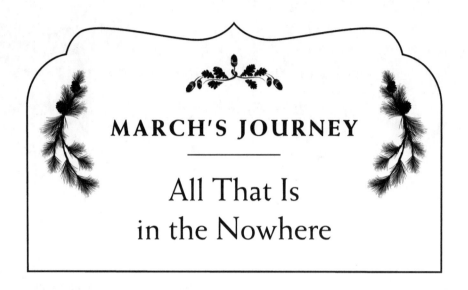

MARCH'S JOURNEY

All That Is
in the Nowhere

I have never found a companion that was so companionable
as solitude.

—Henry David Thoreau

First day the snow is gone from the forest paths, I am putting a saddle on
my horse and going for a long ride to nowhere. It's always the best place,
and every time I go nowhere I always find my Self there. Waiting. And
my Self says to myself: "Where have you been?" And myself says, "I was
somewhere, but it was nowhere. Now I'm nowhere and it is somewhere."
And my Self replies to myself: "This is where the magic is." But both my
selves already knew that.

First day the ice is gone from the Whispering Lake, I am going to
portage my canoe down to its quiet edge and glide out over the glassy
waters, clear like crystal to the very bottom. I am going to quietly dip the

oar into those calm waters and ne'er raise a splash and trek the lotuses and lilies, float like a log at the cove and sing with the peepers at dawn, drift beyond the peninsula and in lucent noon sunshine watch the pitcher plants feast on unwary insects with their unearthly blossoms. I am going to harvest a feast of plantain, dock, and cattail and grill it with venison where I camp on the westerly shore. And I'll bet there, among the lake's many whispers, in the company of brother moose and sister bear, I'll find my Self again, in the nowhere that is the only *where* that matters.

But for now, there is only the long silence of March, and in the highland forests of the Maritimes, it is a fickle silence, never quite able to make up its mind what it is. Sometimes it is the silence that comes with a stormwind. At these times, it is a lonely silence that soughs through naked boughs whistling songs in scales only the winter wights know. Sometimes it is the silence of a warm day when the high sun is strong and melts tufts of snow packed among spruce boughs and lays golden beams across the icicles that dangle from the cottage's roof so that all the world carries the drip, drip, drip of a pensive melting. Sometimes, though … sometimes it is the silence of a still and clear day, where the piercing cold air moves never so much as a breath. On such days, it is as if the creatures of the wildwood join in the silence. I see deer in the hidden meadow that skip over the land raising neither puff of soft snow nor evoking the crunch of hooves on frozen ground. I woke this very dawn to find such a silence, on a day that was very cold and hard. So I meandered from our bed to the wood stove to stoke the fire good and hot to take the chill off the morning, and once that was done, I wandered to the kitchen while the cottage still slept and the dawn gloaming was just hinting at a lucent day, and set tea upon the stove. Daphne would be up soon to make breakfast for everyone, but I'd let her sleep in for now. Partly for her; partly for me. I love all of silence's many personas, and so—tea made—I slipped into a pair of boots and my heavy parka and out onto the covered deck to immerse in the brightening of the world. I had taken only a single step out the door, Willowisp, my Australian Shepherd, at my side, when I caught movement out the corner of my eye to the right. I froze. There, in the silence, was a very large and very still snowshoe hare. As is the way with its kind, it believed in the power of its camouflage. It knew instinctively that if it held very still, animals would overlook it. And hares are very good hiders. Often they go unseen right out in the open. But humans have very special eyes. We see things against the backdrop whether or not they move. And Mr. Rabbit had chosen to freeze in the open with the backdrop of the dark trunks of the Elfwood right behind him. The close-spaced evergreens formed a shady curtain in the new light of day, and the hare's white fur, showing the beginning of losing its wintry hues, clashed against the wood. He stood out.

At the end of a long winter comes fickle March, when the snow comes and goes and tantalizes with thoughts of trail rides on horseback and gliding over lakes by canoe. But the weather never holds quite long enough to do the one or the other just yet.

I stood there for a long moment watching him. I knew the hare knew it had been spotted. Its stillness told me it was wary. And as I regarded the hare in the sharply biting cold, I felt that what I would do with my day was decided. After breakfast, I needed to go to a hillock where the wind had knocked down some trees and harvest some for the last of our winter firewood, but afterward I would head off into the woods and see what there was to see. An inch of snow had fallen a couple days before. Not much, but there would be abundant spoor in such conditions. Tracking would be easy. Who knew what I might find in the depths of the wildwood. But for now the door behind me was still open. Heat was escaping and I was hot at my back, cold at my front, and the biting air was sapping the heat from my tea. I knew the moment I moved the hare would be off, but so it would have to be. I turned to shut the door and looked back and the hare was gone.

I spent the rest of the silent morning writing til Daphne announced a breakfast of farm eggs and ham with crisp, spicy hash browns on the side. I ate, washed, and then set off to get the firewood taken care of. Where I was cutting today, it was too rocky and steep to use horse or tractor. Instead, I had to cut the logs to manageable lengths and carry them out of the woods on my shoulders, toss them over the Hollow Brook, and leave them beside a path. Only then could I use the tractor to haul them to the cottage, and from there I had to cut them down to one-foot lengths and break up the thicker logs with a hefty maul. Most of the wood gathering has to be done in winter because it is safer to walk over a layer of packed snow than to stumble over rocky ground covered in a tangle of exposed roots. The highlands are rough country and it is no wonder few people live here. But that roughness keeps it wild, so I don't mind.

I arrived by tractor at the hillock a little past nine. The sky was a brilliant blue. I clambered off the faithful working machine and grabbed my chainsaw case out of the bucket. I set the case in the snow and withdrew the saw and hearing protection. It's a very large, heavy-duty saw made for serious logging that I bought nearly twenty years ago when Daphne and I lived at our remote Alaska bush cabin, and it's still going strong. But it's a beast and weighs about twenty pounds . . . a lot to swing around for hours on end.

In March snow fades from some of the sunnier places, and in such places a hare's winter camouflage works against it.

I had to cross the Hollow Brook and then climb half the hillock to get to a pile of huge windfallen logs I'd been cutting away bit by bit for over a month. The old trees had fallen in a windstorm several years ago. Still partly attached to the ground by their roots, they had been held slightly aloft and thus had seasoned to perfection. It was a shame they had toppled for they were once beautiful trees, but the rocky ground of the hillock only allowed roots to go so deep and so all the hillside's large trees eventually became top-heavy and fell. But these trees wouldn't go to waste. They would make good firewood and harvesting them would clear the ground so new trees could grow in their place. And after they were burned, the ash they produced would be recycled; we would filter brook water through the hardwood ash to extract lye for soap, and then scatter the spent ash over the gardens and meadows to provide essential nutrients to the soil.

New saplings were already growing where the fallen trees did not cover the ground: maple, willow, alder, aspen, and various spruces and tamaracks were several feet tall. Weaving between the saplings so as not to harm them, I went up and down the remainder of the log pile, lying one atop the other, and cut away their various small branches. When at last the logs were cleared of branches, I began cutting them into lengths that I calculated to weigh around a hundred pounds each. The narrower logs, I cut down to eight-foot lengths. The broadest log was so thick that mere yard-long lengths weighed a hundred pounds. After an hour of cutting, I had cut up all I could move that day and turned off the chainsaw.

That was bloody hard work, and it was the easiest part. Now came a much harder part. I had to pack the logs down the hillock and toss them over the stream. Zero degrees or not, I knew I'd be sweating bullets by the time I was done. I removed the hearing protection and leaned on a young tree to catch my breath. It was then I became aware again of the profound silence. It is odd how one can set aside a marvellous thing like a perfect silence. Just put it aside and fill the gap with activity. But with the saw off and me very still, the silence stole back over the forest as if it had been waiting for its chance. Overhead, the sun watched, clear and cold. The bare winter bones of maples and green-skirted boughs of red and white spruces stood like sentinel-statues. There were none of the ubiquitous black cap finches to clamber and chitter. No busy red squirrels raiding their winter caches. The silence was complete and encompassing.

And yet, here in the wooded depths of the homestead, there was a powerful sense of being watched. And somehow, entirely contrary to the silence, there was a sense of ceaseless movement. Over many years of dwelling in wild places I've learned to trust my instincts. I felt sure some thing, or things, was out there. I didn't really feel in danger, but I knew I wasn't alone. And then the silence was broken. Not dramatically, just with the softest padding over the snow, the easiest scudding of movement beneath the winter-bare boughs. Now here, now there, it seemed to come in random spaces between the minutes, never when it was expected, and from any direction. Something was afoot in the wildwood, but I had no idea what.

There was a pile of heavy logs to move, though, and experience has taught me that it is best to do such jobs when the body is warmed up and ready. The work was extreme. I hefted the logs, one by one, over my shoulder and carried them down the hillside, tossed them over the brook, and left them by the path's edge to haul home later with the tractor. Then I returned to where my saw still lay by the remainder of the fallen trees. And I was still. And the silence returned, stealing over land as if it had never left but was only waiting. And soon enough in its wake came again that sense of being watched, and of furtive movement, ever just beyond the eye.

Wiser men might have thought this a great time to head for hearth and home. I guess I am not that wise. But no one ever grew by running from what they did not know.

I left the chainsaw where it lay in the snow beside the half-cut logs and ventured up the little hill. The hill was skirted by old trees: a mix of birch, maple, and evergreens. At its top, the woods changed abruptly and before me lay a coppice wood of slender birches and poplars between ten and twenty feet tall. They grew thick and I wove between them, automatically making note of which to harvest come summer. Coppice woods were a valuable resource for a sustainable homestead. A coppiced tree is created when a mature trunk with well-established roots is cut. If it is a species that will form coppices, the roots quickly shoot forth multiple saplings from the stump. The saplings grow fast due to their established roots and their leaves feed the rootstock. Coppiced tree roots only ever get the youthful hormones of young saplings and thus never seem to age. They are nearly immortal and the rootstocks can last for centuries if the forester is careful to always leave saplings to feed the roots. And the saplings have so many uses. Young ones make good fence posts as well as wattle to build hurdles and walls. Older saplings make good logs and firewood. And because coppice woods regrow so fast, it is a very sustainable kind of forestry. In fact, coppicing trees is a traditional forestry technique that dates back into prehistoric Europe. The homestead has a few acres of maintained coppice woods that we draw upon regularly.

Here in the thick of the dense coppice woods, I paused, suddenly realizing I was unsure where I was going or what exactly I was looking for. Now and then there were the almost whispered notes of something padding ever so lightly on snow...eerie footfalls that seemed to come from somewhere and nowhere. And the growing certainty of a presence.

No...of myriad little presences.

I knew: I wasn't alone in the wildwood.

Animal? Spirit? I wasn't nervous. I was what you might call cautiously curious, and I found my mind drifting back to a similar day long ago, when I dwelt far-deep in the limitless reaches of the Alaskan wilderness...

◆ ◆ ◆

Our Alaska cabin was fifty miles from the nearest tiny village and over twenty miles to the road. It was truly wild country: the kind where you didn't go to the outhouse without a rifle because you might have to scare off a grizzly, and you didn't go into the sticks without survival gear because if something went wrong, no one was going to come looking for you. We lived on caribou and enormous trout and burbot from lakes, some of which may never have been fished before. We gathered berries and mushrooms from the high tundra. We harvested rhubarb and feral greens from an abandoned cabin whose owner had passed away decades earlier. And we heated our little cabin with firewood we gathered from a glen less than a mile away—a beautiful wood of tall cottonwoods, shady white spruce, little hidden lakes of wild swans and loons and piercing golden sunbeams. The glen was a remarkable place of primal beauty so intense it could melt the heart with its unearthly sweetness during the endless sunlight of the warm months. And it was one brisk September day I found myself in that glen carrying a rifle and moving with the slow caution of a tracker bent on silence and the hunt.

It was a beautiful day, not at all unlike this March day. Sunbeams poured through the dense canopy of tall spruce boughs like spears of molten gold. Scattered birches and regal cottonwoods sported cloaks of buttery leaves not quite ready to relinquish their trees, yet now and then when a gentle breeze blew overhead some fell nonetheless, so that the forest floor was carpeted in brown, red, and gold hues. It had rained the day before, and the leaves still held the dampness, which worked for me, as they were soft and soaked up any sound I might have made. Today I was seeking a bull moose whose tracks I had come across recently while gathering late-season mushrooms. A moose would provide enough meat to see us through the winter and well into next spring. It would make a godsend of hide, as well, that we could tan to serve as blankets or provide any number of other uses.

I had been in the forest since sunup. The only time you really got a sense of a normal day and night cycle in the far north was during the between-times of spring and autumn. Daphne had fed me a hearty breakfast of fried trout and toast and then I had set out. I had been out for hours and hours and figured it was now somewhere near mid-afternoon. I had had no luck picking up the moose's trail, though. Last night's heavy rain had washed it away.

But I'd lived in the wilderness a long time, and I had long ago developed a second sense of where things were, or would go, and I was following my instincts. Yet the whole time I had this nagging intuition that I was following something, but not my moose.

Daphne lies on the small dock in front of the cabin where we lived many years deep in the Alaskan wilderness. The vast lake before the cabin is just beginning to melt and innumerable aquatic birds returning for spring occupy her attention.

Slipping through the dark woods, I passed tracks of wolves and found a sudden descent that dropped to a secluded little lake at the bottom of a sequestered valley. I stood hidden in arboreal shadow and saw the elegant forms of a small flock of wild swans down there, gliding over clear water as still as lead crystal except for the gentle wakes they raised. The lake was too small and sheltered for the slight breeze to stir it in the least. It never ceased to amaze me that here, in the heart of one of the harshest wildernesses on Earth, one could find creatures of such unearthly beauty and delicate grace as those swans below. I watched them for a while, then followed my instincts on, going ever deeper into the vast glen, far into regions I'd never before explored, always moving slowly, careful to keep the wind in my face so as not to betray my scent to anything ahead of me, careful to walk only where the damp duff was thick and free of twigs so as not to make a sound.

And the further I went, the more I had that sense of little presences, movements in the forest. Of being watched. It was an eerie feeling, but not like the wary edge I have felt when encountering a place of danger, such as the haunt of a grizzly. It was more like ... well, more like a sense of cautious anticipation. As if I was about to stumble upon a secret that could be dangerous but didn't want to be.

And then I came across the bull moose's tracks. They crossed right in front of me, heading to my right. And they were fresh. I turned and followed them. The woods were thick and shadows fell from towering cottonwoods. Graceful silver birches filled any space between them. And suddenly I came to something I would never have guessed to find. The woods opened into a tiny grassy meadow, perfectly rectangular, perhaps an acre in size. There were no telltale stumps to mark a woodcut and no scars of removed stones—none of the signs that might indicate this strange clearing was due to the hand of Man. It was as if the forest itself had parted around a sacred space. And at its very heart a tiny hillock rose from the meadow, looking like nothing less than a faerie sidhe of ancient Gaelic legend. And of all places, here in the depths of the Alaskan wilderness. I knew the aboriginal folk believed in faeries ... the Inuqun, who were so like the faerie beings of the myths of the Old World.

I have very good ears, and I heard faint movement I knew right away came from halfway up the little meadow in the woods on the left. Perhaps the moose I sought. I dropped and lay flat on the soft grass, unshouldering my rifle as I did and quietly working the bolt action to jack a shell into the chamber. I could tell by the sound that whatever made the noise was large and growing closer. It would emerge from the woods some fifty yards away; point-blank range for a good rifle. It would be an easy shot. The wind was in my face and the tall grass concealed me. It would never know I was there.

And then I felt again that sense of being watched, powerful and piercing, and the press of a great presence. It was like the light but certain touch of fingers on the side of the neck. Like the touch of strong sunlight on the skin. I felt it to my right and looked that way. And in a nearby birch right at the forest's edge was a tiny boreal owl no bigger than my open hand. It sat there, wrapped in a cloak of silence, watching me with piercing, large eyes. I watch it back, frozen in the moment, and had this sense that nothing that would happen in the next few minutes would be as I had thought, for here I had stumbled into an enchanted place and was only just realizing it.

There was the sound of movement again, from the same location fifty yards up to the left, this time of twigs breaking as something large pushed through brush and fading ferns. I pulled my mind back into the moment, back into the practical. I had to get a moose. We had to eat. I set the butt of the stock firmly into the cradle of my shoulder, rested my index finger lightly on the trigger guard. One shot into the chest at the bone plates of the forelegs would drop the creature on the spot, punch through both lungs, and make its death quick and clean. A respectful death for worthy quarry. In my mind, I began the shaman's prayer I always say over a fallen beast of the hunt:

> *I am sorry to kill you, Brother.*
> *I did so of need and not of want . . .*

But it was not a bull moose that emerged from the forest's edge. Instead, a caribou doe emerged, and then another. Graceful as the wind in white clouds, they ghosted over the tall grass of the meadow and loped straight to the little hillock and broke around it like water. Neither glanced left or right. The wind was in my face. They could not see or smell me. I was a ghost; they could not know I was there. And off to the right of the meadow they went, leaving in their wake only that sacred silence.

And then another caribou emerged from the woods, a huge old buck, the lord of this little herd, there was no doubt. He did not lope across the meadow, but trotted, head held high and proud, a massive rack of antlers upon his brow like a crown. Glancing neither left nor right, he started across the meadow but he did not break around the hillock but surmounted it, and at the very top he stopped, turned his head and looked right at me. He knew! Somehow, he knew I was there! I was just a shadow among the grass. I offered him no scent of Man. The wind was in my face masking even the sound of my breath, but somehow he still knew.

And I had him. He only stood there, still as stone, an arrow-shot away, filling the crosshairs of my rifle's scope. I could take him and end my hunt here and now with enough meat for months. But in my soul, as he looked at me, I knew something far more important than a hunt was transpiring in this sacred moment. It wasn't that I felt it was wrong to hunt of need. Such is a ritual that has gone on since the first life at the dawn of the world. But this moment had become something far more. And so there I lay on the cold, wet earth, in a perfectly square meadow that should not be, in some eerie nexus between the piercing gaze of Brother Caribou and Owl. I clicked the safety of the rifle in place, rendering it impossible to fire, and let it rest over the ground. The caribou only continued to watch and the meadow became bright gold as overhead a marshmallow cloud emitted a spear of sunlight that fell over the lord of the herd.

The moment could not have been more splendid.

And then the caribou leapt down the hillock and trotted to the far side of the meadow, disappearing into the wood where his does had vanished a moment before. I lay there a long time, and the whole time the little owl only sat in the tree regarding me with those keen and relentless eyes. I felt then and still feel to this day that my whole life had led to that moment, a meeting place of shared consciousness suspended in a sunbeam. I believe that was the day I became brothers with a caribou and the spirit of Deer became one of my guides.

But the day was not done with me. The magic was not over. I stood up, shouldered the rifle, nodded to the boreal owl whose great gold eyes said and asked a thousand things. In perfect silence. I turned back the way I had come. The light was failing and I had miles to go to get back to the cabin. But I had not gone a hundred yards from the meadow when I heard movement in the woods. I froze instantly and turned slower than maple syrup flows on an icy day and saw behind me more caribou slowly working their way through the forest. Ever on the move, these creatures are always migrating, seeking new graze, evading their many predators, looking for something over the next horizon. And I thought again how simple it would be to unshoulder the rifle and take down two or three, giving us as much meat as a bull moose and setting us up well to get through winter. But everything has its time, and another part of me understood today was no longer a day to hunt. It never had been. Myself just hadn't realized it yet. But my Self always knew …

So I stood there, still as stone, letting the innumerable tree trunks and scrub around me break my outline, letting myself dissolve in the shadows, letting my scent vanish with the wind in my face. And so the caribou could not see me. Their eyes are not as good as a man's. The herd began to pass around me, not running as creatures afraid—not as prey—but as creatures who also shared this wood, this life, this sacred Earth. They passed and they passed and the light grew ever weaker, and if they smelled my scent as they passed to the downwind side of me, they still took no notice of me. They only paused to nibble this and that, unalarmed.

One great buck stopped just two feet from me and lowered its antlered head to browse. Ever so slowly, no faster than the big hand of the clock moves, I extended my left arm and brushed its fur. It took no notice. It moved on and another passed and I slipped my fingers through its fur. I was just another tree in the forest, my arm a branch to brush it.

And so the herd passed, and some I petted as they went. And how many people can say they have petted wild caribou among the taiga? But I had, in an enchanted forest, in the beams cast by a westering sun. And it was the very essence of magic!

◆ ◆ ◆

And all these years later, upon this quiet day in the north woods of Nova Scotia, the land again had such a feel. There was magic in the wood, amidst sunbeams, shady boughs, and sacred silence. So I wandered through the coppice wood, and from there into a labyrinthine maze of spruce trees. Nearly two decades ago, long before we bought the homestead, the west part of our land had been logged, and the logger must have been drinking something potent, for he had cut out winding paths between hedges of dense spruce, such that one could easily become lost if one did not know to watch the sun or moon to keep one's way. Alas, that strange haphazard maze is much regrown now.

In a clearing at the edge of the Labyrinth, a streamlet born of a not-far-off spring snaked through. It wove between the Five Sisters, ancient maples I often tapped for sugar as the days warmed. They stood tall and wise against a sky of such piercing blue it hurt the eyes in the same way as wonderful candy that is just too sweet makes the teeth ache.

Whenever I walked, the silence fled, the crunch-crunch-crunch of my boots in the dense snow of late winter pushing it away. In the boughs of the many young spruces, I began to see the first hints of activity. Black cap finches flitted to and fro. Red squirrels were up and about, nibbling away at stored cones, leaving heaps of brown-red scales at feeding sites called middens. Tracks of hares were everywhere, dotted with little round droppings like balls of sawdust—signs the hares were eating well. Near the edge of the streamlet, I encountered fresh tracks of a mink that could not seem to decide if it wanted to travel by land or by water, slipping into the stream and going a few yards, then emerging to run along side the stream in its unique inchworm amble. I could visualize the gait of the mink by those tracks in my mind's eye as clearly as if I were watching it with my flesh-and-blood eyes. Thinking of the comical way it inched and slid over the snow—so ungainly on land—made me want to laugh, so I did. And the noise set scurrying a snow-white hare I might have missed had it not moved. It scurried off between the boughs of a copse of mid-sized spruce, and there it stopped, not realizing it stood out there with its white fur against those dark greens and darker trunks.

I knelt to one knee in order to observe the hare. It was plump and healthy looking. The hare's condition told me it was well fed, so we were not over the peak of the population cycle when overpopulation among them leads to starvation. With so many hares about, maybe lynx would be lured in from deeper places in the wild country. And maybe this year I'd finally get a chance to catch sight of the elusive wildcats which I had tracked often but never once actually witnessed with my own eyes. But as I knelt there, watching the still hare some twenty yards off, in my stillness the larger stillness returned, sweeping over like a cloak, and once again it brought that powerful sense of being watched. And again I heard the little movements all around: not the rustling of birds and squirrels in trees, or the padding of hares in soft snow. Just a constant motion, like tiptoeing spirits ever at the corner of the eye.

And I thought: *Why am I out here? What am I looking for?* And I answered myself: *I am looking in the nowhere that is everywhere to find a thing I never lost but did not know I had.*

It was a peculiar thought. A wild, unanticipated kind of thought. The kind you find only in lonely moments of deep silence in far-deep untamed lands, in those rare and precious spaces when you sense the enchantment hidden in the ebb and flow of obvious yet hidden things.

And as if a sudden knowing came upon me, I turned. I looked up. And there it was, sitting in the nook where a great branch joined a stout trunk in one of the ancient maples we call the Five Sisters. A boreal owl, not much bigger than my hand from wrist to fingertips. Golden eyes regarded me with calm and certain interest, in those eyes a wisdom of silences I had known before. It watched me from its perch, and I watched it back.

And so I said to the owl, "Where have you been?"

The Five Sisters are enormous, ancient maples at the edge of the labyrinthine maze of spruce hedges left by a crazed logger a generation ago.

And Owl said, "In the nowhere that is somewhere, the only *where* that matters. And look, I see you brought your Self along."

I felt a swelling at the back of my throat, the shedding of an unknown weariness, the joy of finding renewal. "There were times I nearly lost me, but in those times I always remembered that day I first saw you, and met Brother Caribou, and brushed my fingers through the fur of his subjects. It's kept me whole when times were hard. "

And so there in the golden shafts of a late-winter sun, beneath the arching boughs of great maples and beside the sparkling waters of a spring-fed streamlet where minks play, I found Owl. Or, rather, he found me. And I told him of the years since we first met, of my earnest wife, of my fine daughters, of the simple joys of a faithful dog at one's side and an honest horse under the saddle. Of the pleasures of eating berries from the hedges and the sweet calm of the paddle pushing the canoe. And as the day moved on, I realized myself had really been talking to my Self all along, and Owl—that clever wight—he was only there to make sure we were still together.

Wild Life

The World in a Dead Tree

In life, trees give so much. They provide food for innumerable fungi and simple organisms in the soil. Those organisms in turn look after the tree and at the same time enrich the soil with many nutrients. Above ground, trees' fruits, nuts, and leaves provide for various animals. Lichens, birds, and small mammals shelter among their branches or build homes in the hollows of their trunks. Trees take carbon from the air and transform it with rain and sunlight into sugar. In the doing, they purify water and air by their very existence. And though long-lived, trees—like all living things—must eventually die. But even death is not enough to put an end to the benevolence of trees. Fungi such as the edible dryad's saddle find sustenance in the cellulose of which the tree's wood is made. Over decades, these fungi will reduce the wood to compost and return its nutrients to the earth. And as this process goes about, algae and bacteria will find a cornucopia of nutrients in that developing compost and transfer that bounty out throughout the ecosystem.

But it may take decades for a dead tree to decompose into compost, at least here in the north where biological processes go slower. During that time, many creatures will call the dead tree home. While it stands as a snag, burrowing insects will inhabit it and feed on the cellulose. Woodpeckers will drill it and feed on the insects. Occasionally, they will excavate a deep hole within the trunk to serve as a nest. After the nest serves its purpose, that hole may later house many other animals, including owls, martens, and bats.

As branches topple from the decaying snag, its peak becomes an ideal hunting perch for birds of prey. In the Blueberry Meadow, east of the cottage, I have observed horned and barred owls hunting from the peak of a tall snag that has managed to remain standing despite the winter gales for over a decade, and once even found the eaten carcass of a powerful, predatory pine marten under that snag. I have no idea how an owl managed to kill the far-more-potent marten.

The bones of this pine marten were about fifty feet from a bare old snag where a great horned owl often hunts. There was also a small pile of chicken feathers and bones around the marten, and a few owl feathers. It appears a marten jumped and killed one of our free-range hens, and in the middle of eating the hen the owl got the drop on the marten.

Eventually, though, all snags topple to become logs. Fungi continue their patient, determined work, slowly consuming the cellulose over the years, like the helpful toothed jelly mushroom, a nutrient-rich fungus that tastes something like tofu. As the cellulose is broken down, the soil around the log is enriched with its nutrients and plants begin to gather, digging roots deep into that excellent soil and further breaking down the crumbling wood. Some insects such as carpenter ants still make their homes in the drier sections of the log, and these may become an easy meal for a passing black bear or raccoon.

Long ago this tree was felled by loggers, but the stump was full of carpenter ants which continued to reside in the wood. Recently a black bear stopped in and tore up the decaying stump, eating up the ants for a snack.

As the years pass and the log continues to dissolve, it flattens and the decaying foliage of many previous seasons builds up and composts upon it. It will come more and more to look like a tiny hummock upon the land. This hummock is the last fading memory of the tree. Earthworms and insects are drawn to this rich patch of ground, turning and improving the soil, and they in turn feed countless tiny mammals such as shrews and voles as well as a myriad of birds.

And then the log is gone, and not even a ghost of a hummock remains to remind us it ever was. But even then it still brings good to the land, for its nutrients stay with the soil and enrich many new generations of growth, and that goodness spreads throughout the great, infinitely complex web of life.

Trees are beings who come into the world and share it a little while, and from seed to towering trunk til returning to the Earth Mother, they do only good along the journey of their slow green lives. How gently we should walk among them, with eyes open to all they do for the world.

Enchanted Forest

Gluskabe and the Maple Eaters

Far back in the dreaming dawn of the world, some trees gave very generously. But humans, who are so easily seduced by the easier path, were tempted to laziness by such gifts. And Gluskabe realized if he was to set it right, he must change the fundamental way of things.

In a way, this ancient tale of Wabanaki origin might be likened to the story of paradise lost. It follows a common theme: humans took for granted the free gifts of Nature and unable to bring balance to themselves had to have it compelled upon them. There is a certain sadness in such a tale, despite its almost whimsical telling, that speaks of our kind's repeated inability to learn from our own mistakes.

◆ ◆ ◆

Long and long ago, in the time when great woodlands stretched so deep and tall across the land that a squirrel could travel from Labrador to Florida without ever alighting paw upon Earth, the people known as the Abenaki dwelt in the great Dawn Lands between the northern ice and the southern heat. They grew their food, the good Three Sisters: corn, beans, and squash. The beans fed the corn and squash. The corn made posts for the beans to climb to the sun. And the squash covered the ground so no weed could overrun them. The Abenaki also hunted and fished their green land, and they knew what was good to eat in it.

In those long ago days, Gluskabe sometimes walked the land. He would go here and there, seeing to the well-being of the peoples and the little spirits who were the animals who shared the world with Men.

One day he entered a village and though he looked all about, he could not find the people. Then Gluskabe listened, and he heard the sounds of men and women and children somewhere none too far off, and he made his way to them. Gluskabe found them beneath the boughs of beautiful maple trees, all lying down, all sucking the broken tips of branches still attached to the trees.

"What are you doing?" asked Gluskabe.

The people said they were enjoying the maple syrup the trees gave so generously all through the year. And Gluskabe saw that they were growing fat and lazy and ill-fit to do anything other than suck like parasites from the stately maples. Gluskabe exhorted them to rise and farm, hunt, and fish, and do the things that lead a people to strength and right living with the land. But the people had no heart for it. The maple gave them all they needed. So that very night Gluskabe worked a great change in things. He gathered water and poured it into the hearts of the maple trunks so that it ran from their upper twigs to their lower roots.

The next morning when the Abenaki people went out to the maple grove to feast upon the syrup for their breakfast, they broke off ends of twigs and lay down, but only a thin sap emerged, and it was bitter. Alarmed, they did not know what to do.

Gluskabe came to them and told them what he had done. And he explained to them that he had made it so now they must farm and fish, hunt and live their lives and be strong as a people, for it is the right place of every creature to live well with the land. But Gluskabe was not cruel, only a good teacher, and he told them he would yet leave them with the gift of the wonderful maple syrup, though from here on they must work hard for it. He explained to them that as of now, they could only gather the maple's sap in spring, when it was not clouded and bitter. And they must make vats of birch bark to hold it, and bake stones in a hot fire and toss them in the vats to boil out all the water he had fed the trees. Only then would the sap thicken and once again become the syrup the Abenaki loved.

Gluskabe's work was done, and he left the people. And the people were not at first pleased, but they were the wiser and better for Gluskabe's hard lesson.

—Recounted in the author's words
from myths of the Wabanaki Peoples

Wood Witchery

Sacred Symmetry

Most books on magical practice focus on "what can the magical do for me." And they offer charms and amulets and spells to gain money, influence, friends. But what if this is very much the opposite of the true and deeper ways of magic? Indeed, a self-serving approach to the magical realm makes it little more than one more kind of technology to procure what we want. But what if magic, real magic, is something else entirely?

The Wiccan Rede is a lovely model for thinking more deeply about the nature of real magic. *An it harm none, do what ye will.* I am not a Wiccan, but I find the Rede a beautiful and marvellously complex bit of philosophy. Its full meaning is lost, though, at a casual glance. At first, it would seem to mean do whatever you like so long as it doesn't hurt anyone else. Drink, drug, eat junk food, play video games. Buy a fancy car because it makes you feel good. Live in a giant McMansion because it's posh. Invest in stocks in a fracking company because you'll get rich. Superficially, the Rede would seem to say the sky's the limit as long as it doesn't cause anyone else harm.

But the Rede is far deeper and wiser than that. If we transliterate it into modern vernacular, it would go like this:

An (if) it harm none (not one), do what ye will (whatever you want).

Revised into a modern sentence, it would read: *Do what you desire so long as it harms nothing.* And with such a rendering, we can immediately see it has far broader implications. The Rede is in fact admonishing us to become keenly aware of the outcomes of our choices which ripple outward in ever-expanding circles. Feast now and bring harm to your body through obesity. Buy a decadently large house and a forest must fall to make it. Invest in that hot fracking stock and enable Big Oil to poison another ecosystem. The Rede compels us to examine all our choices and ensure they bring no harm, and so long as that is the case we may do as we desire. It is empowering, liberating, but it also lays immense responsibility on us to choose the path that goes gently and wisely.

It would be rightly observed that it is not possible to get through life without harming a single thing. At the minimum, a person must eat. To do so, a fish must be caught, a sheep must be slaughtered, stalks of grain must be hewn. But the Rede is not naive to such realities. What the Rede tries to do is help us find a lifeway that is in balance. For example, if a farmer who must supply that food opts to take the easy path, he can monocrop a vast field of genetically modified grain, feeding it thousands of pounds of artificial fertilizer and pouring over it thousands of gallons of toxic herbicides, fungicides, and pesticides. Such a field would produce a great deal of grain with a minimum of effort, but it would kill the delicate balance of bacteria and microscopic fungi that enrich the soil. It would destroy pollinating insects such as honeybees and butterflies, and the earthworms that churn soil into rich friable loam. It would kill local birds, raccoons, and other wildlife. The farmer could indeed produce much grain, but grain carrying traces of toxic chemicals, grown on land that has been reduced to a dead canker upon Earth.

Or that farmer might choose a gentler path. He might instead grow grain free of genetic modification. He might interweave his fields with hedges as refuges for wild flora and corridors for wild animals. He might raise livestock on one side of his land and next year sow his crop there, where the livestock's dung has made the soil fertile. Such a farm would absorb carbon from the atmosphere and yield a net of clean oxygen as well as pure water. This is permaculture farming. It is more laborious but it is in ecological balance and promotes the well-being of all the creatures that share the farmer's land as well as the persons who consume his grain. And the Rede recognizes and makes sacrosanct this wiser way.

Many spiritual paths around the world have their own versions of the Rede. The Christian "Do unto others as you would have them do unto you" is probably the most famous. And, of course, shamanry in all its forms around the world is founded upon principles of knowing the difference between need and want so as not to overuse the gifts of Nature. I believe that the Rede's appearance in so many spiritual paths indicates it is an archetype of some of the highest principles of wisdom.

Personally, I have found that when one earnestly seeks the wisdom of balanced living, one becomes part of life's healthy and joyous ebb and flow: stress decreases, health and insight increase, and one begins to perceive the world for what it really is—something green and enchanted and full of marvels. We learn to differentiate that all-important yet oft-elusive difference between need and want. And our minds thus cleared, we can at last experience the pure, green flow of enchantment.

And so this bit of wood witchery is more pensive than practical. Using the methods of whatever path you honor and follow, take time to focus on your tradition's notions of balance. Call it the Rede, the Golden Rule, druidic balance, or whatever else is appropriate to your way. For myself, I think I shall venture into the forest to that quiet place full of the music of flowing water and songs of birds, and sit upon the great stone at the brook's center and journey in spirit into the Underworld and discuss this wisdom with my friends, Owl and Bear and Deer. In that gentle interrelationship ... that is where one finds true magic.

Woods Lore

Gone Mapling

Maples are common trees throughout northeastern North America, and even out west a number of maple species can be found. Once you hit northern temperate woods they become one of the predominant trees, perfectly suited to hot summers with long days and bitter winters with endless nights. There are many maple species, but best known is the sugar maple. It is highly prized for its extremely hard, strong, and easily worked wood. I have built musical instruments from this wood and fully understand why local folk sometimes call it rock maple. It is hard as Earth-forged stone, but it provides strength, beauty, and gorgeous tonal resonance and is cherished by luthiers, especially violin makers. But the sugar maple is also prized for its ability to produce sweet sap. From far and wide, people come to northeastern North America every spring to visit sugar shacks where the great tree's sap is turned into syrup and try hot pancakes with new maple syrup or maple candy made by boiling the sap extra dense and letting it crystallize. However, other trees yield sweet sap, too, and in the far north the humble but ubiquitous birch is a favorite springtime sugarbush. Getting sweet sap and converting it to syrup and candy is labor intensive but not complicated. With a small investment in the requisite tools, anyone with access to some trees can do it.

You will need only a few tools to harvest tree sap: (1) spiles, (2) buckets, (3) a drill or hand brace, and (4) a place to boil it.

A spile is a just a small metal tube, slightly cone-shaped, with a hook at one end. They can be acquired from many farm-supply stores where maple trees are abundant. They can also easily be found online. With a little carving skill, spiles can also be fashioned out of wood, though I recommend going with metal or plastic as forgotten wooden ones will rot in trees and introduce decay. Tapping maples is harmless if done right, but if done wrong it can be detrimental to the tree.

A typical metal spile. Drill a small hole just big enough to fit the cone about one-third of the way into the trunk. Orient it long-side down. Tap lightly with a hammer or stone to firmly set it. Hang the bucket by its eye from the hook.

Traditional metal maple buckets hung from spiles in an old maple tree near the Firefly Brook. I find old trees, especially if they have been damaged in the past, give the sweetest spring sap.

The buckets are just that: containers to hold the sap as it slowly drips out through the spile. A sap bucket typically will hold only a gallon, so it can't overload and pull the spile from the tree as it fills up. Also, a sap bucket is usually slightly cone shaped so it can lean better against the tree's trunk. A well-made sap bucket has a reinforced eyelet near the rim to bear the increasing load as it fills. Maple buckets come with lids, too, to keep bits of bark and other detritus from falling into the sap. If it sounds confusing now, trust me: the whole process of tapping a tree for sap is so simple that it'll all make sense the moment you start doing it.

Tree sap flows winter and summer, as long as the weather is above freezing, but you only want the early spring sap before the tree leafs out. The early spring sap is water and tree sugar. After that, sap gets cloudy and often bitter as the tree begins to move other substances between its roots and leaves. The time to tap trees is just as spring is breaking, when the days rise just above freezing but nights are still below freezing. As a rule of thumb, I tap maples as soon we get three straight days of above freezing weather.

To tap a maple, select a tree of at least one-foot diameter. Use a drill or hand brace to drive a hole about one inch into the tree somewhere between waist and chest height. I prefer the reliable old-fashioned hand brace as there are no batteries to worry about malfunctioning in the cold. There is nothing more frustrating than hiking all the way out to your sugarbushes to start work and discovering the battery of a portable drill has petered out. Also, a hand brace is far more environ-mentally friendly. I cannot tell you exactly what size bit to use because it varies somewhat depending on the spile maker. Use a bit as big as the smallest end of your spile plus 25 percent. Drill bit sizes between ¼- and ⅓-inch diameter are typical. You can put more than one tap in a tree; it depends on its circumference. I tap trees roughly every two feet of their circumference. It will not harm the tree. Animals put thousands of small holes in trees over the course of their lives, so a few maple taps each year will make little difference. The holes will quickly dry out and seal when you remove the spiles after the season. Do not try to fill or cover the holes. It inhibits the tree's own healing process.

After making the hole, use a hammer or the back of a small forest axe (I've even just used a handy stone) to lightly tap in the spile, longest side downward. You want to seat it just firmly enough to seal the hole and support a full bucket, but not set it so tightly you cannot remove the spile at the end of the season. There is a bit of skill in learning to set a spile just right but you'll develop it quickly with practice. You can test the grip of the spile by hanging a bucket and pushing down on it. There should be no play in the spile. If there is, lightly tap it in just a bit more. Be careful not to hammer with too much force or you could split the frozen wood of the tree's outer trunk, which will cause sap to leak around the spile rather than into it. If you do get a leak, do not tap the same tree elsewhere or you might overstress it. Remove the spile and tap another tree.

That's it! Just leave the buckets. Depending on conditions, they can take a day or up to a week to fill. The temperature must drop below freezing by night and rise above freezing by day or the sap will not flow. It flows best when nights are biting cold but days are clear and warm. It flows poorly on clouded days. When conditions are ideal, I check my taps every day. If days are cloudy, I check the taps every three days. Other factors will also play a role in how vigorously the sap will flow, including the tree's size and age, whether it is situated near a good water source, atmospheric pressure, and more. Given how rare ideal conditions are, I find twenty taps will yield an average of enough sap to make a gallon of syrup per week. Sap does not store well at room temperature, so until you're ready to start boiling, store the sap outside in sealed buckets to keep it cold and fresh.

Once the nights rise above freezing and the trees get well into budding, the sugaring season quickly comes to a close. You'll know that time when you get your first bucket of clouded sap. You can use the first clouded buckets of the season but soon the trees will start producing bitter sap. So when you see those first clouded buckets, that means it is time to remove the spiles so the holes can heal. Do this gently, tapping the spiles side to side with a hammer or hatchet and wriggling them around till they come loose. They pop out easily if you have not set them improperly tight. Eventually you will break a spile in a tree. Just leave it. The tree will heal around it, and you would do more harm trying to dig it out.

It takes a minimum of forty gallons of sap to make a gallon of syrup, and that's from a very good sugar maple. If you tap a silver or red maple, ratios can be 50:1 or even 60:1. If you tap birches, which yield a wonderful minty sap, ratios are closer to 80:1. Because of the work involved, we only tap sugar maples, which are abundant in this part of the world anyway.

To render the sap into syrup, simply boil it on a high flame to drive off excess water. Traditionally this was done on an open fire in a *sugar shack*, hundreds of gallons at a time in a vast cauldron. At our woodland cottage, we usually boil it off in a five-gallon, stainless steel pot. Whether outdoors on an open fire or on the stove, we wait til we have collected a good forty gallons of sap then set it to a hard boil, adding sap each time the pot reduces to one-half full. When we add the last sap, we begin to watch carefully for the transformation to sugar syrup.

It is important to watch carefully after you add the last bucket of sap. If you let the sap boil much too long, it will become thick and burn in the pot, ruining all that hard work. If you let it boil a little too long, it will become syrup but will then crystallize over a few days while in the jars. If it is too thin, it will be sweet but watery, and it won't keep. We have found a good rule of thumb is to be aware of when you are near that all-important 40:1 ratio and start watching carefully for a pale tan foam to develop over the roiling sap. When it appears, let the sap boil five minutes longer then take it off the heat. Once it stops roiling but while it's still plenty hot, ladle it into clean canning jars, and seal. The density of the sugar content keeps it from spoiling.

If you want to make maple candy, let the sap continue to boil over a low heat til the sound of the liquid changes. It will start to make a popping sound, the way a pot of oatmeal does as it simmers. Let it cool then pour into forms (like an ice cube tray) and set the forms outside on the snow to chill.

But here's a tip a lot of people don't know: maple sap is a wonderful beverage. Try drinking it right out of the sap bucket and I am sure you'll be hooked. It has a light, delicate flavor and is a marvellous thirst quencher. It tastes like new spring!

APRIL'S JOURNEY

Green Man's Blood

[In] Hungarian mythology, the world is separated into three
layers, the upper world of the gods, where we find the sun and
moon, the middle world of men, and the lower world of the dead.
These three worlds are connected by a tree whose branches
support the sky, while its roots go down into the underworld.

—Theodora Goss

Hungarian Fairies

As soon as the emerging spring brought about three straight days above freezing, Daphne and I set out into the woods to tap maples. The snow was still deep and the going hard, but the sugar season is brief and getting enough sap to make a year's worth of syrup means starting as soon as the sap begins to flow. What happens is that at night the temperature dips and the sap in a tree trunk freezes. This expands the sapwood, which creates suction and draws liquid sap up from the root system. When day comes, the sun warms the sapwood and it contracts, pushing the sap up into the boughs. The sweet sap feeds the budding leaves and wakens the tree's spirit. This slow expansion and contraction of the sapwood deep within the tree—when you think about it—is like the beating of a heart. A tree does indeed have a heart. It beats once a day when spring comes. And it is this slow, arboreal pulse which causes the flow of sap as if it were the Green Man's own lifeblood.

For weeks after setting the taps, the girls and I trekked through the snow every other day dragging a small sled to the maple trees. It was hard going when the sled was empty, and much harder coming back when it held up to twenty gallons of sap, but the days grew slowly warmer and bit by bit the snow receded. About three weeks into mapling season, the snow in the open places was mostly gone. The first songbirds had returned, woodpeckers were tap-tap-tapping the snags, and the grass of meadows was showing the first hint of greening. And much to our relief, with the snow gone, the work of retrieving gallons and gallons of sap became much less onerous. It was far easier to carry a pair of five-gallon buckets filled with sap a quarter mile to the tractor than it was to try to drag a loaded sled through several feet of snow. But we also knew the warm weather would soon end the sugar season.

But one evening, just near the middle of the night, a smear of cloud rolled over the horizon. There were no great winds to announce it. No sudden fluctuations in temperature. In our cottage deep in the highland forest, we had gone to bed to the first sprinkling of ice pellets and thought it no more than a passing frozen rain, and awakened the next morning to find more than three feet of snow had covered all the land. Transformed overnight, the great forest became a domain of ice as winter again sought to reassert itself. But the sun returned the very next day, and with it a determined spring. The sugar season was extended, but it also meant I was back to having to break trail through dense snow to retrieve the sap.

But it had to be done. For a traditional homestead, maple syrup is an essential. We use it for far more than pouring over pancakes. It is the perfect sweetener for our incredibly healthy chaga tea, and we baste it over venison and pork hams, and even cheeses, that will go into the smokehouse. Not only does it improve the flavor, but they seem to absorb the smoke better with a good maple baste. I even use it in lieu of brown sugar in some of the hard cider I brew come autumn, and it adds that certain special something. So, we needed at least five gallons of syrup to get us through a year. Preferably ten. Making that much means collecting a minimum of two hundred gallons of sap; a lot of work at the best of times, but the recent snow would make it a backbreaking task. For even though some maple trees grew close to the cottage, we had to go a good way to get to the best sugarbushes.

You see, not every tree is ideal to tap. Experience has taught me that old trees yield the most and sweetest sap. Especially those near a flowing water source such as a brook or spring. And trees that show the scarring of an old injury (such as an old, healed split in the trunk), will yield sap that is all the sweeter. By tapping only such trees, I have been able to get sap to syrup ratios as low as 35:1. But such trees are rare. Within a third of a mile of the cottage, there are just seven that meet my specifications. Five of them grow in a small, roughly circular glade that I call the Nemeton, the name of the sacred groves of the ancient druids. When the sky is clear and it's a degree or two above freezing by day, we can expect yields in excess of ten gallons every other day from just those five trees. They are huge, ancient matrons of the forest, and they are blessed to grow beside a vigorous artesian spring that flows year-round. Well fed, with deep-running roots and branches that ascend well above the neighboring trees, it is no wonder they provide such fine sap.

◆ ◆ ◆

Two days after the great late-spring snow, my younger daughter and I headed out to the west side of the land to gather the sap at the Nemeton.

There is a dirt path running along the southern side of the homestead and we took the tractor down it. Normally, we would just hike such a small distance, but there would be a lot of sap to haul back. And we both knew that by the time we got it out of the woods, we'd be bushed.

When we reached the little trailhead, I parked the tractor just off the path. We climbed off the tractor and each took in hand an empty five-gallon bucket. We waded through the icy stream, our knee-high, -40 C rated winter boots keeping our feet dry, and climbed the embankment on the other side. Entering the forest, we could see we would have our work cut out for us. The Nemeton was several hundred yards away, the old sugar maples towering over the other trees with branches uplifted as if praying to Father Sun. The going was all uphill, over ground that was treacherous with fallen logs and hidden depressions. But to make it worse, the deep snow had been warming by day and freezing by night, and we both knew that would give it a tricky crust. It would seem to support us and make for easy walking, then break and try to trip us the moment we trusted it.

Natalia looked me up and down as if appraising. I knew what she was thinking; the same thing I was. I'm two hundred pounds, and with the winter gear I was wearing, pushing two-twenty. The snow crust was going to break every other step for me. She smirked and said, "You know, the advantage of being a girl is I'm light enough to walk on top of this stuff all the way there." Then she stepped off the embankment and the crust gave way and she face-planted most ungracefully.

I rolled my eyes and tried to keep from chuckling. I almost succeeded, but soon she and I were both laughing. "Come on!" I told her, stepping out in front of her. "This is one of those times where brute strength is going to be more useful than a light touch." I marched off the embankment down into the snow. I was heavy enough the crust couldn't hold me most of the time, and I forced my way ahead, breaking a path she could follow more easily. But it was bloody hard work. The snow was the dense pellet kind, more like wet sand than the usual deep winter fluff. Our going was slow. I'd push forward fifty feet or so then stop and pant for a bit. I'd liken it to the exertion of climbing a vertical cliff with a fifty-pound pack strapped to one's back.

Natalia said, "We should have worn snowshoes."

I shook my head. "They would sure float us on the way in, but on the way out, when we're carrying the sap, even snowshoes wouldn't float us. We'd just end up tripping and spilling all the sap. No, the only thing to do is break a trail all the way there. We can walk that trail back out, carrying the sap safely, and we can re-use it over the coming days. It'll get a little better every time we walk it."

As we moved away from the brook with its hedge of hardwoods, we came to open ground. Natalia pointed and delightedly yelped, "Look!" She was pointing at the fresh tracks of hares, probably made that very morning. The tracks scampered here and there, the hares easily floating over the snow with their big feet. They had been nibbling away at the bases of trees, stripping back the outer bark for the nutritious cambium beneath.

"A lot of hares this year," I told her. "A whole lot of hares." I noticed movement off north, in the sky, and pointed. "See that bald eagle? It lives here, just beyond our land back in the Rusalka Wood with its mate. I've watched them for years, they and their young, sailing over the wild meadows and hunting. It will be a good year for them."

Natalia said, "I've noticed lots of hare tracks at the cottage, too."

I nodded again. "I know. I've seen them." As we walked, I explained the hares' population cycle to her. They were starting to put our fruit trees at risk, so Daphne, her mother, had in autumn wrapped foil around the base of the fruit trees to protect them from the hares. In spring she'd have to remove that foil so moisture didn't build and cause mold to set on the trunks. "But it won't be enough," I told her. "They always seem to find ways to get at the trees if not stopped."

In the shelter of the dense spruces, the snow is shallower and softer. Natalia and Willowisp pause to examine numerous hare tracks as we make our way to the great old maples to retrieve today's harvest of sap.

Natalia knew that meant I'd have to hunt the hares. We liked them and were happy to have them around the rest of the homestead, but when their numbers became so high they began attacking the fruit trees, they had to be culled. She wasn't squeamish about that, though. She'd grown up in the Alaskan wilderness and understood such things.

The eagle I had pointed out began to spiral as it rode thermals to a higher elevation, then it leveled off over the meadow again, continuing its hunt. "The eagles and falcons, and the owls and wildcats and coyotes, and the martens, will help bring the hares' numbers down. We'll leave it to Nature for now and see what we have to do as needs require."

We continued pressing toward the Nemeton. We had been at it over ten minutes and only covered a hundred yards, such was the effort of breaking trail in the deep snow. Often, there were little clefts and declines in the ground that the snow hid, now and then sending us for a tumble. As we went, I had Natalia practice carrying her bucket low to the ground so that if she felt herself losing balance, she could press the bucket into the snow as she went down. A fall in deep snow would not hurt her, and the precautionary technique would keep the precious sap from being lost.

We came across another little thicket of white spruces, and their needles were dark against the bright contrast of the sunlit snow. Tiny twig tips and shattered cones lay beneath the spruce, evidence red squirrels had been at the trees. But Natalia paused again and pointed to a pile of teardrop-shaped pellets. "More hares?" she asked.

I shook my head. "No, those are whitetail deer droppings." I withdrew my folding knife and flicked the blade open, then used it to break open a pellet. "You see how it looks like its made of sawdust? That means it was made sometime between late autumn or over the winter, when deer are having to settle for eating lichen and twig tips and whatever else they can find to fill their stomachs. There is lots of cellulose—the stuff that makes up wood—in that kind of browse, and when the deer pass the pellets, the droppings are basically just little packets of sawdust. Sometimes I collect them and use them for starting campfires. They burn like rolled-up newspaper and catch a spark if you break them up to use flint and steel on them."

"So a deer left them last autumn?" she asked.

I shook my head. "No, this deer came through here not long ago. In fact, sometime within just the last couple days. Otherwise, the pellets would not be sitting on top of the snow."

We pressed on and forged our way to an old rock wall, the remnants of a Scot's homestead long since abandoned and vanished. We scurried over it. I paused to clear brush from the rock wall so we could make the return trip with less chance of tripping over tangling branches. The snow here, on the open side of the slope, was less dense and Natalia forged on ahead the last fifty yards to the first of the great old maples.

Natalia pauses at the first two of the Five Sisters, the ancient maples in the Nemeton that provide the majority of our sap. Notice the black taps in the tree on the right with hose stretching away. These are a new style of plastic spile. An airtight hose is attached to them and the sap runs down the hoses to buckets on the ground. This eliminates the risk of buckets blowing off trees in winter storms and reduces the amount of detritus that trees are always shedding getting into the sap. It's getting harder and harder to find traditional metal buckets and taps these days because this new style is very effective. In the second photo, you can see a pair of three-gallon recycled ice cream buckets being used to collect the sap from two of the large trees. On a single sunny day, a single tree will nearly fill one of these buckets.

At the tree, she inspected the sap buckets for debris. Trees always shed bits of bark, and no matter how leafless they look after a long winter, there are always desiccated leaves sequestered among their tangling branches, as well as winged maple seeds and dried lichen. After I'd finished clearing most of the snow and snarled raspberry canes from the stone wall, I glanced toward her and saw she was using her fingers to pick out some bits of bark. I approached Natalia as she finished and poured one of the collection buckets into her large carry bucket and covered it. "That's how you do it!" I told her earnestly, and waited for her to reset the collection bucket, then we continued on to the next group of old maples, growing right beside a streamlet created by an artesian springhead where a thick patch of aquatic mint grows.

I walked to the farthest tree, set down my carry bucket and lifted the collection bucket's lid to inspect the sap. There was no detritus in it. I poured the sap into my five-gallon carry bucket. Maple sap has a scent that is distinct, like maple, but also like vanilla. It is very pleasant. "Smell that!" I said to Natalia and moved so she could lean over and draw in a whiff.

"It smells like the forest!" she declared.

I nodded. "It is the forest. The pure essence of spring and earth and sky."

I looked up the trunk of the massive tree. How many times I had visited this little place in all the seasons. Various tasks brought me out this way. In spring, it was the gathering of maple sap. In summer I often came to the Nemeton to pass the days among June flies and songbirds, deep in thought, and to watch wildlife. I had built a small camp not far off, a small place to listen to drums and burn incense of sumac and pearly everlasting as part of shaman rites to commune with the spirits of Nature. In winter I hiked through to track the activities of wildlife at the far west of the Elfwood. A pack of coyotes lived not too far away, as well as the bald eagle family, and the park-like open woods here were also home to innumerable hares, red squirrels, rodents, deer, and even the occasional fisher and bobcat. In autumn I had ascended the tree more than once to scout the terrain for deer, and a few times I had even passed days in it with my bow if it seemed some deer were coming through.

I reached out and laid my palm gently upon the ancient tree's bark. It was rock hard and cold as the day, but I liked to imagine I could feel it's arboreal heart pulsing slow but sure with the coming and going of the sun.

The old maple was a mini-ecosystem in itself. There is an amazing complexity of life that grows in the company of every tree, and the old ones are virtual avatars of the whole web of life. A tree's root system is as big as the visible part of the tree. Deep roots punch down into the depths of the earth, through the topsoil, down into clay and gravel and weaving round and about bedrock. In those depths, a well-rooted tree finds secure strength to hold it against mighty wind storms, and it finds water to sustain it through even the driest seasons. But there is more going on in those unseen places than merely good footing and water. A whole subterranean world exists in symbiosis beneath the tree—one so rich and complex we are only now on the very cusp of awareness of it. In a cubic yard of undisturbed forest soil, there can be some fifteen thousand species of bacteria, fungi, and protozoa. They play innumerable roles in improving the soil and protecting the tree.

Some of those subterranean fungi grow in the form of tiny threads no thicker than a single cell, but some form large ropy clusters. They live in a mycorrhizal relationship with the tree. They grow next to or even slightly embedded into the tree's stringy feeder roots and form extensions for those roots, seeking out and transporting nutrients to the tree: minerals, nitrogen, phosphates, and other things a tree finds essential. The tree transports these basic nutrients to its leaves where they are blended by sunlight into food. But a tree does not make all this food for itself. It sends as much as 40 percent back down and out through its root system. The food disperses into the soil, and it feeds the surrounding bacteria, protozoa and mycorrhizal fungi. Some of these fungi, you may know. The delectable chanterelle and the equally delicious but lesser known penny bun are two. This infinitely complex, delicate balance of interwoven life around a tree's root system takes decades to form and perfect. It is sobering to consider that when you see a tree, the wealth of life and activity going on below ground where you cannot even see is literally more complex than the mind can grasp, and all that amazing complexity is absolutely essential to the well-being of every living thing in the world. It is the strength of cohesion, community, harmony—perhaps the very origin of the notion of love.

But this remarkable web of life is not only below ground. I could look at the maple in front of me and see that, for around the great old trunk was a complex collection of lichen and algae. The algae appeared as just a pale greenness lower down on the side facing the streamlet where humidity was highest. The lichen grew up the trunk and well up into the branches in all manner of shapes and sizes. Some were like patches of tiny ferns. Some resembled dark clusters of tiny cones. Others looked like dull-hued corals and beards of old men.

Actually, lichen is a bonding of two kinds of life that come together to support one another in a profound symbiosis. One part is a fungus— the basis of any mold or mushroom. The other part is plant-based: cells of algae if it's green; cells of cyanobacteria if it's bluish. The fungus provides a tough shelter for the plant part and effectively collects water and nutrients. The plant part, in return, turns those nutrients into food that it shares with the fungal cells. The bonding of fungus and plant makes the lichen an extremely resilient organism, and it can grow in some of the most unlikely places: upon bare rock surfaces, high up in the Arctic, coating old stone walls and even upon the rugged bark of ancient maples. Windblown dust and mist on humid days are all a lichen needs to survive. Thinking of that lichen reminded me of a good marriage—something I have been privileged to experience over the last twenty-three years of my life. Two beings come together in love, work to make each other better, and from that union a whole is created that is much greater than the sum of the parts.

I looked into the spreading boughs of the old maple and recalled an autumn I had climbed into this very tree, secured my backpack to the trunk with a rope, and was so comfortable I had allowed myself to fall asleep. I awoke late at night to the soft hooting of an owl in the nearby Rusalka Wood, a great haunted grove of ancient deciduous trees that began a quarter mile further down the mountain valley. There was a full moon that night and the welkin was clear as a crystal ball. The sky was a vast firmament of twinkling stars and through the branches I could make out the constellation Orion, peaked by huge, red Betelguese and Bellatrix, and off its shoulder the beautiful star, Aldebaran. On very dark, clear nights one could spot within Orion the Great Nebula and the galaxy of Andromeda appearing like faint hazes. But that night the full moon drowned out the subtler celestial bodies and created throughout the forest a hoary illumination, casting all the trees and ferns in hues of silver contrasted by sharp ebon shadows. The branches undulated in a gentle breeze, unseasonably warm, as if moving to a languid tune, and the preternaturally bright moonlight wove through the half-bare branches and fell over the ground swimming in the way light moves at the bottom of pools.

There in the autumn darkness, yet rich with lingering summer, I watched little brown bats, and some much larger species of bat, flit around the tree, hunting moths and other late-season insects. In the tree opposite me, I espied a cavity in a rotten branch and knew a woodpecker family had made of it a home during the spring. And in a frost crack that had opened out in the side of the trunk, there resided at least one red squirrel. Aloft in the branches was a small bird's nest, long abandoned, and I did not know the species that had made it. But what I did know was this one great old tree was a World Mother in itself. Trees only give. Of all the creatures of Earth, they must be the angels.

Back in the present, I emptied more collection buckets into my carry bucket and re-hung them on their spiles. Maple sap continued to drip rapidly from the spiles, tapping into the now-empty metal buckets. I stepped back away from the tree, taking in all its vast, magnificent form. I had a sudden sense of it as a person then. A wondrous, kind, and patient person whose very nature was benevolence and generosity.

I stopped my backward steps, turned and looked at the other great old maples, and also took in the plethora of surrounding white spruces, and the mix of alders, willows and birches that are so common throughout the forest. And I knew then—all trees share in this kindly nature. They are the scions of life, the nexus between land and water and sky. They are magic given form—the foundation of the living Earth. And these towering maples, they were like the great oaks of Europe, tall, broad and majestic among their arboreal kin. No wonder the druids of old saw such great trees as sacred. And we too were sharing in their arboreal goodness. What we were doing—it was more than just tapping a tree for sugary sap. It was, when seen well and true, a communion with the Green Man's own life essence.

Natalia and I finished and began the trek out. It wasn't easy going, but at least it was downhill and there was now a broken trail. We made it back to the brook without incident and I carried the heavy buckets across while Natalia skipped over steppingstones. I walked over to the tractor waiting just off the path, fired it up, and drove back to her. She helped me load the sap buckets on the deck then climbed on with me and we started heading back. The powerful little tractor didn't even notice the nearly hundred pounds of additional weight of the sap.

We passed innumerable trees standing in the quiet anticipation of spring. Each was slowly waking with the land, countless arboreal spirits small and great. And already they were sharing their goodness with us, and with so many other creatures interdependent with them. What could we mere mortals do for them? We could care for them. We could live wisely and kindly with them. And we could get to know them. They are the denizens of the enchanted forest, and they have hearts and souls. Slow and green to our quick and red. But we are brothers and sisters of the Earth Mother all the same. And in our communion, there is magic!

Wild Life

The Resurrection of the Brook

Brooks course the forest like blood vessels through a living being, yet in the fickle course of early spring, the banks are rimed with ice even as the land seeks hard to become green again. The wildwood rouses slowly, yawning with great groans of cascading snow-melt. It stretches as boughs of birch and maple shake off icy cloaks. But its reveille goes slowly, cautiously, eons of history having taught the north woods to emerge patiently from its long sleep, for some trees and creatures stir too soon and when night falls with a north wind they succumb to the cold, as happened one year to a huge old poplar near the cottage. That too-soon awakened tree perished in an evening's ice storm, and it has long since gone to the warming of our hearth. But the death of the old tree was a stark reminder that the spring resurrection is a perilous moment for green-sapped and red-blooded creatures alike. They are eager for fresh food and warm sun. Eager for a new season's decadent warmth—and who can blame them—but winter cedes its hold resentfully, and occasionally tries to reassert itself.

A muskrat lives similar to its cousin beaver, but it prefers to whittle away at plants smaller than trees.

At this time it is a marvel to regard the resurrection of the brooks. Only a week or two before, they had been locked in ice. Only at the places the water was deep and the current strong were the brooks able to continue their flow. Their banks were lined with treacherous ice and wherever the brook water raced over stones and kicked up spray, icicles soon came to cover overhanging limbs of trees.

But no matter how much winter resists, spring comes. Coy and shy, flirting with warm sunbeams dappling through tattered clouds now here, now there, spring slowly spreads its influence. While nights yet remain winter's domain, the days of April become resolutely tepid. Sap flows more and more eagerly through the boughs of trees and awakens the insects within. Pileated woodpeckers venture forth and begin their staccato search for those arboreal insects.

As the ice recedes, the brooksides become busier with the activities of beavers and muskrats who emerge from their dens to find new forage. Beavers favor smallish trees that they quickly cut down using their powerful front teeth. They limb them, drag them into the brooks, and move them to feeding areas. Often I have found these trees floating along the banks of the large Rusalka Brook deep in the Hollow, not far from a beaver lodge. After the beavers are done with them, they have been stripped of bark and cambium, branches and even nubs of branches. They are smooth as if roughly sanded and often nearly perfectly straight. I pull them out of the water and sometimes use them as walking staffs.

As spring gains momentum, snow along the braes melts and rushes down into the brooks, which double or triple in depth. The racing water draws air along with it, and because it moves it is especially effective at melting the remaining ice along the bank. Trees near brooks often green up a bit sooner than those further from water.

When the ice clears, wildlife and anglers turn their attention to fishing. The star of the brooks of the northeast is the speckled trout. A diminutive fish that rarely grows more than twelve inches, it is nevertheless a favorite of anglers for its fine meat and the tremendous fight it puts up when caught. I confess to having caught and enjoyed a few myself, though their life cycle is far more fascinating. They are an indicator species and tell us how healthy the land is, for they will only flourish in the purest of regions. If the speckled trout fail in a place, it is most likely due to the depredations of the human species upon the environment.

Speckled trout females find gravelly places in a stream where water percolates through the stone and there lay their eggs which are fertilized by males who draw up alongside them. The eggs hatch in about fourteen weeks. As soon as the new-hatched fry consume their yolk sacks, they begin to feed, at first on nearly microscopic creatures, but soon progressing to the larvae of insects. As they grow larger, they prey upon more mature insects and will eventually feed upon other fish and even voles and frogs if given the chance.

But speckled trout also provide food to many creatures in the ecosystem, and young ones may be preyed upon by other fish, star-nosed moles, even spiders. I have even observed a tall snag at the edge of a birch copse where a great horned owl is fond of perching at the very top. He hunts the surrounding meadow, but I have seen him sometimes whooshing down to the little brook and, to my surprise, emerging with a fine speckled trout in his talons. I hadn't known til then that a horned owl fished like that...like an eagle or osprey.

The brooks of the forest truly are its blood vessels, carrying water and nutrients while providing invaluable habitat for many creatures. They even provide travel routes for species such as beavers and minks, and they are brilliant examples of the interrelations between all living things, for so many creatures' lives revolve around them. They might be likened to the trees for all the good they do.

The yellow-bellied sapsucker and the downy woodpecker look a great deal alike. I am not an expert on birds, but I am sure this is one or the other.

Enchanted Forest

The Water Sprite's Wife

Water is a complex material, existing at any time of the year as solid, liquid, and gas. Like the land, it is the abode of wild flora and fauna and myth bequeaths it numerous spirits, some friendly toward humans, some not, but most disinterested and utterly alien in thought and purpose. Most noteworthy, water seems to hold a unique place as a soul grapple, for in many old legends if a person dies in or near water the soul cannot move on promptly to the afterlife but is caught within water's alternate reality. The myths that speak of the alternate reality of water are ancient, an example being the Celtic tales of the Land Under the Sea, with its own sun and stars, forests and cottages, peoples and palaces. The watery Otherworld is not the proper realm of human souls, so they cannot rest if caught there. Yet it is not a wicked place, either. It might best be likened to the shamanic Underworld. With water's mythic ability to hold the souls of the departed, one could almost think of it as a counter-psychopomp.

Folklore out of eastern Europe has many legends of water's alternate reality and eerie entities. Most noteworthy are the legends of the rusalkas. In some of the old legends, the rusalkas are never-human spirits—they are fey beings entirely of the Otherworld. In other legends, human children and women who perish before their time near water are said to become rusalkas. Whether of mortal or never-human origin, some rusalkas are said to be malevolent, others are merely lost and prankish. Some are just playful, lonely beings who make failing attempts to find love and companionship.

Out of Russia comes this brief faerie tale of a mortal girl who became a rusalka and was married to a water sprite. I should note that at the opening of the tale, where it says the girl was *drowned*, this may not literally mean death by drowning. Concepts of life and death are more relative in the magical/shamanic perception. I once spoke to a Yupik boy who told me his uncle "hung himself til his head popped off" and then traveled the Otherworld. A considerable amount of questioning later revealed that what he meant was his uncle, the village shaman, had a trusted friend asphyxiate him as part of a ritual that led to a powerful spirit journey. In the magical perspective, such metonymies are common.

◆ ◆ ◆

Once upon a time a girl was drowned, and she lived for many years after that with a water-sprite. But one fine day she swam to the shore, and saw the red sun, and the green woods and fields, and heard the humming of insects and the distant sound of church bells. Then a longing after her old life on earth came over her, and she could not resist the temptation. So she came out from the water and went to her native village. But there neither her relatives nor her friends recognized her. Sadly did she return in the evening to the waterside, and passed once more into the power of the water-sprite. Two days later, her mutilated corpse floated on to the sands, while the river roared and was wildly agitated. The remorseful water-sprite was lamenting his irrevocable loss.

—W. R. S. Ralston
Songs of the Russian People

Wood Witchery

Waterways of Power

All Nature is sacred, but there are some places that are especially enchanted. Since deep prehistory high mountaintops, windswept vistas, certain coasts, and forests of ancient growth and deepest green have drawn folk seeking spirit and magic. Walk though these places and you can feel the flow of enchantment. The sense of magic almost crackles in the atmosphere. At such places, the veil between Earth and the Otherworld is thin, so legends accumulate over time as visitors touch now and then upon the deeper green truths of reality. As in the berry flats of Newfoundland, where folk are said to sometimes vanish and reappear a few days later with little memory of what happened save strange music and unearthly cavorting with not-quite-human entities. Or certain sacred valleys of the west where shamans go to converse in secret with ancient spirit guides. The wildwood about our homestead is thick with legends of Acadian, Gaelic, and Mi'kmaq origin, tales of the megumoowesoo spirits and faerie folk and moldering ghosts, and certain remote, pristine places virtually sparkle with eldritch power.

Springs, pools, and brooks hold a special place in old myth as places of power. Around France and the British Isles there are regions where one can hardly find a waterway that doesn't have preternatural legend attached to it, and at many such places it is traditional to leave little bits of food and small gifts for the spirits. I find such places to be extraordinary sites for hikes and camps. Any day I pack out to a remote location like to the Hobgoblin Spring on the slope west of our cottage, I always find that I experience wondrously restful sleep and insightful dreams. I wake with the sun next day feeling utterly renewed.

In many places it was considered beneficial to wash in the waters of such places. Such waters cleansed and purified body and spirit. Some waters were even said to work healing. I have found it to be a very powerful ritual to wash my hands and face in the waters emerging from the mouths of sequestered springs. These waters have been filtered by Earth and are especially pure, have coursed ages through quiet dark over stone and crystal.

Simply dip your hands in the water and pour it over your face and hair. Do it in honor of whatever gods you serve and ask that the water cleanse your flesh and spirit. Ask that the light of the dawn sun may enlighten your renewed self. Seek wisdom first in such rituals and let every other good thing follow in its course.

Woods Lore

Healthy Working with Wild Water

I love wild waters. I grew up with wild waters in the Deep South, building rafts to explore the bayous, fishing the swamps for catfish, and catching crawfish in the murky streams. When my wife and I lived in the far north of the Alaska wilds, the lake in front of our cabin provided our drinking and cleaning water, and I often fished it for enormous lake trout and burbot. I wandered the interconnecting chain of little rivers and lakes on a flat-bottomed boat and on calm summer days I would simply stop, drift, and stare up into the cerulean sky and revel in the gentle sound of small waves lapping the hull. Here in the woods of east Canada, I spend a good portion of each summer wandering sequestered lakes by canoe, sometimes casting about for pickerel and perch, sometimes observing the antics of muskrats and beavers, bald eagles, and curious otters. Wild waters are as much a home to me as the woodlands themselves, and I oftentimes think I must have had a slough of ancestors born with paddles in their hands.

Wild water is beautiful, and it offers so much. Chances to wander remote places, see wildlife, encounter spirits. But with all wild water, wisdom must be exercised. In the lovely, whimsical tome, *Faeries*, by Brian Froud and Alan Lee, the authors noted: "Water has always been of importance in faerie lore. Its ambivalent nature as provider of food, nourisher of crops and taker of lives makes the divinities associated with it particularly potent." Water is sacred, cleansing, eternal—like liquid crystal. But it can also be a medium of potent danger. It is important to exercise wisdom when dealing with wild water.

In the previous essay I wrote about dawn ablutions. I do such at crystal-clear brooks and springs in Canada, but even in this country—known for its vast wild lands—waterways can harbor unseen threats. For example, here in east Canada, beavers frequently make use of brooks and little rivers as well as lakes. Though the water can look crystal-clear, beavers are known to carry the illness giardia. Before you poured water from a lake or brook over your head in these parts, you would want to make sure there are no beavers upstream. Of course, water from a springhead is almost certain to be pure, having just emerged from Earth, which has cleansed it.

Waters from vigorous brooks can usually be used safely for ablutions because as the water splashes and sprays over stones and down little falls, it is aerated, a process which purifies it. Still, you should not drink such water. Even if you are certain there are no beavers upstream, the sad truth is the main contaminant of groundwater in today's world is industry and modern non-organic farms. Both use numerous toxic chemicals, which have a terrible tendency to escape into waterways.

It wasn't long ago a man in the wilds could stop and drink from most any clear brook if he knew beavers weren't upstream, but now it is best to be prepared to purify water you will get on your face or use for drinking or cooking. A good compact water filter is the best solution. When I am going on a trip where I anticipate needing more than a couple quarts of water, I carry a compact but extremely effective Katadyne filter that uses a ceramic shell around a silver oxide core to cleanse water of all possible biological and chemical contaminates. This is overkill as where I live is pristine, but I have learned through experience it is better to be safe than sorry. I drank contaminated water once as a child and underwent several very painful days of infection afterward. As the old saying goes, *An ounce of prevention is worth a pound of cure*. To me, that filter is worth every ounce of the two pounds it adds to the weight of my gear.

A lesser but effective measure is to carry water purification tablets, such as *Aquatabs*. Such tablets use chlorine or iodine to sterilize water of any pathogens. They are very effective but only against waterborne bacteria and viruses. They can do nothing to cleanse water of chemicals such as herbicide runoff from a farm ten miles up the way.

An old method for purifying water going back to pioneer times was to use bleach and silver. We used this method at our cabin in the Alaskan bush. Use two drops of bleach per quart of water (eight drops per gallon) and place a sterling silver object, such as a coin, in the container. The bleach will kill any biohazard and the silver—toxic to any microorganism—improves the effectiveness. Be sure the object is real silver. Modern coins may look silver, but they are mostly of some non-silver alloy.

In the world before Man, pristine watercourses naturally purified water as it flowed through gravel and sand, went uninterrupted among cleansing plants, and sprayed over stones and falls. It is a tragic shame that humans have decimated so many waterways and polluted the environment to the point that even traditional sources of fresh water must be held in suspicion. But until the world is made whole once again, being cautious with water is essential. I do not believe that preparing water for safety in any way reduces its effectiveness as a ritual cleanser, though it does, it's true, reduce the appeal and simple beauty of just dunking a bowl into a pool and pouring the cool water over oneself. But acting with wisdom is in itself a spiritual merit.

MAY'S JOURNEY

Contentment

Only participation in Nature can produce the intimate knowledge
necessary to guide us in establishing a sustainable lifestyle.
—Samuel Thayer
Nature's Garden

The Hollow is situated on the north slope of a little valley atop a broad
Appalachian mountain, so even though our latitude is equivalent to that
of Maine, our climate is more like that of much more northerly Newfoundland. It is not til May when the days begin to feel truly warm again,
for throughout April any cloud-shadow evokes frosty spirits. This fine
May day the sky was a clear cerulean. Daphne is a good and eager forager, and she and I had decided to venture into the woodlands lying west
to discover what bounty the spring might provide. So she donned her
hat and knife and jacket and a small pack and I did the same, adding a
few other odds and ends to my gear: the quintessential compass in case

we lost the sun, flint and steel and tinder kit, and a hearty lunch, along with my ever-present bowie, and we set off to wander. Our plan was to hike down to a broad brook, make our way south up to the highest ridges and explore the hardwoods and high meadows, then turn east and go to the evergreens lower down. Each direction would take us to a different ecozone that might offer its own bounty.

By the time spring arrives we are all craving fresh vegetables, but it will be weeks yet til the gardens start yielding greens. So one bright May morning Daphne prepares to set off into the wildwood with me to harvest wild ostrich ferns, spring beauties and whatever other goodies we can find.

After a hearty breakfast of farm-fresh eggs, bacon, and Labrador tea, we set out. The sun was only a fist-span over the eastern horizon. (This is a woodsman's means of reckoning time. Hold your arm out to the side, full length, and make a fist and turn it vertical. If it is a.m., face north or south and hold your fist to the east. If it is p.m., hold out your fist to the west. The bottom of your fist should be level with the horizon. Note where the upper part of your fist is and move your arm up til the bottom of your fist is even with where the upper part was. Repeat until the upper part of your fist is parallel to the sun. Each step represents about 7.5 degrees, or roughly a half hour's movement of the sun. It's not precise, but it serves for basic determination of time in the woods. Often, for example, when my daughters go hiking I will tell them, "Dinner will be served when the sun is two fists over the horizon.") Golden early sun, tinged with just a bit of the night's chill, spilled over the land as we exited the cottage through the library and made our way through a thicket of young raspberry canes and rose hip growing amid a latticework of willow and alder saplings. We reached the old stone wall at the tall trees of the south hedge and clambered over, then crossed the Hollow Brook by way of large steppingstones I had set in place years before. On the other side we turned right, following the dirt path westward. As we went, we took note of everything around us, for the land was full of goodness, ready to yield itself to the skilled forager. Waterleaf and cucumber-tasting blue-bead lily grew to either side of the stream, as well as various wild mints. Indeed, we could hardly take a step anywhere near stream or pond without crushing mint, which caused a cool, mouthwatering fragrance to waft through the air.

On the open ground of the path, young wild carrots vied for space among new dock and field shamrock (also called meadow sorrel). Though rare here upon the mountain, we passed a couple linden trees, sporting new growth of tender leaves that taste like lettuce but with absolutely no bitterness. We paused here and there as we went to gather a bit of this and that. The land was so abundant that we had to be careful as we went so as not to fill our packs too quickly. There were certain prizes that we needed to save space for later on. But as we gathered, Daphne and I mused over the difficult history of the Maritime provinces. When pioneers first came here, they often suffered starvation. This highland country is stony, wet, and cold, and it resisted their European style of life and farming, so most people abandoned this land long ago. A local Gaelic speaker once read Daphne and I a poem written by one of the early Scots settlers of these parts. He described the land as all barren with nothing to eat but "the bare potato." But the real dilemma for the Scots settlers had not been the fecundity of the land, but a refusal to adapt and live by its terms.

Soon we had filled several of the cloth bags we carried with wild greens. We hung them among tree boughs beside the trail to retrieve later and continued our hike. There were other prizes to forage deeper in the wood.

The first half mile were softwoods and mixed young hardwoods immediately behind the cottage. A couple decades back, before we bought the homestead, this forest had been cut over. It had been a sloppy job and the concept of sustainability had been nowhere in the mind of the loggers. The land was slow to heal, but we have been here almost a decade now and we could at last see its rejuvenation was well underway. Willows, alders, aspens, and birches which had been mere poles when we first arrived were now stout as my arm and pushing twenty-five feet tall, and some as much as thirty. One area we passed through, spanning a couple acres, was so thick with young alders and aspens that we often had to squeeze between the new trees.

"I'll have to get up in here with a felling axe," I told Daphne as we trekked through the thicket of trees. "The growth is much too dense and the trees will choke each other out."

Daphne, ever practical, looked around. "What'll we do with all the excess wood?"

"We'll use the treetops for hay. The goats will love it. The alders we'll set aside to season and use for the smokehouse come butchering time.

We'll have surplus, so we can smoke any cheeses you might make early, too. The extra wood, and all the willow, can go into the fences where we want to make the new meadow for the goats." We planned to open up a couple acres of tangled brush just north of the Blueberry Meadow next summer, in a sheltered area just beyond the gardens. Doing the project the old way, according to the sustainable methods of permaculture, would take a couple years. The first step was to measure and fence off the area. I'd fence it using natural resources, drawing from the abundant saplings to create a traditional pole and wattle fence, like has been used in the British Isles since the dawn of agriculture. Then we'd set piglets out there to dine on all the small scrub and roots and grubs. They'd turn over the ground and prep it nicely. The pigs would later become bacon and hams, and we'd set a hearty, old breed of cow—perhaps the highland variety—in there to work over the things the pigs had overlooked. While the cow was busy, I'd build an open shelter of tied hurdles for the goats— a run-in for them to take cover from storms—and then introduce the goats to their new site in the spring of year three of the project. Permaculture takes patience but it is minimally intrusive upon the land, avoiding the need of foreign materials and wastage of fossil fuels to make and transport them, as well as promoting the strength and health of the soil by adding nutrients and developing a sustainable localized farm ecology. We knew from experience that such a meadow would sustain our little flock of dairy goats for years while the old goat meadow rejuvenated under the ministrations of our poultry flock.

We emerged from the thicket and found ourselves entering the old hardwoods where the Hollow Brook met the broader, larger Rusalka Brook that ran along the west slope that forms the boundary of the Hollow. The trees here were great and tall, ancient maples mostly. It was a shady, friendly place we visited often for family picnics or just to walk and enjoy the quiet peace of a secluded wood and its wildlife. And such a place is a wealth of opportunity for a knowledgeable forager. Weaving among the great old trees, it was easy to maintain a westerly course by keeping the sun at our backs, and soon we came to a small path in the woodland made many years ago by a farmer, but long since abandoned. These days the path was just ribbon of grass that wove between the trees.

"Look!" I said with glee and pointed to a snag. A half-dozen enormous mushrooms grew on the side of the dead tree. Daphne is not a mushroom forager and leaves it to me to find them. She is happy to cook and preserve them. That's good enough for me. I love mushrooming and I love her cooking. I unshouldered my pack and drew my bowie.

The dryad's saddle is an easily identified edible polypore that grows on dead and dying wood. Polypores are a safe mushroom group as there are no toxic members. If a polypore is inedible, it will just be tough or bitter. The dryad's saddle can become huge, as it has in this photo, but it also gets tough as old leather if left on the tree too long. But even a big one will still sport a tender, tasty outer band that can be sliced off, so long as it is still growing and hasn't shed its spores.

The mushrooms were dryads' saddles, and some of the largest I'd ever come across. Some field guides list them as mediocre in flavor, and I cannot understand why. When harvested right, they offer a clean, rich flavor similar to the *Agaricus bisporus*, which is the common store mushroom, but with a richer, heartier taste. Cooked with a little garlic, bacon, and butter, they were to die for. But they toughen quickly and will become as hard as wood within a couple weeks of reaching peak size, so they must be harvested young or one must learn to identify the tender part and slice it away. These were still flexible and I was sure all but perhaps the point at which they connected to the tree was tender, so I used my bowie to slice them entirely from the tree. I always keep it very sharp for just such tasks. I had more cloth sacks in my pack and stowed them. (With few exceptions, one should never stow mushrooms in plastic as it can cause rot to start setting in within minutes.) The mushrooms were so large they filled half my large daypack. We had not even been hiking two hours and already we had found more than two week's worth of wild food. And it was only the bare beginning of the spring green-up!

I shouldered the pack, cleaned and sheathed the knife, and we continued onward to the Rusalka Brook. Some sixty years ago a woman was murdered and her body was found in that brook. Such things are exceedingly rare in the peaceable backwaters of Nova Scotia, and to this day local folk still talk about it as if it just happened. They may have a different name for the brook but I call it the Rusalka Brook because whenever I ride one of the horses this way, the animals shy hard of it, and upon evenings I have hiked through these secluded woods and near the banks, I have often heard following footsteps among the trees, though never was a person to be seen. But I have never feared the brook or its spirit. In all my years, I've never met a spirit more dangerous than a living person, and I've always found otherworldly beings to return courtesy for courtesy. So I make it a point to live well with the land's spirits and they live well with us.

In the last hundred yards from the brook, where the land suddenly swept downward at a steeper angle, the woods abruptly transitioned from ancient maples to towering white and red spruces, scattered hemlocks and pines, and tall, graceful birches. The ground changed from the ubiquitous stony clay of the upper reaches of the Hollow to clay and sand. Ferns grew everywhere on this shaded slope, and ferns— in particular, young fiddleheads—were what we were after. But the ferns growing here were cinnamon and interrupted ferns, inedible and slightly poisonous.

Fern fiddleheads are a popular dish around northeastern America and eastern Canada. But there is only one kind of edible fern in North America. All the others are toxic to some degree. But the edible fern is commonly called the "fiddlehead," and it is an unfortunate appellation because all ferns start life as a fiddlehead, and this leads to much confusion among novice (and sometimes even advanced) foragers. Fortunately, the other ferns are only mildly poisonous and eating them rarely leads to more than stomach upset and headache, and then only if a fair portion is consumed. But the noxious varieties taste insipid, bitter, and utterly foul. Yet, rumor has it that fiddleheads are utterly delightful; a true wild food gourmet's delight, and so strong is the power of suggestion that I have personally known several persons who choked down the noxious varieties all the while praising their qualities. One person even emailed me an image of some fiddleheads she had spotted growing in a nearby wood with the text: "Look how tasty! I just picked these and am looking forward to turning them into dinner." I wrote her back and warned, "Um ... those are cinnamon ferns. Think of the bitterest thing you've ever eaten and add a headache to it, and that's what you'll get if you eat those." She wrote back: "No way! I've been eating these for years. The headache's just because I eat too much." What more could I add to that logic? At least it wasn't fatal delusion.

A tantalizing but toxic fern in the fiddlehead stage of growth. Actually, only to a novice might it look tantalizing. If you become adept enough at foraging edible ferns, you look at this and just think, *Eww!*

Ostrich fern fiddleheads tend to grow in clusters from well-drained, sandy soil near water, as illustrated in this photo, taken from our secret harvesting place we call the Island of the Ostriches. They are smooth, have no silky hair cover, and sport only a bit of brown papery scale at the sides of the tightly packed leaves in the fiddlehead, though the scales are loose and often fall away before harvest. Most distinctively, ostrich ferns have a deep groove down the stalk, much like celery.

A while back I gathered some cinnamon and interrupted ferns. They were scrawny things, not nearly the size of the edible fern, but I gathered enough to make a dish and Daphne and I cleaned and steamed them. It was just an experiment. I was trying to understand if we were overlooking some merit in these plants. We even drained the water twice to eliminate the bitters. Even so, they were so vile we spat them out, and that is notable because we are vegetable lovers, prone to eating greens many others would reject. But I thought, *Maybe we prepared them wrong.* So I gathered another batch and this time Daphne steamed them, then fried them in bacon. The fat from bacon will bind with a plant's bitters and neutralize it. But the ferns even made the bacon insipid. Even the dog was hesitant to eat the bacon after.

But suggestion is a powerful thing, so people keep harvesting the wrong kind, choking them down and telling themselves how good they are. Actually, this happens a lot among novice foragers. That deep desire to find something good probably leads to more misidentifications than anything else.

The term *fiddlehead* refers to the shape of the fern when it first springs forth: a delicate stem gracefully curved and surmounted by a globe of tightly curled, tender leaves. All ferns begin life in this way, though only the ostrich fern is edible. And, fortunately, it is easily identified and none too hard to find, if you know the trick of it. And for those who understand her, the wildwood is more than willing to share her abundance.

The ostrich fern is the largest of the North American ferns. It is easily distinguished from all other ferns in several ways. It prefers to grow on sandy soil but will tolerate a little loam and clay, though the soil must be well drained. While other ferns may be found anywhere, ostriches love water and will only be found nearby. It is a deep green and sports a brown papery scale on either side of the bundled leaves, though the scale often falls off before harvest. Most distinctively, it has a deep and pronounced groove down the entire stalk from crown to leaf, much like celery. Also, it tastes sweet and wholesome, even raw, unlike any of the other North American ferns. While uncommon, where it grows it tends to thrive in great colonies. If you find a patch, much can be harvested in a short amount of time and its taste is truly delectable. Some have likened it to asparagus, though I would not do so. It is sweet, tender, and delectable raw or cooked, but its flavor is uniquely *ostrich fern*.

We knew a secret place in the remote wood where a whole colony grew and that's where we were headed: a place I called the Island of the Ostriches. Trekking down the slope, we entered a clearing. Tree stumps were scattered all around, about knee height. One might have thought loggers had been at work in here, and that would be right, though not human loggers. Beavers had a lodge further down and fed on the young trees near the brook.

Intrepid beavers have harvested a medium-sized striped maple at the edge of the Rusalka Wood.

Innumerable and often colorful birds make their home in the wildwood.

Taking advantage of the beavers' clearing, we made faster time and soon reached the island. It was a large teardrop of land in the midst of the wide brook—almost a river here—and the water forked around it, meeting again on the far side. In most places the brook was deep, but there is a shallow bank of sand on the upstream side and we made our way there and crossed. The little island was thick with ostrich ferns. A few were precocious and had already grown into mature, shaggy ferns several feet high and broad. They would keep growing and by midsummer would be nearly as tall as I. Mature ostrich ferns are too tough to eat, but most were still in their fiddlehead stage.

Even in their juvenile fiddlehead stage, ostrich ferns can stand two feet tall. Many were thick and dark green and only a handspan or two tall, though, and many more were yet only knee-high. Daphne and I removed our packs, pulled out several more cloth bags from them, and began harvesting. The day drew on and became rapidly warmer, and soon was as hot as a high summer's day. The sun reached its zenith and strong light spilled over the sandy little island. It was too early in the season for blackflies or mosquitoes, though, and the work was pleasant. We stripped out of our jackets and Daphne, who enjoys going barefoot, slipped out of her boots and socks, as well. She is a redhead, that rare red and green that wilts in strong sun, and during the warm time of year she is always trying to find that balance between enough clothing to protect herself from the sun while staying adequately cool.

I could see she was withering in the heat, though, and suggested she go for a swim while I finished gathering the harvest. I am Cajun and grew up in Louisiana's sweltering heat and humidity. Nova Scotia at its hottest and dankest was at best mild by my standards, and I thought nothing of continuing the work. Daphne stripped and slipped into the clear stream at a place where the sandy bottom formed a little pool about four feet deep. The current was brisk, still fed by recently melted runoff, and the water was chilly. She was only in there a few minutes before she had had enough and came out of the water and sat on the sand, soaking in the warm sun on fresh-chilled skin, reveling in the songs of spring birds.

I finished harvesting as she rested. She has a preternatural sense of timing, though, and as I began to fill my last bag, I heard her shifting about. She dressed, then rummaged through the packs for our food and water bottles to prepare a picnic just as my stomach began to rumble. So, I set the last sack down and sat beside her. We ate hearty sandwiches of homemade bread and relish with thick slabs of local bacon and tangy mayonnaise that Arielle had contrived. We drank cold tea of dried staghorn sumac berries harvested last summer. We shared a salad she had prepared of pickled garden vegetables, to which I had added tart forest shamrock. And then we lay, her head on my shoulder, in a sunbeam and napped an hour. Never was a lunch or a rest more sweet and perfect than there in the forest with my best friend. I woke before her and left her sleeping while I wandered about the island, looking at this and that. I noted tracks of minks and coyotes and even deer that had ventured through the brook. In grassy thickets young frogs hid, waiting for rainy days and twilight when they would sing their courting ballads. I noticed common water striders playing their eerie, insect games in still places upon the brook, frolicking over the water as easily as a man runs across the land.

The forest had been so good to us this day, but there was yet more before us. I returned to Daphne and our packs and woke her. I gave her a moment to stretch and shake off the grogginess and then we shouldered our packs and moved on. We carried our harvest in the cloth sacks in either hand through the woods to the path and there left them. Later in the day, I would return on horseback and pick them up.

It was weeks after I took this photo that I realized there weren't two water striders in the image, but in fact four, moving as one in the act of mating.

Daphne and I decided to curtail our plans to explore the eastward evergreens because we had already gathered so much, but we did decide to enter the deep hardwood forest and venture up onto the ridges since we were already at their foot. We crossed the Rusalka Brook at a rickety old wooden bridge then left the path. The land rose immediately westward to our right, but we had not gone a hundred paces when I espied an enormous chaga growing on a birch in wet, shaded ground at the very foot of the slope—perfect chaga ground. I had brought a hatchet for just such a possibility. It was about nine feet off the ground, but the tree trunk forked four feet up and I clambered up to the fork and used the opposing trunk to brace myself while I chopped the chaga away from the tree. Daphne gathered the bits that broke away as I worked and laid them on a bed of bracken to air dry a bit while I finished getting the whole fruiting body. Chaga is hard and cutting it away while being careful not to harm the host tree took a while. Then I spotted a second chaga, almost as large, a bit further up. I climbed higher and began chipping away at it. This work took longer because I was now at a very awkward angle, and I ended up breaking the chaga into little bits as I cut it away. But it didn't matter. They would dry and serve just as well. I scraped the last of the chaga mycelium away from the trunk with my bowie, then swung off the tree and leapt to the ground. Daphne was putting it all in a sack, which it nearly filled, a good harvest of about ten pounds. Six months worth. I stowed the sack in my pack and we continued on.

With that accomplished, we pressed on up the slope into the vast forest of old maples. These were the deep hardwoods, rich with wildlife. As we went, I pointed out spoor of various woodland denizens: droppings of porcupines, middens of red squirrels, nests of owls in the high canopy and hanging nests of finches on the lower boughs of small and mid-sized trees. Here and there we passed rare nodding trillium, which is a pleasant-tasting edible that grows only in deep forest shade. However, like many forest plants, it grows exceedingly slowly, and it is very fragile. Pick so much as a single leaf and the entire plant will die, so we leave it be, except for the occasional photograph of this lovely, unusual plant. However, it is not due to foragers that nodding trillium has become scarce but due to an overabundance of whitetail deer. With a paucity of natural predators, deer thrive and spread quickly and eat back all manner of foliage. If left unchecked, whitetails can render both woodland and meadow barren. And all throughout the wood were the spoor of deer: gnawed lower branches, antler rubs, hoof tracks, and droppings. I decided then and there to hunt one in this vicinity next season. Culling one would do the forest good.

As we ascended the top of the ridge, we began to feel a cool breeze blowing from out of the north. Lower down, the rising land had shielded us from it, but here it was palpable. It was just strong enough to make the treetops whisper and keep the dense woodland air from becoming close.

"Do you smell that?" Daphne asked.

I paused and sniffed. There was a fragrance in the air, something delicate and wonderful. It was like honey and fresh fruit. No…that isn't right. It was sweet and fruity, yes, but not like anything I could put a finger on. And it had a certain…I don't know a word for it…It was as if *fresh* has been rendered into a fragrance and floated through the woodland. And the higher we went into the hardwoods, the more pronounced it became.

We reached the heights and the slope flattened out like an island in the sky. And ahead we saw a spray of small, delicate flowers. Pale white petals overlain with light and dark stripes of lavender surmounted slender stems that were surrounded by deepest green leaves. Tiny but gorgeous, and marvellous in their thousands, they stood only ankle tall, and beneath the high canopy of the hardwoods, barely leafed out, sunbeams poured over them, illuminating the woodland in ethereal sprays of gold.

Daphne, who is from small town British Columbia and is newer to wild foraging than I, had never seen the like. She gasped for the beauty. "What are they?" she asked.

The ephemeral spring beauty appears only in the shade of old woods, and only for a couple weeks in spring. They spend the rest of the year in quiet dormancy in tiny tubers the size of a pea below ground. The delicate blossoms are ambrosia for intrepid bumblebees.

I knelt, pulled one up, and popped it into my mouth, blossom, stem, and all and chewed contentedly. It tasted sweet and herbal. I smiled at her. "Some call them spring beauties," I told her. "They are ephemerals. They appear before the trees leaf out and are gone just a couple weeks later. They crop up before most any other plants and drink in the cool early spring sunlight. They are pollinated by bees and feed them sweet nectar in exchange, and then they vanish to sleep the rest of the year as tiny tubers underground. The tubers can live up to twenty years."

With my hands, I scooped into the soft duff of the forest floor. A webwork of fine roots came up with the earth, popping with little snaps as it broke away from the ground. I spread my fingers slightly apart and shook so that the dirt quickly sifted away and left in my hand a tiny tuber about the size of a mere pea. I held it out for her to see. "They have another name because of the little tubers." I doused the tuber with some water from a bottle and cut it open, revealing a firm flesh. I gave it to her to try and she nibbled at it. It was very much like a raw potato in texture and taste. "They are also called faerie spuds, and you can see why."

Then she popped a spring beauty into her own mouth, blossom, stem, and leaves, smiling at the mildly sweet, herbal flavor. "These are good. Are we going to harvest them?"

I stood up and looked around. They grew in broad patches between the roots of the great maples, but here and there I could see little holes in the soil too, earth piled roughly to a side of each. I shook my head. "We can take some. Enough for a meal for the family, so everyone can try them. We'll get the spuds and tops and two very different dishes can be made. But ... " I pointed out the various holes, "deer made those holes. They are eating the plants but they seem to want the faerie spuds even more. And it takes years for a patch to establish itself, and like many understory plants, they are slow growers. They cannot be harvested too heavily. We'll take no more than ten percent of any patch."

She nodded. We always aimed to harvest sustainably, bringing the permaculture philosophy by which we operated the homestead into our wild-country foraging. And so for an hour we gathered spring beauty tops and their faerie spuds. Always moving, we went from one patch to another so as to minimize the effect of our foraging. A healthy patch could rejuvenate itself with ease, so long as its numbers weren't too far reduced. When we had a little bag of greens, blossoms, and spuds, we stood up and stretched. In truth, the work had not been hard—it was just a little tedious. But harvesting is always a little tedious; a process of picking and picking and picking til the job is done.

"You know," I said as I slipped the herbs into her pack because mine was full, "there are a lot of myths that the way the ancestors lived was so very hard."

Daphne smirked. "Yeah, I remember that in school." She vociferated as if quoting a line from a textbook she had studied long ago: "Life was a brutish struggle, and early Man worked every waking moment to clothe and feed himself."

I nodded. "Of course, we know that's all nonsense nowadays. Numerous anthropologists and archeologists put those theories to the test and found that, on average, early people only needed to work a couple hours a day to obtain the necessities of life. There were exceptions, of course. If they relied upon the salmon harvest, when the salmon were running they had to work day and night to catch fish. If they relied on wild grains, they had to gather them during the harvest season. But by and large their lives were a lot easier than those of persons these days."

We started hiking down from the ridge. It was steep in some places, but we could easily just skirt around the drops. As I picked my way over a fallen log, she said, "It makes you wonder why folk ever decided to change things."

I could only nod. On the way home, we postulated how and why the world had become the materialistic, desperate, warring thing it is now.

Maybe the need to store food against famine had given people an instinct to acquire far more than they needed. Maybe, as human numbers grew, territoriality had launched folk headlong into an unending rush to outdo one another. Maybe most folk just followed the whims of a more avaricious minority. While these questions might seem academic, they were of great interest to us as Twa Corbies Hollow was created to experiment with permaculture and develop and share ways to live green while living well. Of course, that whole concept of "living well" depended on how you defined it. Was living well getting as much as you could? Or was it knowing when you had enough and being content with it? In my work as a psychotherapist, I knew from experience that contentment was a concept a great many people are very blurry about.

We hiked home debating the merits of one point or another and at the steppingstones across the Hollow Brook, I gave Daphne my pack. She was heading up to the cottage to start dinner. I went on to the Blueberry Meadow and whistled for Aval, my horse. He trotted over, I led him back to the wood shop where his tack is stored and quickly cleaned and rounded his hooves and saddled him. Then I put on his halter, to which I clipped a couple leads to either side. Aval is an enormous heavy horse standing nearly six feet at the weathers. But he is a gentle if exceedingly powerful giant and tremendously helpful around the farm, whether it's helping me haul firewood out of the woods or scout out the locations of deer. Today, he and I would just ride out and retrieve the day's foraging. I slipped a foot into his left stirrup and slightly leapt as I hauled myself up into the saddle. It's harder than it sounds with such a tall horse. A slight tug on a rein to turn him and a tap to his flanks and he was sauntering proudly down the drive to the dirt path. There we turned right and after a few minutes of paced walking to warm him up, I tapped his flanks firmly and he launched into an easy canter. At the trail leading to the Rusalka Brook and the Island of the Ostriches, I dismounted and let him browse while I grabbed the sacks of fiddleheads and mushrooms and tucked them into saddlebags, distributing the weight evenly to either side.

Then, just because it was a beautiful spring afternoon, we rode a bit further on. As always, Aval hesitated at the Rusalka Brook. He crossed brooks elsewhere without problem, but he was always twitchy here. I spoke soothingly to him and stroked his neck from the saddle, lending him confidence, and after a moment he trotted quickly over the haunted brook. We turned up the dirt path which wove like ribbon between the trees, and rode uphill a mile to a trailhead, invisible unless you knew it was there. I steered him into the forest and instantly we were surrounded by tall, ancient trunks and overarching boughs. The sun was westering and shadows lengthening, already lending the forest an eerie quality of bright patches woven with ebon shadow. Aval, like all equines, was nervous here in the wood. His kind evolved in arid country, on open plains, and instinctively they knew forests to be places of predators and unexpected dangers, where an animal whose primary defence was outrunning danger could not move very fast for the many obstacles. I could feel the tension in him as we made our way through the darkening wood, and now and then I spoke soothingly to him which set him at ease, though at one point we flushed a pair of grouse and Aval nearly spooked and would have galloped for home had I not pulled him into running a circle til he settled.

Yet the forest was what it always was: place full of sunbeams and shadows, mysteries and secret lore, things knowable and a place to become lost in faerie tales. The forest is the forest; a home if you understand it; an alien, fearful thing if you are ignorant of its ways.

And the air smelled fresh and new, an indescribable sweetness that could only come a short two weeks each year when the spring beauties emerged. I passed one broad patch after another. I knew Daphne and I could come up here for the next few days and make a huge harvest in this place, setting aside many pounds of faerie spuds in our larder and making lovely salads and greens til our gardens began yielding. Daphne could even sell some at the farmers' market. But whether we were harvesting deer and hares, or wild foliage, we always made it a point to understand what the Earth Mother had to offer and not take more than she could give. We would leave the spring beauties—tempting as they were—to grow and make the world beautiful.

For what we had was enough. And we knew it. And that is contentment.

I rode Aval on into the forest, enjoying the play of light and green shadow, smiling as I watched Aval's alert, curious ears twitch this way and that as he became accustomed to this place, so different from his sunny meadows, aware that he was starting to feel confident and enjoy himself.

"The truth is," I told him as we trotted, "living well with Nature ... all by itself, it is contentment."

Wild Life

Musical Frogs

In the forests of the northeast, small frogs called peepers are one of the first creatures to awaken from winter. No sooner does the snow vanish than these diminutive frogs begin their choruses along the banks of brooks, ponds, and vernal swamps. I've always considered us fortunate that the cottage is situated at the edge of a hill with a spring-fed pond and a vigorous brook not fifty yards away, because every spring we are serenaded by these musical frogs.

There are actually several kinds of peepers deriving from a complex of two subspecies. They are well camouflaged, rarely bigger than an inch long. They hide well, though if one walks slowly along the bank of a body of water where they are known to sing, they can be spotted in the grasses or climbing up sedges, and now and then they are spooked into hopping away into the water where they can be seen swimming among clusters of eggs clinging to submerged twigs and leaf detritus. They help create balance by consuming abundant moth larvae, small spiders, midges, and other soft invertebrates.

In fact, it seems that much of their role is in relation to balance, for peepers are an indicator species. They are very sensitive to environmental change and degradation. Peeper populations are monitored, and if they decline it is a sure indicator that something is amiss. All frogs share the trait of being indicator species, and sadly, around the world frog populations have been in decline for more than a decade, without a doubt the result of increasing global pollution. And though scientists are aware that human activities are the cause of the problem, by and large humans do nothing about it. In a documentary about climate change that I saw several years ago, a scientist opined that evolution has designed humans to be excellent at coping with problems of the relatively immediate future (say, as far off as a few decades), but addressing global, multi-generational problems such as environmental decline is beyond the scope of our current evolution. I cannot recall the source of that information, but I am a psychotherapist with a specialization in behavior psychology and I must concur. And though we humans don't like to face this dangerous shortcoming of our own nature, the truth is the grossly unsustainable way we live in this era is killing our world and we ourselves, little pieces at a time. But because the damage builds slowly, we let ourselves ignore it, carrying on with business as usual.

Frogs are sometimes mentioned in magical and spiritual tomes. They are, like the butterfly, creatures of profound transformation. They begin their lives as tiny fishlike beings and go through an incredible metamorphosis, gills becoming lungs, fins becoming feet. A frog is a true symbol of the transformation that occurs over the course of life, but unfortunately, this remarkable little being is often overshadowed by the more luminous butterfly that is more apt to capture human imagination.

Thus, frogs have suffered in folklore. A frog is not something a person aspires to, but something they aspire from. A princess kisses a frog and it becomes a prince. A witch curses someone who becomes a frog. The simple fact is frogs do much, teach us much, but they get a bum wrap.

Enchanted Forest

Candle Flicker Spirits

The folktale below is one that is popular in the oral tradition of the Cajuns of central Louisiana. I heard it often as a child, though I do not know if it has before been set to writing. Set in spring when the livestock fences are annually inspected and repaired, a pair of boys encounters the mysterious faerie or ghost beings of the woodlands called the *feux follets*. The names of the boys vary in the telling. The *feux follets* are dangerous creatures, though no one knows if they intend harm or if, rather, their nature is simply dangerous to people, just as lightning is dangerous without intent. And it is only through wisdom in the ways of Nature that the boys weather the encounter.

◆ ◆ ◆

The farmer had two sons who worked hard to help him look after his meadows and fields. He kept cattle, pigs, and a mixed-market garden, as did many farmers of his day.

One spring day his sons went to the back of the meadow to tend the fences and a storm arose. Being honest, hard-working boys, they kept at it. A warm rain would do naught but soak them, and while it fell it would keep the mosquitoes at bay. So they walked the fence, looking for places the wire had been stretched and repaired it, and also found places where the posts had come loose and redug them.

Their work took them down to the edge of the great forest that abutted their land, and as they worked one saw a glimmer in the deep rain-cast shadows of the black oaks. He called to his brother, "Etienne, did you see that?"

"See what, Gaston?" asked the brother.

And Gaston explained he had seen a glimmer in the forest, but Etienne thought he meant only to trick him. And so they continued to work.

Minutes later the glimmer reappeared, this time at the very edge of the forest. What they saw was a little flame a man's chest height above the ground. It looked for all the world like a candle flicker drifting through the air and burning despite the rain. Goosebumps pricked the skins of the farmer's sons, for they knew in an instant what this being was; it was one of the *feux follets*, the spirit lights that haunted the woodlands, swamps and bayous of the Cajun lands.

The *feu follet* ghosted toward them. They had heard that the *feux follets* sought to touch the living, and that if they managed to do so, the shock of the touch of something so otherworldly could kill. No one knew why the *feux follets* sought to touch the living; perhaps to taste for a moment what it was like to be alive again, perhaps out of malevolence. The truth was, no one even knew what the *feux follets* were. What the farmer's sons knew is they must run for their lives.

And so they fled, abandoning their tools and running afoot through the rain, racing for all they were worth, and should one glance behind, there was the *feu follet*, always just a bit closer. And soon it was just behind them and in a moment it would touch the brothers. But they knew the old lore and saw a stream, seasonal and often dry, but it was now flowing hard with rainwater. The boys leapt across the stream and fell to the ground on the other side, panting. They saw the *feu follet* stop at the stream's edge and come no further, for it is well known that such beings cannot cross moving water. And so in the storm the little candle-flicker spirit drifted away as if carried by the wind, and the lucky farmer's boys made for home.

—A common oral folktale of the
Cajuns of the Louisiana bayous.
Told to the author as a child
by numerous sources.

Wood Witchery

Living Well with Spirits

I was born in New Orleans. My father was a private eye and my mother was a blonde bombshell beauty queen. I know, sounds like the makings of a bad hard-boiled novel, doesn't it. My father took to the horse tracks; my mother had enough. A Cajun, she returned to the bayou country and there I grew up with the castaway French that are the southern Acadians, a people who had kept much of their language and traditions unchanged for centuries but who had been profoundly impoverished and altered by an age of hardship in North America.

They were a magical-minded lot and looking back, I consider it a privilege to have grown up as one of them. I was raised in a world where folk didn't believe, they *knew* the dark forests and misty bayous were the haunts of otherworldly beings, from the slave zombies of evil bokor (wicked sorcerers of the *vodun* tradition) to the *Père Malfait* (pare mal*fae, translating to "ill-made father"), something like an unseelie Earth-elemental of the bayou lands, to the lonely ghosts of fallen soldiers of the American Civil War. I grew up with constant instruction from my grandmother, cousins, friends, and elders in how to live wisely with these many entities. Don't get me wrong: I am not claiming to be a hereditary witch or have special insight. Nor do I have psychic powers, and it wasn't as if persons sat me down and *taught* me. It was more that bits of lore were imparted through the very way we lived. If my grandmother saw I was heading into the woods to harvest wild persimmons and she sensed a storm coming, she would be sure to warn me to get back before the *feux follets* appeared, and if they approached to jump a ditch of running water as they could not cross it. When my friends and I went into the bayous to catch catfish, they showed me how to watch for alligators that floated like logs and taught me to watch likewise for the *Père Malfait*.

But this was not to say I was taught to fear the backcountry. We accepted and even loved these entities. They were just part of the unique and special character of the land. Just as the far north is loved by its folk while it is home to both the graceful caribou and also the powerful grizzly. We learned to be at peace with our land's marvels and perils through living wisely with them.

A large part of living wisely is simply being courteous. And especially with entities of the spirit world, courtesy matters. Perhaps this is so because while our world is more affected by action, the spirit world seems more affected by intent.

Lessons admonishing courtesy to the otherworldly beings appear in all cultures and go into deep history. In Japan, Shinto practitioners took care to honor their ancestral spirits by speaking to them from time to time, and they left gifts for the kami at their shrines. In the western islands of ancient Europe, the Gaels long held traditions of setting out a little food for the land's wights. It was traditional for a Scandinavian shepherd to leave a bit of sheep or goat milk in the hollow of a stone. If someone dropped food, it was left on the ground. When farmers harvested, they often left behind a little of the crop in the fields.

At our woodland homestead, Twa Corbies Hollow, we carry on many of these practices. We leave the first of the goat milk for the barn bruanighe (BREW*nee, Gaelic for the helpful faerie called a brownie), and we never close our barn by night, and though coyotes and bears are abundant in the forest all about, our goats are never bothered by them. We always leave a little of the garden's harvest and I don't think we have ever lost so much as a corncob to one of the many local raccoons. And when I venture into the wildwood, whether it's purely for pleasure or for some practical purpose like wild-food foraging, I bring courtesy with me. If I stumble into some beautiful place, I speak a word of praise to the sylvan sprites who keep it hale. If I go to the great flat-topped rock I call the Shaman Stone to set out upon a spirit journey, I leave a morsel of bread and cheese or some other food for the spirits that haunt that sacred, powerful place. I play the fiddle and some days, when the mood strikes, I'll meander out to a meadow and strike up tunes just to entertain the slow spirits of trees.

And what do I get for it? Things just seem to work smoothly at the Hollow. It's as if luck is bent toward us. Just two weeks ago I had to plant a new matted-row strawberry garden, over a hundred fifty plants on four twenty-foot-long, four-foot-wide beds. Strawberries like to be planted early in spring because they thrive in cool, moist conditions and are virtually immune to frost, but I had to delay planting til late June in order to tend more pressing concerns of the homestead. But two days before I was planning to plant, the weather turned cool and rainy, lowering the temperature of the soil and moistening the beds. The day we were to plant, the weather became mild but sunny, perfect for setting them, and we put the plants in their rows. Three days went by, allowing them to benefit from the sun and spring to life. And just when I was thinking I should water them, another three days of cool rain set in. Now, the barely started new strawberry garden looks like it's been planted a month. Things like that happen for us all the time. We live well with the land; it returns kindness for kindness, courtesy for courtesy. But the truth is I would do these things even if

I got nothing for the effort save the satisfaction of having done something right for the green world. Does courtesy need any other justification?

Those things listed below have been traditional forms of courtesy toward Nature's creatures and spirits for millennia:

1. If eating outdoors and a morsel of food falls to the earth, leave it. Let it become a gift to the spirits.

2. If you are outdoors and find something that is renewable as well as lovely or useful and wish to harvest it, leave at least half so that it may grow back quickly.

3. Take note of hollows in stones and when you are by that way again, leave a little gift. A crust of bread, or a little beer, milk, cheese, or some natural candy. Leave something that would be a rare but wholesome treat for Nature's entities.

4. If harvesting nuts or seeds, take a moment to plant a few so the mother plant's labor is fulfilled.

5. If hiking or camping, do more than just pack your garbage out. Try to leave each place as it was before you were there. "Leave no trace," as they say. Restore the ground as best you can so it looks like you were never there.

6. If you encounter something that enriches you, whether it is a pool or a beautiful flower or a tasty wild mushroom, let the spirits of the place know you are grateful. Never thank, for it is taboo in faerie lore. I have often wondered why this is and can only posit that spirits would be offended if it was implied they gave gifts only to receive gratitude. But it is fine to

take a moment to speak your appreciation. You never
know who or what is listening, and a kind word is a
true and potent treasure.

◆ ◆ ◆

Perhaps it seems that these things are too simple to be magical. One thing
a lifetime spent deep in Nature has taught me is that the most powerful enchantment is rooted in little things. A moment's courtesy to right a toppled
plant, taking home an injured bird to mend its wing, or leaving a morsel
for the shy, little spirits of natural places—enchantment grows out of these
things like a great maple grows from a tiny one-winged seed. It grows in
its own way and reaches fullness in its own time, but it is there. And small
courtesies are its start.

Woods Lore

Wild Food Foraging

Foraging is one of the most essential and fun skills of woodsmanship (or as it is commonly called these days: bushcraft). Living in a large forest as we do, every year we commonly harvest hundreds of pounds of wild foods, which provide about 20 percent of our diet. These foods range from chaga fungi for tea and huge boletes for mushroom steaks, to Jerusalem artichokes for starches, to wild cherries for jams, to staghorn sumac tops for a healthier, tastier alternative to lemonade. We forage so many kinds of wild foods that I could not possibly write about them all in this book. But we are going to take another look at ostrich ferns to teach you the basics. Ostrich ferns are easily identified and taste wonderful, and have the advantage of having no dangerous look-alikes, so they are a good plant to introduce the skill.

But why write about foraging in a book on the spirit and magic of Nature? The truth is I know of few better ways to immerse oneself in Nature than by foraging. It teaches one to see the land. Really see! Often when visitors come to our homestead, they will wander around with Daphne, the girls, and I on Nature hikes and conversations go something like this:

Us: "And over there you'll see a pileated woodpecker."

Visitor: "I had no idea! How did you know it was there?"

Us: "And if you look down that glen, you'll see a patch of wild cherry trees."

Visitor: "My goodness! They just look like bushes."

Us: "And up that way are nearly transparent edible mushrooms called *toothed jelly fungi*."

Visitor: "I see a log."

Living by the land opens the mind's eye to the patterns of Earth. One begins to sense her subtlest nuances on a deep intuitive level that isn't really psychic but goes so far into intuition it might look like it. One night, for example, Daphne and I were taking a walk down a path in the Rusalka Wood and as we passed the brook I paused, cocking my head to a side. Daphne asked what was wrong. I said, "Something doesn't feel right. It feels…unwelcoming here. We aren't wanted." I had a small but powerful LED flashlight in my pocket and withdrew it, flicked it on. The beam fell upon a patch of tall poison hemlock, one of the most toxic plants on Earth. It is an unfriendly plant, and even consuming a small bit would cause seizures and a painful death. Deeply unseelie creatures, they did not want us there. I sensed them because some part of me detected a break in the normally benevolent pattern of the forest. Perhaps it was a subtle waft of noxious odor. Perhaps I caught a glimpse of their tall shadows within the deeper night. I could not tell you. But I knew something was out of place and unfriendly as we passed through.

I have found that persons who live distanced from Nature lack this sense. However much they might love Earth and want to be a part of it, no matter how much they may have studied through books and documentaries, such a sense just is not there. I am not writing this to disparage anyone; it just is. Allow me to offer an illustration. You can read all you want about how to play the fiddle. You can study all the books on musical theory and form and technique. You can watch masters give lessons. But until you put your hands on a fiddle and start practising, you can only know *about* playing it, you cannot actually *play it*. Developing a deep intuitive sense of Nature is just like that. You have to enter it, become part of it, live by it. What better way to do this than by foraging?

If you take up foraging, be forewarned: it has a way of becoming a lifelong passion, and no matter how much you learn there is always more. If that appeals to you, then by all means, proceed!

So, back to the ostrich fern...

As you already read, ostrich ferns are North America's only edible fern. Because they are often referred to by the unfortunately misleading name fiddleheads, and all ferns start off as fiddleheads, many people end up eating ferns that are not ostriches. The forager has to learn to tell ostrich fiddleheads from all those other fern species, such as the interrupted fern and cinnamon fern, which often grow nearby.

When identifying any plant, you need to be well aware of what it looks like at the stage of growth when it's good to eat. You confirm each of its identifying traits one at a time, as if putting together the pieces of a puzzle that will all together form its identity. Normally the forager would use a field guide to do this, and to use a field guide the forager must learn some botanical terms. I am going to avoid most of those terms now for simplicity, as they are beyond the scope of this book, but refer you to a resource later for study.

Puzzle Piece One:
Know Where Your Plant Will Be Found

Ostrich ferns are very picky about where they will grow. They insist on partial to full shade and sandy, well-drained soil. They want a source of clean flowing water nearby though they do not like "wet feet," i.e., their roots in perpetually wet ground. They prefer to grow among hardwoods or mixed conifers and hardwoods. I tend to find them in forests of mixed birch, maple, spruce, and pine. While they are picky about their ground, when you do find a colony, they are usually profuse, and even a small patch can yield grocery bag sized sacks, and gathering goes quickly. Daphne and I can gather fifty pounds in an hour from a single small patch without even trying hard.

Puzzle Piece Two: Color

Ostrich ferns are a uniform dark green, certainly greener than other ferns and in fact one of the greenest things in the forest in early spring.

Puzzle Piece Three: Morphology

The ostrich fern emerges from a crown (plant base at the center of a root mass) that is situated above ground. Often the crowns have dead shoots from previous years and even spent spore stalks growing out of them, desiccated from the previous winter.

Young ostrich ferns will be in their fiddlehead form, with a stem that ends in a graceful curve leading to tightly curled leaves. It very much resembles the neck and scrollwork of a fiddle, hence the name.

The stem has a deep channel running its entire length, like celery.

Puzzle Piece Four: Smell and Taste

Smell and taste play important roles in plant identification. Break off an ostrich fern and smell its base. It should have a clean, sweetish, vegetable smell, like asparagus but not pungent.

Put a tiny amount on your tongue, say a bean's worth. Chew and taste. If it's bitter, spit it out promptly. An ostrich fern will taste sweet and like a vegetable, maybe a bit like a broccoli stalk. Unlike all other ferns, which are especially insipid raw, you wouldn't mind eating ostrich ferns raw.

◆ ◆ ◆

Now you have put together all the pieces of the puzzle and confirmed the picture is indeed that of an ostrich fern. A couple additional notes on ostrich fern harvesting.

You can harvest and eat them even if the fronds are nearly fully uncurled. As long as the plant feels rubbery, tender, and flexible, it is good. When a vegetable feels rubbery, it is in a growth stage and has little tough cellulose in its structure. This rubbery, edible area is called a meristem. When we eat vegetables, we are eating the meristems.

Some people just harvest the curled tips. That is incredibly wasteful as the whole shoot is good and most of the nutrition and flavor is, in fact, in the shoot. To harvest, break or cut the shoots from the bottom about two inches above the crown. Don't cut any lower so as not to damage the perennial crown.

Never harvest more than 50 percent of the shoots from any single crown so that it can still produce leaves and keep growing year after year. And only harvest from a given ostrich fern colony once per year so as not to overstress it.

Look-Alikes

Many edible plants have look-alikes. In the case of the ostrich fern, all other ferns must be thought of as look-alikes. They are easily distinguished because they have fuzz or lack a deep channel or have scales up and down their stems. (Not to mention the insidious taste.)

◆ ◆ ◆

Ostrich fern fiddleheads are excellent as a garnish with salad, or steamed and topped with a little butter or cheese. They can be used in many other ways, too. At the end of the previous journey, I came home to discover Daphne made what we call *woods and garden soup*, a hodgepodge of the seasonal bounty of our gardens and the greens we foraged that day. It was nutritious and tasted wonderful, and that's what it's all about.

Now you not only know how to put together the puzzle pieces that allow you to distinguish the ostrich fern but how to disqualify its would-be imposters. With this knowledge, and presuming you are confident to identify ferns in general, you are ready to forage your own ostrich ferns. These basic skills of identification generalize into all other foraging. To learn more about wild-food foraging, I highly recommend beginning with *The Forager's Harvest* and *Nature's Garden*, both by Samuel Thayer. They will introduce you to the essential botanical terms and concepts, the process of identification, and thoroughly review dozens of wild edible plants found all over North America.

Daphne made this simple meal at the end of our day of wildwood foraging. A hearty dish we call *woods and garden soup*, it contained various garden vegetables along with our fresh forage.

SUMMER

Into the Green

JUNE'S JOURNEY

Goldilocks & the Hobgoblin

"I am the hobgoblin of the pool," the voice replied.
"But I cannot see you," replied Jegu.
"Look carefully into the reeds and you will see me,"
    the voice answered. "I am disguised as a green frog.
I can take any form I wish. And I can make myself invisible."

—Elsie Masson
The Country Bumpkin & the Hobgoblin
Folktales of Brittany

Summer was settled in, the days having been balmy and pleasant since early May. In fact, this year was proving to be exceptional from the agricultural perspective and every week saw a day or two of friendly showers followed by periods of cyan skies with a mild breeze. Already, Daphne and I had harvested bumper crops of wild forage: ostrich ferns, hosta spirals,

dryad saddle mushrooms, cattail shoots, tender dock and plantain, linden tree leaves, shamrock and sheep sorrel, Solomon's seal, and so much
more. The gardens were also giving us early season bumper crops, chief
of which were perennial asparagus, radish greens, and early lettuce. We
had been enjoying fresh greens regularly for over a month now.

Spring is an exceptionally busy time around a farm, and we had
been going nonstop since the first hints of thaw. At that time, animals
need to be shooed out of the barn in order to clean stalls and air it out.
Chicken coops must be repaired from winter damage and thousands
of yards of fence have to be touched up from snow damage. Meadows
must be fertilized and seeded, and horses need their hooves trimmed
and teeth brushed. The gardens must be tilled and planted; the fruit
trees pruned and fertilized with manure tea, which we make from the
animal droppings. On and on the tasks go, occupying us from sunrise
to sunset. As long as there is light in the months, we work. So by the
time June rolled around, I was ready for a break. I wanted to get into
the woods and romp. Natalia enjoys our forest forays, too, and usually
we end up camping out together several times during the summer. So
we decided to venture south of the cottage into the old-growth maple
woods which we share with a pack of coyotes, several black bears, innumerable martens and fishers, and many other woodland denizens.
We had no particular goal except to visit the forest and relax to the
music of a hidden brook in the light of spilling sunbeams.

So at the beginning of June we packed our backpacks, equipped
ourselves with knives and hatchets, and ventured into the wildwood for
a couple days. This was the perfect time of year for it: before the biting
flies were out in force and when many wild animals were on the move,
taking advantage of the tender, early browse, often in the company of
their young. We headed out shortly after daybreak on a pleasant June
morning somewhere between warm and cool, with sun on our backs
and adventure ahead of us.

A long-abandoned homesteader's trail makes for easy going much of the way to our campsite at the foot of the great forest.

It only took an hour to reach the campsite. A good trail led much of the way there. A half-century before, the trail had been a path to one of the homesteads that used to exist out here, but it has long since been abandoned, leaving only a couple meadows that are rapidly going back to forest. The trail that is in the best shape is an old farm tractor route. Only a shadow of it now remains, and it makes me happy to see the land healing and going back to its natural state, but it also makes for easy trekking to remoter places. It has become a major game trail, too, and often I wander up and down this path where it is not uncommon to find spoor of marten, coyote, black bear, and see any number of eastern birds from the elusive snipe to the sadly now-rare eastern bluebird.

You can blame the rarity of the eastern bluebird on Shakespeare, and I kid you not. You see, over a century ago, a Shakespearian society in greater New York decided to hold a festival, and to mark that festival they chose to release a pair of each of the birds mentioned in Shakespeare's plays. Of course, this was done in the naiveté of the early twentieth century when people really had no idea of the ramifications of introducing alien species to foreign ecozones, but nonetheless the terrible consequences of their action were irreversible, for one of the species released was a pair of European starlings. The starling is a darling songbird that is delightful to watch, but it has the unfortunate habit of preferring to nest in sites required by the eastern bluebird, and being bigger and a bit more aggressive, it gets them. And so today, over a century later, the eastern bluebird is a rare site and starlings are everywhere. Seldom anymore do the bright songbirds grace rural fences and low tree branches, brightening the land with their sky-blue and ruby hues and delicately sweet songs. Some folk have made efforts to support the eastern bluebird's recovery by putting out nesting boxes for them and checking to ensure they are not taken over by European starlings, but it is like a finger in the dam, for the starling is prolific. I know it will disturb some readers, but I would like to see the starling become a delicacy and heavily hunted. It is the only way I can see that a real opportunity might be made for the return of the eastern bluebird.

Natalia and I especially hoped to catch sight of the bluebird on our trip. The country was at the edge of broad meadows dotted with thickets of white spruce that they seemed to favor, so our odds were good.

As we hiked we noted tall heaps of wood ant hills. I explained to Natalia that wood ants actually made for a tasty and readily accessible survival food . . . if you knew how to get and use them. The trick was to find a hill in the sunshine and lay out a tarp, say ten feet by ten feet, beside it, and fold over the edges, weighting them down with a few small stones. With a small spade, shovel several times deep into the hill and set the earth onto the center of the tarp. Hundreds of adult ants and their juvenile grubs will have been transferred with the soil from the hill. It's the grubs that are edible. The grubs are soft and pale and have very little tolerance for sunlight, and the adults will carry them beneath the folded edges of the tarp to shade them. You can then go around the edges and scoop them up. These can be fried in an iron skillet with just a bit of butter or oil and salted lightly. They taste much like shrimp. Natalia made retching sounds as I described the process, but that was okay. She'd never been marooned on islands or cast-off in remote wildernesses or so poor you couldn't afford to buy food, and I'd been through all those things in spades. At such times, you reach a point where even gnawing on trees starts to sound appealing. And if she should ever face such a time, the knowledge would be there.

Finally, we reached our intended campsite, right at the edge of the Rusalka Brook and the edge of the old forest where the great trees stretched dark, broad boughs that kept the brook ever in green shadow. An ancient rickety wooden bridge passed over the brook, so old and rotten it was ready to crumble, but we had figured out in previous years that if we were careful to walk directly over the right side, it was passable. Natalia called it the Troll Bridge, and I suppose if any bridge were likely to have a troll scuttling about beneath, it would be this one.

We set about pitching camp. We were both experienced and it didn't take long to select a patch of ground where we'd catch the morning sunbeams to warm the tent and where any precipitation would flow downhill from us should it rain. In minutes, we cleared the site of brush, laid down a protective tarp and set my old tent over it. Then we espied a boulder with a roughly flat surface nearby and using my hatchet we gathered an armload of small twigs, plenty adequate for the efficient, tiny wood stove that I had brought along. We dubbed the boulder the

Green Man's Kitchen and set up. Natalia made a simple lunch while I stockpiled a couple gallons of water from the brook, a simple process using a powerful, compact pump and ceramic/silver filter. Chances were the brook water was perfectly pure, but we could not be sure if beavers might have built a lodge upstream. If so, the water might carry giardia, so filtering it was a good precaution. When I returned to the campsite, I found Natalia had whipped up a nice soup and sandwich combo for the two of us.

The day was yet young, barely 11:00 a.m., and we proceeded without hurry, just a dad and a daughter in the company of the wildwood. We ate and talked and told stories and shared tips. After dinner we crossed the bridge and went to a bed of sphagnum moss so green it almost hurt the eye, and I showed her how to use the filter and explained why it was important, and had her fill up a couple more liter bottles that we could pack with us on our hike. She took to it quickly, as I knew she would. She has a gift for bushcraft.

I gave her a gift she wasn't expecting: her own magnesium rod and steel. Natalia, ever practical, said, "Why do I need this to start a fire? I can just scrape the spine of my knife across chert."

That was true. It wasn't absolutely essential. But I drew the steel across the magnesium rod and it created an impressive shower of sparks. "It'll just go faster," I explained. "The sparks are hotter, so they catch easier. But most importantly, it'll work even if it gets wet."

Natalia nodded but wasn't sure. I think in her mind the less you had to carry, the more fun you could have. Why bother carrying steel and rod when a knife and rock would do? She'd never been in a situation where you were wet and cold and your life depended on getting a fire going while your chilled hands felt like flippers. I had. I would explain that to her later. A good woodsman is always prepared.

An ancient crumbling footbridge, long forgotten, is the only way to cross this forest brook. Ages ago my younger daughter dubbed it the Troll Bridge, and if there is a place a reclusive troll may dwell, it is surely here.

There is something deeply soul-satisfying about outdoor cooking.

Our stomachs full and ample water stashed at camp against the building heat of the day, we set out. Packing light, we took only our knives, a compass, and pair of flashlights in case we didn't get back til dark, along with an empty daypack and a hatchet. The pack and hatchet were for any foraging opportunities that came up along the way. I had a deep desire to find some wild oyster mushrooms and perhaps mayapples, which are rare this far north. And if I found any fresh birch bracket, a common woody mushroom that grows only on birches, we had numerous uses for it, too. I had recently read that young bracket isn't bitter and can be sliced thin for cooking, and I wanted to test that theory. Older bracket has a plethora of uses, too, chief of which is it is a potent antiviral/antibiotic medicinal. It can be crushed to powder and applied to wounds for its natural sterilizing and styptic qualities. It can also be boiled to make a curative though unpleasant-tasting tea. And it can be cut flat and used to strop blades that require extremely fine honing, like my old-fashioned straight razor. Used at the last step of honing, it can give that finishing touch that renders a razor truly shaving sharp.

At first we veered south and followed an old game trail, and it wasn't long til we came across spoor of coyotes, deer, and a family of black bears that often passed through here. Natalia asked if we might be in danger as our camp was set so close to their game trail. It was an excellent question. I explained to her that only in myth were coyotes any real danger to people, and while bears occasionally could be, eastern black bears knew to avoid people. We'd just give ample warning that we were there by creating lots of human scent in the vicinity of the camp. Going to the bathroom not too far from camp would accomplish that. And after dinner, cleaning our cooking and eating utensils thoroughly in the stream would remove the worst temptations.

We entered a glade halfway up the hillside. I watched carefully for various foods we might forage for tonight's dinner. In this place, I mostly expected to find meadow sorrel, wild chive, and dock, but I was elated when just within the forest shadows on the opposite side of the glade I espied mayapples. We hurried over, climbing the odd fallen log and dodging thorny canes of raspberry and jabbing thickets of wild rose.

In the center of the field, we realized just how hot the day was becoming. The sun had reached the meridian and taken on much greater force. A cool morning had evolved into a cooker of a summer day, and it was baking moisture from the soil that was being trapped among the trees, making for stiflingly humid conditions. We paused to remove our light jackets, which we wore mostly as protection against underbrush. And as we did, Natalia noticed the ground had been trampled in a regular pattern, and said, "I think deer come here."

I was proud of her; she was learning to *see*. True *seeing* is at the heart of the art of tracking: becoming almost unconsciously sensitive to the subtlest clues in the land, making sense of them and reading them like the words of a tale. The mayapples weren't going anywhere, so I dropped to a knee and sought among the ground for other clues. Here and there were deer berries (the little round pellets of deer droppings), and I pointed them out.

She said, "They're dark and shiny. They must be fresh."

I shook my head. "Remember that it's been moist. And they are mostly sheltered among these tall grasses. They could actually be weeks old. Deer droppings are leftover, indigestible cellulose, a lot like sawdust, so they don't disintegrate fast. But look..." I pointed to some discreet marks made by the deer's cloven hooves, deep enough in the soft ground to show the dewclaws higher up the foot. "They probably came through during or right after that rain a couple nights ago because these tracks were made when the ground was soft. That's why you can see the dewclaws, which ordinarily never touch the ground," I explained. "And you can see three distinct sets of tracks. Two were probably does moving together. They often stick together. This set is very large. It's an old buck."

"They're a family?" Natalia asked.

I shook my head. "Deer don't stay in family units like eagles, sweety. In the warm months, does tend to stay in little groups that may include their young. But bucks older than a year tend to either wander alone or stay in loose all-male groups. It looks like this was a pair of does that came through together and whatever buck keeps this territory may just have happened to be with them." I went on to explain that I'd seen that kind of behavior many times before. A group of does will wander about browsing and one or two bucks in the area will follow them at a distance. I didn't know why since it was far out of breeding season. Maybe the bucks were just keeping tabs on where the does were. "No way to tell," I summed up. "But they are calm and well fed and healthy."

"How can you tell?" asked Natalia.

I swept my arm over the tracks, indicating their pattern as a whole. "The tracks are moving at an even pace, no wobbly motions that would indicate a very sick deer. They are deep, so I assume they are well fed and of good weight. And the tracks are closely spaced, so I assume they are moving calmly."

"But you can't be sure?" she asked.

I shook my head. "Tracking is a blend of knowing the animal and educated guesses," I explained. "That's why I call it an art as well as a science."

She was fascinated by the lore of tracking and we spent five more minutes examining the deer spoor as they progressed across the little glade. I explained that deer tended to use the same paths over and over. That way they created a network of trails all over their territory, and they know each and every turn of them intimately. If a predator ever tried for one, the deer would be able to flee quickly along its winding network of trails, and it would know every hiding spot along the route. That was why few predators except ambushers like wildcats and pack hunters like coyotes ever tried hunting them. Deer were fast and brilliant at elusion.

With the heat increasing rapidly, we made our way to the glade's edge and entered the embrace of green forest shadows where we finally came to the plants I had taken at a distance for mayapple. Except up close it turned out they weren't what I had hoped. They were something as remarkable, though they would not bear the uniquely sweet-tart fruits that grew on the otherwise direly poisonous mayapple plant (which is not for nothing also known as American mandrake). This was a patch of nodding trillium, now much larger than those I had encountered elsewhere the previous month. Much more mature now, they resembled from a distance the mayapple with their broad drooping leaves atop stems like umbrellas, sheltering a blossom roughly resembling the mayapple blossom. But up close the difference was apparent. I sighed. I still hoped to find a patch before the harvest season. If I did, I would gather all the fruit, collect the pulp, and then replant the seeds in the meadows around the homestead where they could flourish in ideal conditions.

Natalia and I pushed deeper. Not much farther on, we came across a sad sight, a clutch of eggs lay broken upon the forest floor. A couple were still semi-intact but several were fully broken up. I am not an expert on birds, but they were plain off-white and about the size of chicken eggs, so I believe they were from the nest of a great horned owl. We counted five in total.

"What happened?" asked Natalia sadly. "Did they hatch?"

I shook my head and pointed to a portion of shell with a residue of yolk and dried blood in it. "I think, in this case, a hunting mammal found the eggs. Any number of tree climbers could have done this, though my first guess would be that this was the work of a fisher. It's large enough to eat all these eggs in a single feast."

Natalia suggested, "Maybe some of the owls hatched and pushed the shells out of the nest."

I shook my head. "No, this isn't how eggs hatch. A chick opens up the end and pushes out."

A tree-climbing predator—probably a fisher—found a treasure trove of food, a whole clutch of great horned owl eggs. In this image, you can see the egg was eaten, not hatched, by the hole gnawed into the side of the egg. When an egg hatches, the chick pecks out a circular escape hatch at one end of the shell and pushes out of it, so that it looks like the egg was opened by a can opener. In this case, something has clearly broken open the side of the egg to feast on the protein and nutrient-rich albumen without spilling the precious contents.

I could tell that the idea of a fisher eating owl eggs disturbed her, but she has lived on a farm and in the woods long enough to understand the way of Nature. "Things have to eat, Natalia. We gather chicken eggs every morning. And, you know, those eggs would hatch if we put them in the incubator for a few weeks."

Natalia nodded. "Yeah, but it's still sad in a way."

I nodded. It was. But it was Nature's way. It is not ours to judge. I said, "At least they were just eggs when they got eaten. Sometimes fishers will find nests with young birds in them, and they won't hesitate to eat chicks any more than eggs."

"Eww!" Natalia blurted and I laughed. With a little good-natured teasing to lighten our spirits, we pressed on. We spent the rest of the day meandering through the forest and found various clues of its secret stories. We found a grove of mighty sugar maples far bigger than all the rest and wandered for a time amidst their vast trunks. We encountered a lone wandering buck and stood silent and still and watched him pass. He looked strong and healthy, and I wondered if he might have been the very one whose tracks we encountered earlier in the glade.

We found a sparkling streamlet that emerged from a spring further up the ridge, and sunlight seemed to gather around it like a veil of golden hues. Natalia espied the tiny frogs known in the eastern north woods as peepers and tried to catch some. She managed to avoid getting wet and muddy, and I attribute that to the superpowers that come with being a girl. A boy her age, i.e., me, would have been wearing a coat of mud by the end of a round of chasing frogs.

We found a lonely glen near the top of the ridge where the land leveled out. There I harvested the stalks of some wild carrots to add to our dinner. Unlike domestic carrots, where you mainly want the roots, the seed stalks of their wild cousins are the best parts, if you can get them when they are still tender, before they produce seed. This is because the roots of wild carrots rarely get to grow large due to the stony, hard packed character of untilled soil, so a wild carrot's energy goes into its top in the second year of its two-year life cycle. This results in tops that have an intense fragrance and taste that is more carroty than the carrot. They are delicious by themselves and go well with salads and stews.

Natalia aims to catch peepers in the forest brook, and somehow manages to avoid picking up so much as a smudge of mud.

Wild carrots have a bad reputation because sometime back in the 1970s a great number of books on wild-food foraging were written to capitalize on the interest generated by *Stalking the Wild Asparagus* (1962) by Euell Gibbons. Gibbons was a true expert but most of the copycat writers were anything but. They were, in fact and at best, novices trying to turn a quick buck on a new fad. As a kid, I had acquired some of their books and was more confused after reading them than before. The plants they recommended were often bitter and vile. Their preparation instructions only made things worse. Often one book's identification information contradicted another's. Sometimes I would bring plants home that I'd studied in those books and my grandmother would take one look and shrilly declare, *"Couillon! Tu vas être malade si t'en manges!"* (Idiot! You'll be sick if you eat that!) And if my grandmother—who had grown up on the bayou's forage—told me not to eat something one of those books recommended, I was going to take her advice. Especially since those authors warned in their books' introductions that they were not responsible if someone actually ate the very plants they were recommending!

If all that weren't bad enough, those authors borrowed from and referenced one another—a case of the blind leading the blind. At some point one of these amateurs mistakenly noted that wild carrot resembles the deadly poison hemlock and should be avoided. Another amateur cited this in his book and then it was cited elsewhere, creating a chain reaction of misinformation about the dangers of wild carrots (which, by the way, are genetically the same as our domestic carrots).

Yet the wild carrot is about as difficult to distinguish from poison hemlock as it is to tell an apple from an orange. Even if you totally discount the fact that poison hemlock is a large, stout plant four to six feet tall while wild carrot is a small, delicate plant that grows low to the ground excepting its graceful seed stalks, they still otherwise in no way resemble one another in appearance, smell, or taste. Wild carrots smell and taste sweet, wholesome and carroty, and their stems are solid. Poison hemlock smells noxious and its stems are hollow. So, with no fears of mistakenly eating poison food, we added the carrot tops to our dinner menu. We also added a few handfuls of wild strawberry blossoms for next morning's tea, as well as some wild oyster mushrooms, and some cucumber-tasting twin-bead lily and tart shamrock. The beauty of foraging is the wild country becomes your grocery and your apothecary—and that's how it should be.

Though we had hiked several miles in our tracking and foraging, getting back to camp was fast and easy. We had hiked a zigzag path up the ridge and returning was merely a straight downhill shot, but by the time we arrived we were ravenous. We'd been nibbling wild forage throughout our wanderings, but nothing beats a hot, hearty meal, especially when you're doing outdoorsy stuff and burning the inner fires bright. I got the wood stove going and started cutting vegetables and mushrooms while

Natalia went to the brook and scrubbed out the pot, which she had left soaking from the earlier meal, with clean stream-bottom sand.

◆ ◆ ◆

Dinner came with a turquoise sunset and featured locally sourced sausages and whole-wheat bread and goat cheese that Daphne had made. After, we built a campfire and roasted marshmallows for dessert and washed it down with cold brook water in which I had tossed sprigs of wild mint. It darkened and the fire played over the trunks of trees, revealing fey shadows in the dancing light, and now and then glowing pairs of eyes of watching animals: raccoons, porcupines and other small forest denizens. We chatted beneath the summer stars and I showed Natalia how to spot various constellations. Nearby was a spring that fed a small pool, and peeper frogs sang for us. And so we retired to our tent near midnight, reading by candlelight until the frogs serenaded us to quiet dreams.

At first light, I opened my eyes to sylvan poetry. Glimmers of a sunbeam touched the top of the tent and caressed the boughs of young evergreens beside us. Songs of summer birds filled the air and echoed among the forest. Natalia was already up and had made tea for us. I stretched then crawled out of the sleeping bag and met her at the Green Man's Kitchen where I was handed a mug of black tea laced with strawberry leaves and blossoms we had gathered the day before.

After tea, we decided to wander up and down the brook while it was still cool. A brook is its own little ecozone and both water and banks are host to many creatures and spirits not found elsewhere in the wildwood. Behind half-submerged stones were still troughs where we might see the shadowy turn of a trout. In broad, calm eddies, water striders skimmed the brook's surface, playing whatever games preoccupy insectoid minds. Climbing over a log, we came upon a piece of driftwood lying half-buried in the sandy bank and upon it was a beautiful dragonfly with crystalline wings, and though we approached very close it made no movement to flee or hide. I explained to Natalia that it could not fly yet because it was still cool at the edge of the brook in the shadows of the woods. It had to wait til the forest warmed enough for it to take flight and begin its daily hunt for biting insects. Nova Scotia is renown for its summer hazes of black flies and mosquitoes, and dragonflies are revered as heroes of the natural world.

We went back to camp an hour later and I set about making breakfast. Natalia hung about to help by breaking twigs down to finger length. The stove burned these very efficiently and could run for ten minutes on half a handful of such fuel. While she broke the twigs, I chopped onions, slit open a sausage of spicy red pudding, and sliced half a small loaf of bread and leaned it upright so that it could toast from the residual heat the stove threw. We chatted idly as we worked and she mentioned she was very hungry. I dug in my pack and found some sweet puffed wheat cakes made with dates and raisins and handed one to her. We usually ate only local food, so this was a rare treat, and Natalia smiled and skipped off to play along the brook's edge.

"Don't go far. Breakfast will be ready in twenty minutes," I called to her, then smiled. I was happy with how the outing had gone so far. Natalia and her older sister worked hard at the homestead, for everyone has his or her share of tasks on a traditional farm, and I believe firmly that it is good for children to learn the value of honest work. But a break is a good thing, too, and this was quality daddy-daughter time. And she was really enjoying herself. Tracks of bear and spoor of martens amazed her. She loved the camp food and drinking cold water from the brook laced with wild strawberry blossoms. She reveled in the night sounds of the wildwood.

The symmetry of the tent, the deep hues and spicy fragrance of evergreens, the timeless notes of myriad songbirds. I've done it thousands of times, but waking in a tent in the forest remains a delight and wonder every time.

In the cool of morning, this dragonfly with wings like spun crystal remained stone-still as I photographed it from only inches away.

Yet, wondrous as all that was, there came an especially touching moment that morning when a young life showed old wisdom. Every parent wants to know he has left something lasting and meaningful with his children. Something more than just a material inheritance. For those who follow the old ways, we want to know we have left them with lasting traditions that are more than just acts of repetition. We want to know we have given them a sense of where they came from, roots from which they can grow with wisdom into who they shall become. And such a moment bloomed into being as Natalia rambled while I cooked our breakfast.

Fifteen minutes later, I called out that breakfast was ready. She returned to camp shortly, and I noticed her cake was gone—odd, for she is such a slow eater—and asked if she had finished it.

"Oh, no," she replied primly. "I looked into the hollow of a tree and there were mushrooms in it. They grew together all weird and looked like the face of a hobgoblin. I thought the goblin might like the rest of my cake so I left it there for him."

I smiled and nodded, though I kept how touched I was by that simple act to myself, for Natalia is very bashful of praise. You see, it is so rare our daughters get such things as those cakes. The kids eat very healthy, fed a varied diet of farm-fresh produce, meat and eggs we raise, and wild fruit and vegetables foraged from the forest. It is only once in a blue moon they get to indulge in something like a sticky sweet cake made with non-local ingredients like dates and raisins. This was a rare, special treat bought especially for our camping trip. I'd bought these particular cakes for other special occasions and Natalia had a particular love of them. Yet for all that when she saw the hollow of a tree and imagined the face of a hobgoblin in the shape of the mushrooms that grew in its shadows, she recalled the tradition we've always practised of being generous and courteous to the spirits of the land and left her rare and much-favored treat for it.

Some say you shouldn't teach kids traditions but let them find their own way in the world. I say that's nonsense. A life without tradition is a life without context adrift in a sea of meaningless action. Teach a child the value and meaning of a path of love, balance, and respect and you can do no naught but good. I saw the flowering of that in the moment when my daughter showed she took to heart the lessons my wife and I had sought all our lives to impart. She knew to live kindly with the land, to respect the wisdom of harmony, and to value unbidden courtesy. In that moment, Natalia found her way into a faerie tale and created a happy ending for all of us.

So I tossed her a bottle of water that I'd had cooling in the brook. It was laced with wild chamomile. "Drink up! You look thirsty. Let's eat," I said, and dished up her food.

We sat in the shade near the Troll Bridge and all the while she offered idle chat while she dangled bare feet in the clear water. After some time, she said, "Something on your mind, Dad?"

I shrugged. "I was just thinking. You're a great kid. It's a privilege to be your dad."

Natalia rolled her eyes. She could never figure out how to handle praise. "Can we catch frogs?" she asked.

"That sounds perfect," I answered.

And so we caught frogs!

Wild Life

Meadow Lights

Fireflies are Nature's own willowisps and all around the world they light up meadows and forests with an ethereal luminescence that may appear as blue, green, amber, or even red. For many adults, some of their fondest memories are of chasing fireflies on warm summer nights and creating faerie lanterns—glass jars filled with the gathered creatures who shine a cool light that is both eerie and magical. And, like many children, when I was a boy I often wandered twilit meadows filling my own jar. I remember distinctly that those fireflies of the Deep South were a cool blue like starlight. But here in the woodlands of Nova Scotia, one of the most common fireflies is *Photorus fairchildi*, and its light is very different. It is so bright that if one flies by overhead and lights up, I can make out nearby trees. These fireflies love places of standing water: spring pools, vernal ponds, even long-lived puddles that regularly appear in depressions are sufficient. There is a pond near the cottage we call the Firefly Pond, and the reason for its name is no mystery; every spring from late May through June fireflies will congregate there, sometimes in thousands upon thousands. Sometimes I will go to the edge of the meadow and shine a bright flashlight swiftly over the pond then turn it off and the fireflies will light up all at once in reply. It is amazing.

It is equally amazing to come upon firefly larvae. Last summer Daphne was making dinner and wanted to make a Bluenose favorite: mashed new potatoes with rich spring butter. It was a bit early for new potatoes but she asked me if I could pop out to the Potato Patch and check if any were ready. I always plant three kinds of potatoes, an early variety for new potatoes, a mid-season variety for big tasty midsummer chips, and a late variety that keeps very well through winter, and I figured the biggest of the early plants should be ready enough. I went to the Potato Patch and found the biggest plant and started digging it up. As I was unearthing the potatoes, I noticed little glowing grubs in the soil. I carried one into the house for further examination. I am much more expert in mammals than insects so I contacted another naturalist friend and emailed him a photo and he informed me it was a larva of the fairchildi firefly.

I went back to the garden and carefully dug about and discovered the soil was full of the larvae. Maybe it was just close enough to the Firefly Pond, and just moist enough, to be ideal habitat. And after reading up a bit on them, I decided I was glad to have them in the garden, for it seems the larvae are carnivorous and eat the larvae and eggs of other bugs. That worked for me. Our large organic gardens are designed to attract insects and birds that prey upon garden pests. The remarkable firefly has become part of that dynamic.

Fireflies produce the most efficient light known to humans. Nothing we make, not even the vaunted efficiency of the LED, even comes close. The firefly's light is cool, clean and 100 percent energy efficient. They are a shining example of the remarkable creativity of Nature when left to her own devices.

But there is far more to them. Around the world they present other amazing behaviors. Most interesting is synchronized flashing. The fireflies I knew as a child flashed here and there in no apparent order. Here in Nova Scotia, it is much the same, but when they are very thick now and then groups of them will get very active all about the same time. Hundreds may light up within seconds of one another at one corner of the Firefly Pond, and then others may light up at another corner. But there are places in Asia where the fireflies flash by the tens of thousands in perfect synchrony. Why they do this remains a mystery.

Fireflies are important parts of the ecosystem. As larvae they are predators, feeding upon other insects and their eggs. As adults they are pollinators, feeding on the nectar of blossoms. Yet little preys on the firefly because they taste foul and, if enough are eaten, are poisonous. Just as poisonous creatures make themselves known in Nature with their bright colors, fireflies make themselves known by their lights which tell potential predators: *beware!*

That such a small creature can bring so much wonder into the world; this is enchantment incarnate, and why I have long said that, when it comes to natural magic, it makes little difference whether there is a scientific or preternatural explanation. It is no wonder that naturalists with advanced degrees in the sciences and small children alike are equally enamored with the firefly.

Enchanted Forest

The Ellylldan's Path

With early summer being the time of fireflies, this seems the perfect place to consider the glowing spirits that British folk call willowisps, who, like earthly fireflies, also prefer to abide above water, often in the vicinity of swamps and bogs. Throughout Europe there have been many sightings of these elusive elves. Some folk thought they were hateful, seeking to draw fools into bogs to drown. Others thought they did not mean harm but that folk were just drawn to their light like moths to a candle flame. Most folklorists, however, perceive them as mischievous faeries who intend no more than pranks by luring the unwary into tricky wetlands. In fact, the Cymric (Welsh) word for the willowisp is *ellylldan. El* may be taken to mean "elf," and *dan* means both "fire" and "lure." The word ellylldan is very likely a composite meaning "elf-fire-lure," and well describes what willowisps are best known for.

Out of the Vale of Glamorgan in southern Wales comes this old legend, recounted by Iola the Bard and written down by Wirt Sikes in the nineteenth-century tome: *British Goblins.* This tale portrays the old British

disdain of their wild wetlands, which may be likened to the modern apprehension about wild places, but at the conclusion of this tale we do not
see a malicious willowisp, just a person haphazardly mesmerized by the
spirit's wondrous elf-light. In the end, it would seem the wisp had little interest in its mortal pursuer. Just as we are barely aware of the Otherworld
all around us, perhaps and ellylldan is barely aware of the mortal world.

◆ ◆ ◆

One night, when the moon had gone down, as I was sitting on a hill-top,
the Ellylldan passed by. I followed it into the valley. We crossed plashes of
water where the tops of bulrushes peeped above, and where the lizards lay
silently on the surface, looking at us with an unmoved stare. The frogs sat
croaking and swelling their sides, but ceased as they raised a melancholy
eye at the Ellylldan. The wild fowl, sleeping with their heads under their
wings, made a low cackle as we went by. A bittern awoke and rose with a
scream into the air. I felt the trail of the eels and leeches peering about as I
waded through the pools. On a slimy stone a toad sat sucking poison from
the night air. The Ellylldan glowed bravely in the slumbering vapours. It
rose airily over the bushes that drooped in the ooze. When I lingered or
stopped, it waited for me, but dwindled gradually away to a speck barely
perceptible. But as soon as I moved on again, it would shoot up suddenly
and glide before. A bat came flying round and round us, happing its wings
heavily. Screech-owls stared silently at us with their broad eyes. Snails and
worms crawled about. The fine threads of a spider's web gleamed in the
light of the Ellylldan. Suddenly it shot away from me, and in the distance
joined a ring of its fellows, who went dancing slowly round and round in a
goblin dance, which sent me off to sleep.

—Wirt Sikes
British Goblins

Wood Witchery

Sacred Landscapes

There is a wee place in Maine wherein is a wee forest, and in that little forest a wee child might find many a wee cottage. And by no means do I mean to say a cozy dwelling for mortals. No, but a fine little place indeed, fit for the wee spirits of the woodland to call comfort and home. These are the faerie cottages and every year more seem to find their way into those Maine woods. Some are as simple as piles of moss and stone. Others are elaborate little hand-carved cottages that seem to have sprung up out of faerie tales. They all share in that they seem to have emerged from the land itself.

Of course, human folk are setting out those cottages, and some do it for the beauty, some for the fun. Yet some do it for the tantalizing pleasure of giving a gift to the Good Folk. But whatever the motivations, there is a certain rightness in their actions, for it makes of the forest a sacred space, one which welcomes and honors Earth's spirits.

A faerie house is a bit of whimsy, a bit of fancy, and a beautiful way to honor the wights of the wild places. (Photo courtesy of Sara Valentim.)

Far to the east there is another people that honor spirits of Earth by creating sacred spaces in a similar way. The people are the Japanese who follow the path of Shinto, an ancient religion that perceives Nature as sacred and filled with sentient spirits they call *kami*. Some kami are great and are the equivalent of gods. Some kami are like barely sentient elemental forces of sea and wave and mountain. Other kami are smaller, faerie-like spirits of woodlands, waterways, clouds, and pools. These are much like the European wight, or the North American aboriginal Inuqun. Practitioners of Shinto set out thousands of little shrines throughout their beautiful mountains and woodlands to create sacred places where the Earth's kami are welcomed and honored. In effect, they make of their beautiful countryside a sacred landscape.

Good comes of such practices on so many levels. They draw people out of doors to experience the wonder contained in natural places. They instill respect for the land, both on the plane of material environment and spiritual Nature. And spending time with the Earth Mother heals us. This is a demonstrable fact. Japanese scientists have been studying the tremendous healing power of simply being in proximity to forests, and their work has resulted in the creation of woodland paths throughout Japan where folk may walk among the trees to rejuvenate their bodies and spirits (see "Your Brain On Nature: Forest Bathing and Reduced Stress," by Eva Selhub and Alvin Logan, *Mother Earth News*). Such things are tremendously healing for Earth, too, because if ever she is to be redeemed from the environmental devastation our species currently wreaks upon her, people must not only know the cost of the harm they cause, they must also understand on a soul-deep level why they should care.

As you can imagine, I am a great believer in the value of creating sacred landscapes. And it can be done in so many ways. An organic garden created to blend in and enhance local ecology. A shrine to honor the land spirits (which is really what Maine's woodland faerie cottages are). Tending and enriching some place of magical-spiritual significance. In fact, anything you can do to enrich, beautify and honor the land becomes an act of creating a sacred landscape.

I hope there is a bit of land you can tend. If so, here are some tips:

1. Plant things that enrich a site's ecology. You would select plants that benefit wildlife from pollinating insects to birds and mammals.

2. Create shelter and habitat for local wildlife. So many animals are struggling today under the relentless encroachment of humans who voraciously devour every vestige of habitat for endless strip malls and suburbs. Creating space for them is an important act

of kindness that is sacred in itself. Many people set out birdhouses, bat houses, and shelters such as log piles for small mammals. As well, they create pondsand pools for frogs and turtles. You will have to investigate what lives in your local area to determine what to create.

3. If you have acreage, create Nature corridors. Until the era of industrial farming, which began more or less in the middle twentieth century, farmers created hedges around their fields and pastures. In these hedges grew all kinds of wild plants and wildlife used them to move about and shelter. Industrial farms aim to squeeze maximum productivity out of every last square inch of the land and so have done away with hedges. Restoring hedges will create immeasurable benefit to flora and fauna, literally creating corridors of biodiversity and enriching the Earth Mother.

4. Create sites meant to host the spirits of Nature. It could be as simple as planting wildflowers around a lonely pool or as complex as planting and maintaining a grove of trees in a circle to enclose a private space in sylvan beauty.

5. Within these sites create shrines or altars. Depending on the path you follow, these can be simple or complex. My Shaman Stone deep in the forest is an example of an exceedingly simple site. Nature put it there and it requires no care from me. I just visit it from time to time and leave little gifts of food for the spirits. Or a site could be as complex and beautiful as a Shinto shrine or faerie cottage or Wiccan altar. Follow the wisdom of your path.

6. If you have a large acreage, set aside land to be wild. Let it be a sanctuary for all the flora and fauna of the natural world. We have set aside over a hundred acres of our own land to this purpose. It is only a drop in the bucket of the world, but if more landowners did this, imagine the benefits this could work for the environment.

7. Invite others to share in what you have created. Let them experience the immense fulfillment and joy of interacting with Nature and some of them will go on to pay it forward, creating their own sacred landscapes and doing their part to make a better world.

Woods Lore

Catching the Light Show

In North America, fireflies are mainly creatures of the east and are rarely seen west of the Mississippi River, though entomologists at Brigham Young University have recently reported finding them hovering about ponds in Utah. At the time of the report, it was unknown if what they found was a heretofore unknown species or if somehow eastern fireflies had migrated westward. East or west, as a lifelong admirer of fireflies, I believe they are one of the great wondrous beauties of Earth. To me, fireflies rival meteor showers and thunderstorms...well, maybe not thunderstorms. I love a good storm. But so do fireflies, and they seem to put on their best shows just at the onset of one.

Of course, to see fireflies you need only be in an eastern North American country meadow upon a summer night. But if you want to see a truly dazzling show, I'm going to tell you how to find it.

Fireflies like open ground but with forest edges or hedges none too far away. They like the humidity just before storms, too, so they prefer sites where the trees block prevailing winds so they can take to the air.

They also need clean standing water close by, so you'll find the greatest gatherings right around ponds or vernal pools. They also require that the grasses and sedges around the body of water are never cut or grazed. This is because fireflies shelter among the grasses by day, and by night the males hover about over the grasses while the females climb them. In this way they can see one another's light and distinguish male from female.

An absolutely ideal site would be a small clearing in a forest with a pond in the middle, surrounded by uncut grass, the whole area on low ground so that even during storms wind can never stir up the area too much. Our homestead's Firefly Pond is just such a site, and that is why they cluster down there by the tens of thousands.

If you have ever gone into the countryside to watch a meteor shower, you know that the best vantages are hillsides facing the direction of the shower, and the best times are a.m. hours when there is no moon. Well, there are vantages and times that present the best firefly shows, too. You'll want high ground facing the pond, and you'll want to get there just at sunset, for fireflies put on their best show in the first couple hours after the sun goes down. You'll also want to note the weather. Fireflies love humidity. They provide dazzling shows just after a rain, but for truly dramatic displays, time your firefly watching with the coming of storms. If you can be in a well-sheltered firefly site just hours before a big nighttime storm, you are in for a treat.

Bring a small, powerful flashlight, the kind that throws a concentrated beam. I always carry a couple flashlights in my pack (it's good to have a spare if you're going to be in the woods through the night) that can throw over 900 lumens, but a light that throws even a twentieth of that is fine. I sweep the beam quickly over the grasses around the pond then switch it off. Within seconds the fireflies return a brilliant display of bioluminescence. It is magnificent, but I only do it a couple times any given hour so as not to interfere too much with their nocturnal mating rites. When we humans approach Nature, it is ever incumbent upon us to do so with gentle courtesy and cautious respect. The old adage, *do no harm*, applies as much to the little wild creatures as to anything else.

JULY'S
JOURNEY

Like Stars on Earth

Sad such a wonderful lifestyle died in so few short years for this
thing mis-assessed as progress.

—David (last name unknown)
From commentary made on
the author's website (2014)

Secrets abound within the depths of the forest, shy and subtle, and they do
not yield themselves readily. They are coy. They are careful. They choose
cautiously those to whom they will reveal themselves. And it has been
my experience that some places hold more secrets than others. Across the
ages such places have come to be known as sacred, full of mystic energies,
the foci where the green world and the Otherworld come together. And
such places are pregnant with possibility. Anyone who passes through may
experience an inexplicable frisson. An especially attentive person might

glimpse some fey creature. A witch may find a rare herb without even trying, as if dousing her way to it. A shaman may find himself absently talking
to a spirit and hardly realize he is not dreaming. For in such places the real
world touches upon that of faerie tales, and in many an old tale such forests
were called enchanted.

I have known many such places in the course of years spent in the
wilds of the world. There are places in the subarctic where the Inuqun
dwell. In the Scots highlands are ancient rolling hills and shining lochs
thick with legends of otherworldly events dating back millennia. I
have climbed Scots mountains and at twilight you can virtually feel the
magic like a fine web in the air. And in the forest around Twa Corbies
Hollow are many magical places. Sequestered at a deep woods waterfall
there is the Shaman Stone that virtually beckons one take a seat upon
it and make the spirit journey and parley with the beings of the Underworld. None too far east lies the Old Wood where I know a Green
Man walks and wards the creatures of that ancient forest of maple and
birch. And southerly lies the vast stretch we simply call the Wildwood.
Broken only by the occasional farmstead or tiny village, the Wildwood
spans from the Hollow to the sea and is home to rural folk of quaint
traditions and a host of wildlife.

Far out there lies a half-lost lake deep in the sequestering forest. We
call it the Whispering Lake, and to reach it one must travel many miles
over dirt paths and lost byways that are barely more than poor trails. The
last leg of the journey is a rugged, broken old path that was made decades
ago, perhaps by a long-since-departed homesteader. The trail is rocky and
so pitted it is fit only for hiking and horses. The girls and I make a tradition of going out there several times every year to canoe and kayak, and
this high summer week Natalia and I decided to set out there and spend a
while, wandering and exploring by canoe and kayak.

We planned to camp on the far side of the lake. The terrain around
the lake was far too rugged to pack in our gear, being in one place bog,

another dense forest and yet another impassible rocky country. But it was a perfect excuse to get some practical use out of our boats. Natalia is partial to kayaks, and the year before, our friend Jenny had bought two for her own children who, it turned out, did not care for them, so she gave them to our daughters. Natalia found herself the proud owner of a nearly new kayak and she loved using it at every opportunity. I am partial to canoes, which are far more practical for the actual business of living in the bush as even a small canoe can carry a substantial load of gear with ease. So we loaded the old farm truck with our gear and set off down the ever-diminishing paths into the far depths of the Wildwood.

Miles later we reached the head of the trail, turned, and carefully proceeded at less than a snail's pace to avoid cracking the bottom on jagged rocks and pit-sized potholes. After we had gone a short ways, we pulled to a stop. From there, we unloaded our packs and gear and carried them down to the lake's edge. Then we hiked back up to the truck, got our boats, and portaged them back down. Moving Natalia's stout little kayak was easy. It weighed less than forty pounds and was only a dozen feet long. The canoe was substantially longer and weighed almost twice as much. We carried it together for stability. We wore tall boots because the path was pockmarked with deep puddles full of rainwater that never seemed to dry.

It was a beautiful summer morning, on the warm side, and we were sweating pints by the time we were able to set my boat down in the water. But Natalia is eager and outdoorsy; she could hardly wait to get on the lake. She donned her flotation vest, snagged her paddle, and shoved into the water, paddling in gleeful circles in the summer sun as I loaded gear onto my canoe, taking my time to ensure everything was well balanced and secured. When I had settled everything just as I wanted, I pushed off, climbed into the rear seat, and we started a patient paddle to the far side of the lake that would be our home for the next few days.

The sky was graying when we grounded our boats, and we worked fast to get the tent up in case it should decide to rain.

"Whee!" cried Natalia, as she paddled ahead of me, thrusting her oar into the water and made her boat turn almost on a dime. Then she paddled behind me and did the same. Compared to the sixteen-foot canoe laden with a couple hundred pounds of gear, her little boat was a nimble sparrow to my stately albatross. Finally, she tired of the game and pulled up beside me. Paddling in rhythm, she asked, "Where are we going to camp?"

I told her, "Remember last month? We came out here and circled the entire lake and then pulled out on that peninsula for a break? I saw a flat bit of high ground in the shelter of the trees. It'll be perfect." But no sooner had I finished speaking than Natalia had lost interest and paddled ahead again. She had seen a fish jump in a little cove that was thick with lotuses and she wanted a closer look. It was in the direction we were going, so I let her wander ahead and continued to ply a steady course for the peninsula. And while Natalia was darting her kayak from the rings of one jumping trout to another, I was able to line up on the landing spot. I started paddling hard, building up speed in order to let the canoe's momentum ground it up high on the wet grass. Natalia looked up from her game just in time to see the canoe coming to a stop.

"No fair! You sneaked!" she cried and raced my way.

Wherever we're going, she likes to get there first. In her nimble little boat, she should have easily won, too. But she got sidetracked and my large, stately canoe had arrived before her—a classic case of the tortoise and the hare. Even so, her little boat was so fast and nimble that I was just finishing pulling the canoe higher onto the grasses when she made land beside me, still declaring it was no fair.

The sky was graying, so I felt compelled to get our camp set up promptly, but I paused to take it all in. It was July, the very heart of summer, and the green around us was so intense it was dazzling. Cicadas sang. Frogs croaked. Songbirds vociferated from the treetops. Natalia could sense it, and she froze beside her kayak. Here was primal beauty, timeless and encompassing. Welcoming or hostile, depending on how you lived with it. We just circled slowly, taking in the sight of the expansive lake, the little peninsula of old evergreens that we would call home for a few days, the glades and glens and high hills lying across the lake, the deep, dark forest beyond. It really was, I realized, like something out of a faerie tale.

"Do you think there are bears here?" Natalia asked.

"The big, bad wolf, too," I replied.

She giggled. She knew as well as I that neither black bears nor coyotes nor coywolves represented any real danger to humans who lived wisely with the forest.

We began the work of making camp. That began with using our hatchets to clear a bit of a path to the campsite, which was a naturally flat area of ground between two huge hemlocks. Deer and moose tracks let us know some other creatures occasionally visited the peninsula, though I wasn't much worried about either. Deer were no danger, and moose could be dangerous, but it was neither calving time (when cow moose could be aggressive) nor the rut (when bull moose might charge). Besides, we would take steps to see they turned away before any kind of confrontation could develop.

Once we made the path and brought all our gear over, setting up camp went quickly. We laid a tarp over the ground and set a second aside to serve as an additional shelter should rain set in. Then we put up the tent. Natalia went in and laid out our sleeping bags and night gear (reading lights, books, toiletries) while I gathered firewood: large for a proper campfire, and small for the little cooking wood stove. There was plenty of wood about, and by the time Natalia emerged from the tent I was already getting on to the next task.

I had taken a hundred foot length of rope and tied a short bit of a dead branch to one end to add heft. Then I tossed the branch high into a tree. It made it over a bough about twenty feet up and the end fell down the other side, dragging the rope with it. As I gathered up the excess coils, I told Natalia to bring me the food, which was all stowed in a sack.

"What are you doing?" she asked curiously as she hauled the sack over.

"I'm making a bear hang. Putting our food high up where it's safe."

She sniffed. "I know what it is. I thought you said there were no bears here."

I cast her a sidewise glance. "Um ... no, exactly what I said was the big, bad wolf was here, too. Which means that not only are there black bears around here, but there are coyotes and coywolves. There are also raccoons and wildcats and wolverines and other critters that would be happy to get in our food. So, unless you want to spend the next three days eating nothing but shamrock and wild dock, we need a bear hang."

As if on cue, a coyote howled somewhere off in the distance. Odd, too, since it was early in the day. Natalia looked off into the woods dubiously. "I know they don't hurt people, but they still scare me."

The weather turns fast in Nova Scotia, and by the time the camp was made, the sky had cleared, offering a beautiful vista of pristine country.

I smiled at her as I hoisted the sack up then tied off the loose end of the rope to another tree. "You should always be respectful. Sometimes you should be wary. But you shouldn't be scared. The animals have no interest in people. They are just here to live, same as us. Respect them and they'll respect you."

She nodded but said, "It's one thing to know it, another to *know* it."

I reviewed with her the various strategies we would use to keep wild-life away from camp, then we enjoyed a lunch of sandwiches made with thick slices of Daphne's bread, vegetables from our garden, and cheese from the goats. Natalia could hardly wait to get back out on the water, so after ensuring she took a break to let the food settle, we set off to circle the lake and see what had grown since we last visited in late spring.

I've always known intuitively that any land-bound water is magical. Nothing sounds more magical to me than the sighing of a waterfall or the babbling of a stream or the secrets of rain whisper-falling in a green forest. A small lake like this one is large enough to offer the lapping rhythm of waves, but small enough at a mere mile-and-a-half in diameter to have the close and personal feel of a pond. And it is a nexus for all the life around it for many square miles. This lake exists in the high country; it is at the meeting point of several slopes and various brooks flow into it. Many kinds of ecological zones come to a confluence in this place: open water, wetlands, forest, meadow—and all the varied life of such places. And I wanted Natalia to develop a sense of the magic and richness of such a focal point.

We shoved our boats out onto the water and paddled to the right, following the lake's edge and came first to a swampy wetland where a stream entered the lake through rocky high ground. Sometime in the last century the land here must have sunk because this area was thick with great dead trees. They were fallen over, creating a tangle of branches and logs in the shallows. It was great shelter for trout and they rose to the surface to snatch at flies, then darted deep again to avoid the bald eagles that haunted these parts. Natalia weaved seamlessly among the tangles and my much larger canoe, now relieved of its heavy load of cargo, was almost as nimble. In fact, the canoe had an edge now that her boat couldn't match. I could scoot into the middle of the boat, centering its weight, and make it pirouette in place, allowing me to get into tighter places than she could. I could also lean my weight to one side, causing the canoe to cant at some 45 degrees, which created less drag and allowed me to paddle much faster and more nimbly. I could also sit back on the bench and allow the boat's full length to settle into the water, which coerced the canoe into wanting to go straight with ease, a phenomenon canoeists call *tracking*. Thus, I could leisurely paddle only on the left side, which greatly reduced the overall energy required to paddle, whereas Natalia had to constantly paddle on one side then the other to keep her kayak on course. A kayak is a nimble boat design and it handles windy conditions better, but it is for good reason the canoe has been for centuries the choice for freshwater long-distance travel among Canada's *coureur de bois* (French for woodsmen). So, playing to the strengths of each of our boats, we wove between the debris of ancient trees and made our way to the far bank where we slowly paddled beside the lake's edge where the calm water was only inches deep. There were frogs in plenty, bullfrogs and tiny peepers, but in Nova Scotia they only sing in spring and now they wandered quietly about their tasks. About thirty yards back, in the center of soupy ground as much water as earth, was the smallish mound of a muskrat colony, but there were none to be seen just now. But most fascinating were the carnivorous pitcher plants growing right at water's edge. The oddly dull yet brilliant purple-red-brown colors of the peculiar drooping blossoms lure insects. The insects, attracted to the carrion-scented nectar within the pitchers formed by the unusual leaves at the plant's base, wander down into them and then find they can't get back out. Small hairs facing downward grow from the inner walls of the pitchers, allowing the insects ingress, but preventing them from finding footholds to exit. The nectar is potent with enzymes that would then break down the trapped insects and digest them.

One grew right at water's edge and we paused to examine it more closely, grasping reeds to pull our boats right up beside it. Then Natalia spotted movement further up where a distant high outcrop hosted a dense grove of young evergreens. Forgetting the pitcher plant, she thrust her oar into the water and was off. Suddenly, she yelped and dove her paddle straight into the water, flatting the blade. It worked like a brake, stopping her on a dime, but turning her kayak so sharply she almost tipped herself over. A moment later I heard a sound like a large stone plunging smoothly into water. A handful of seconds later, there was a loud slap, like enormous hands clapped a single time. I saw a bit of spray just port of her boat and knew it for what it was at once: a beaver. Natalia blurted, "The beaver came out of the woods and started into the water and got right in front of the kayak! It was so close I almost ran into it. I think it thought I was a log til it saw the paddle move." Then she started giggling as if nearly bumping into an enormous beaver and rolling her boat was the funniest thought she could have imagined. She's crazy. She takes a lot after her dad. We both laughed.

A moment later the beaver surfaced and scowled at us, then dove again, slapping the water again with its large, flat tail, close enough this time to send spray over me. I laughed all the harder. This was how beavers alerted their colony-kin that there were strangers in their water. There were at least two lodges on this large lake, so it was no surprise to encounter a beaver. Clearly, it had been in the copse of young evergreens doing what beavers do, cutting trees for food. We played a game with it for a little while, following it at a distance, trying to predict where it would emerge next. The water was clear as crystal, but the brilliant sky shone blue over it and hid the beaver well. But a little breeze began to kick up so we decided to go back to the lake's edge to take advantage of the shelter of the trees.

Onward we paddled, passing by an expanse of open slope rich with wild blueberries and cranberries. A third beaver lodge we had not known about was tucked back in a swampy thicket of lilies. We paddled onward and soon were at the far side of the lake.

Here was an expanse of wetland country a fifth the total size of the lake. It was riddled with clear, narrow channels that ran between rafts of aquatic grasses. Just beyond the grasses were tall reeds and cattails and numerous lotuses and lilypads. As wild-food foragers, this is rich land to us. The lotuses are few, so we harvest from them only lightly, but they grow into alien-looking seedpods that yield large, meaty seeds that are nice for a rare treat. Further south in North America, they grow in such abundance and so rapidly they could be a staple food source, but are largely overlooked as a crop. Some of the floating blossoms that people often refer to as lilies are actually wapato and they have tubers down in the muck. However, the real prize is the cattails, which are common and grow in vast swaths. Every part of the cattail is useful, and what is useful depends on the season. In spring the young shoots can be cut from the water and steamed or fried for a flavor like peppery asparagus, cucumber, and celery. End of summer, the young heads can be cooked but I don't know what you could compare the flavor to; it is unique. Later in autumn, the heads will become covered in dense, yellow pollen, which can be shaken into bags, sifted to remove any bugs, and serves as a high-protein flour. And in winter before the freeze-up the cattails can be pulled up at the roots, yielding starchy tubers that serve as a potato replacement. I pulled my canoe up beside a growth and used my folding knife to cut several at the waterline. Normally, I would pull them up from the rootstock and use more of the plant, but there were leeches here. The leeches fed fish and birds but I didn't care to get one on me. I tossed the stalks into the midsection of the boat. When we got back to camp, I intended to grill them with the venison steaks we planned to have for dinner.

These wetlands also sheltered countless small fish such as trout and perch, as well as peepers and bullfrogs and their tadpoles, and any number of insects. Ducks and wild geese lived in the thickets, nesting on little islets or near water's edge. Natalia and I paddled up one of the many channels that zigzagged between the grasses. We pushed til the channels became very narrow and shallow—places the water was only inches between our keels. There we became very quiet and motionless, letting ourselves drift back to the lake with the gentle current. Quiet and still, the wetlands came to life all around us. We heard the cries of wild geese and ducks. Off starboard, a mated pair of loons splashed about and one emitted the haunting call that is quintessential of the north country. Muskrats that were hidden in the reeds came waterside to ramble, and one swam beside us for a while, curious perhaps if we were some oddly shaped logs. Several hundred yards south, we heard loud splashing in the wet and reedy lands near lake's edge—probably a moose. I hoped we got to see it. Moose are growing ever rarer in these parts. The forest service blames their decline on a worm that whitetail deer carry but are immune to, yet is fatal to their larger moose cousins. And that may be so, but poachers sometimes wander the woods, too, shooting moose opportunistically even though their numbers are low. Whenever Natalia or I espy a moose, we tell no one in order to keep their locations secret and safe.

But by the time we had drifted back into open water where visibility was better, whatever it was had moved off. All I knew was it had been large. But it could just as well have been a black bear, which are plentiful in these parts and inclined to take a dip on hot days. We aimed for the north side of the lake and skirted the shore back to camp, passing a mix of young evergreen and tall hardwoods. I noted numerous sumac and wild cherry trees, and some dogwoods, all of which bore fruit we might later come back and harvest when it was ripe.

The breeze subsided and the air became very calm. I let myself fall several hundred yards behind Natalia so I could observe the wildlife better. What I would do, she could not match in her kayak due to the

side-to-side way it had to be paddled. There is an old aboriginal technique of paddling that is inefficient but almost soundless and motionless. One dips the paddle in the water and strokes slowly back, then
instead of withdrawing the paddle from the water it is turned sharply
so the narrow angle of the blade is facing the direction of motion, then
the paddle is brought forward. When again in position, the paddle is
angled broadside and stroked back again. This is called sculling and
it propels the canoe slowly but without raising a splash. It takes a fair
bit of skill and the first time I ever tried it, I nearly rolled my canoe by
failing to angle the paddle correctly, which torqued the boat to one
side. But paddling like this, I sculled ahead ever so slowly. In the calm,
I saw shy, rare eastern bluebirds, which had eluded us on our last camping trip. Downy woodpeckers worked their way over various live trees
and snags. Colorful ruby-crowned kinglets and scarlet tanagers and
common grackles put in appearances. A barn owl napped in the shady
heights of a tall, leafy birch. Chipmunks rambled and I encountered
two more beavers going about their business, dragging the floating
hulk of a small tree through the water. It was idyllic.

About twenty minutes behind Natalia, I made it back to camp. Eager
to try her new fishing pole, she was already down at the opposite end
of the peninsula where the clear water dipped rapidly and various small
trout were rising for flies. But I wasn't counting on fish. She was a complete novice and trout are small, anyway. I rarely bother to fish for them if
I am planning to live off the land. And if I did seriously need to eat fish for
calories, I would improvise a fish trap—a survival skill I'd have to teach
her one day. I snagged a light lunch of a sandwich from our bear hang,
and let her fish for an hour. Then, as she'd had no luck, I suggested she
try again in the evening. For now, we were going foraging.

A sun ring appeared overhead. It happens when fine ice crystals are
high in the atmosphere and sunlight refracts through them like a prism.
They indicate rain is coming in a day or so. Tomorrow we might have to

set up some tarps as additional rain shelters. Ah well, that was tomorrow's problem ...

We meandered into the woods upland following an old game trail. The woods were in places towering evergreens of white spruce and hemlocks. Springs were everywhere, so thick that in places the ground was swampy. In those places the woods became denser, comprised of water-loving willow and black spruce, the latter a scraggly tree that always looks like it exists at death's edge. After a half mile we came to a high meadow filled with summer flowers, and it wasn't long before I found what I was looking for: tart dock—an edible herb that can grow quite large. This late in summer, they mostly had tough leaves, but even in high summer tender young leaves can be found if you dig among the dense large leaves. I harvested some of those tender leaves and saw some plants were already sporting tall stalks covered with seed. I harvested those, too. I could rub the seeds between my hands to remove the calyxes, winnow them by tossing them in the air, and derive seed meat that was like fine grain. I also gathered stalks of wild carrots. Dock is tart, carrots sweet, and cattails are peppery. All together they would make a great green mix to go with our steaks.

I noticed wild Jerusalem artichoke also grew here, but I didn't want to harvest them at this time of year. The starchy tubers tasted like artichoke hearts if harvested extremely late in autumn, really just before winter sets in in earnest, but they were hideous if harvested too early. For a starch, we had plenty of Daphne's homemade loaves.

The day was getting late when we returned to camp. As the sun neared the horizon, I made a small fire in the little wood stove and grilled the venison steaks, then the vegetables in the gravy. As always, Natalia was fascinated by the stove. It was about the size of a small coffee can and weighed about the same. It was cleverly shaped to suck in air as it heated up. The superheated air sucked the smoke back into a secondary combustion chamber where it too was burned. It was called a rocket stove because once it heated up, the flame emerging from it looked a little like a rocket flame. They are very efficient. They burn hot and long with just a smidgen of fuel. I used one made by Solo Stoves, and it had no moving parts, never wore out and created no waste such as spent fuel tanks. I could cook a whole multi-course meal over it using only a couple handfuls of tiny twigs. But Natalia was perplexed.

"Why carry something like that when there is all the firewood we want back here in the woods? It's just more weight."

I poured her a cup of tea brewed from forest shamrock I snagged nearby. It had a lemony flavor. "When people think there is a lot of something, they never consider it must eventually run out. Beavers are everywhere now, but just a hundred years ago they were trapped to make hats for fashionable folk in Europe; trapped til they almost went extinct. There are plenty of beavers now mainly because the fashion died out before the beavers did. If you aren't careful not to overuse something in abundance, all too quickly it can become scarce. And if it vanishes, it never comes back. That is a terrible thing. Perhaps the worst thing."

A ring around the sun heralded coming rain.

She nodded. We had talked about environmental care many times, but I always made it a point to reinforce the lessons with real world experiences.

Soon enough, the steaks were ready. We ate, chattering amiably about this and that as the sun continued to lower. When we finished the meal, we washed the dishes thoroughly in the lake to drive off any food smells that might attract animals in the night. I double-checked our firewood supply. We had enough to burn for several hours, plus plenty of piled green ferns and bracken we could throw on the coals so it would smoke all night. I liked black bears, but I really didn't want to wake up in the middle of the night and end up spooking one in the course of answering a call of nature. A spooked animal is a dangerous animal. But even more, I wanted to discourage clever raccoons which might well find some way of defeating our bear hang and getting at our food supply. I decided to double-check the bear hang, perhaps use a long pole to shift it even further from the tree trunk which a raccoon might climb. Natalia came with me.

It was the last light of day as we walked through the tall woods, and it made for a dazzling surreal landscape: pools of congealing dark contrasting sharply with the bright gold of end-of-day sunbeams slipping almost sidewise among the boughs. The bear hang was in an especially old grove of hemlocks. They did not make a tight canopy, so when we had put up the bear hang near midday with the sun overhead it had seemed a bright but unremarkable place. Now, the little hemlock grove was cast in wine shadow, and as we walked over the forest duff Natalia and I gasped. The ground was covered in young bunchberry plants, small with deepest green, waxy leaves that seemed to pull the coming night around themselves like a cloak.

"It's eerie here," Natalia commented.

I nodded. "Like it's dark here, even though the sky is still blue." Frissons danced along my spine as I realized this was a twilight place, a haunt of woodland wights.

The breeze crept up again just then, soughing in the evergreen boughs and waving them so that they opened just enough to admit a burnished final beam of the lowering sun. It sprayed over the preternaturally dark bunchberry and illuminated their pale blossoms like a carpet of Earth-bound stars. Wordless, Natalia and I watched the magic. Breeze touched boughs; sun touched blossoms. The light swam in the flow of the breeze through the branches. It was a magic formula that set the forest floor a'twinkle.

"This is a sacred place," I told Natalia. "Can you feel it?"

I don't think she was as comfortable with words in the presence of such awe and merely nodded. Finally, though, she swallowed, and asked, "What do we do?" She meant, *Are we intruding? Should we strike camp?*

I shrugged and said, "We'll leave a bit of bread and cheese for the spirits. I'll tell them we respect them and love this place of old magic. The spirits want us to know the land, not fear and avoid it. They'll understand."

Natalia nodded. She'd seen things in this wood: fey lights, shadowy movements, the way good things happened around the homestead that defied rhyme and reason. She and her sister even said they'd seen an old homestead that appeared and vanished at times, far off in the forest. She knew the reality of enchantment and how it touched betimes the wild places.

I voiced a quick word of respect then checked our bear hang, using a nearby pole—remnants of a young, fallen tree—to shift the sack a couple feet further from the trunk. And as the sun slipped beneath the horizon, Natalia went back to camp to prepare the evening fire. The campfire was our way of being good neighbors and announcing our presence to the wild creatures, but Natalia also really liked the fact we'd soon be roasting marshmallows over it.

I left a bit of bread and cheese, taken from the bear hang, among the luminously white bunchberry blossoms and said, "For the Good Folk and the Old Wights. Our gift in turn for this good place."

"Look!" cried Natalia from camp, a hundred yards away. She did not sound alarmed, but yet more amazed. I rose from the small act of the offering and hurried back to the camp and saw her standing beyond the tent at water's edge. The eastern horizon glowed a remarkable silver hue as can only be seen in the true night of remote lands. Across the lake the full moon was rising in a clear and perfect welkin of pomegranate and plum, casting an exquisite cool light that was reflected and intensified by a lake so calm its surface was like glass. And in that fey light we could see a single muskrat floating not fifty feet from us, facing us, studying us, like the incarnate eyes of the spirits of this place.

I cast a glance toward Natalia, and in the dazzlingly clear moonlight her own eyes were aglow with wonder. And I knew she was aware then how precious were places such as this lost pristine lake, for they have power, the most precious kind: the magic that is rooted deep in the Earth Mother. She did not know that I had had another motive for bringing her on this outing. As well as fun, this was education...the best kind. And as the muskrat regarded us and the wondrous moon drew ever higher, I knew that she had learned lessons today no words could impart, for she too could feel the flow of enchantment. It had hidden among the many beauties of the wildwood; it was found among blossoms that shone like stars upon the Earth. And like the many colors of twilight that hallowed the rising moon, it was oft-overlooked unless one stopped to truly *see*.

After a long while, as the moon drew higher and the colors faded to ebony and starlight, we left the lakeshore and returned to the pile of firewood where we sat on stones we had pulled up to serve as seats. Natalia sat quietly as I struck sparks from my steel and set some dried mushroom to smouldering. I wrapped the little coal in brittle, dry lichen and blew it into a tiny flame which I set at the base of the twigs. Soon, the little spark grew into a comforting campfire casting shifting warm light over the sheltering trunks and boughs. Natalia sat pensively, watching, thinking. And I knew as I stuck marshmallows on twigs today's experiences were going deep into her young shaman's soul.

Wild Life

Bunchberries—Ubiquitous Boreal Apples for the Woodsman

Being able to identify what is edible in the wild changes one's relationship with it entirely. Prior to such knowledge, it is a barren place and visits are limited til one's supplies are exhausted. But for the one who can forage wild foods, the land becomes a welcoming place and everywhere is home. And one of the friendliest, easiest to find and identify yet oft-overlooked wild foods of the north woods is the bunchberry. Anyone who lives at sufficiently northerly latitude has probably seen the bunchberry, pictured on the next page. The further north you go, the more common it becomes, happily sprouting anywhere there is adequate moisture and forest shadow.

The bunchberry is a low-growing, gorgeous plant sporting glossy, veined leaves that are typically oval and come to pointed tips. It is a dwarf form of the dogwood and grows by means of a slender stem emerging from underground rhizomes and often grows thickly matted along the forest floor. By June it produces lovely small flowers of pale white. The flowers are actually composites of many smaller blossoms, and each will later become a small red berry that will grow in tight clusters with tiny, firm seeds.

Easily identified, most foragers in the north are aware they are edible but largely ignore them because the berries' flavor is so mild. Indeed, if eaten only one at a time, one might describe them as tasteless. Trust me—they are worth harvesting. You just have to eat them right to appreciate them.

They are easy to harvest, with their bright berries offered in clusters above the low-lying leaves as if inviting a forager. Just sweep your hands through the clusters, fingers slightly spread, and swipe the berries from several plants at once. You can get a whole handful this way. Pop them all into your mouth and munch away. By the mouthful, bunchberries offer a pleasant, mild apple flavor, though not quite so tart as apples. No need to spit out the seeds, either. They won't harm you. Think of them as texture, like poppy seeds on a muffin.

Bunchberries survive intense winter cold and keep well. Typically ignored by insects and animals, you can often find them from the time they are first ripe in August right into the thaw of the following spring. As long as they are bright and firm, they are good to eat.

On long hikes or camping trips, I love to make bunchberry tea. I simply harvest enough to fill a mug, mash them, and add them to a pot over the campfire or stove. I add an additional mug or two worth of water and let it come to a boil, then remove from the flame and let it steep a few minutes. It will have a mild apple flavor, and if you have it on you, a dash of cinnamon and brown sugar goes great with it. If you have the skill to identify some other useful forage, such as Labrador tea or wood sorrel or chaga, they also go well steeped into bunchberry tea.

The bunchberry is a diminutive relative of dogwood that grows low to the ground in northern woods and produces mildly apple-flavored berries that grow in tight, prolific clusters.

Enchanted Forest

The Gwragedd Annwn y Llyn
*(Gor*ah*geth An*noon ee Lin)*

The Welsh (Cymric) faerie lore is a beautiful mythology and faerie spirits of lakes feature prominently in it. This tale, which I have titled "The Gwragedd Annwn y Llyn" (Elf Ladies of the Lake) to distinguish it from other Cymric tales of elf maidens of watery abodes, stands as one of my favorites and became the root concept behind the Brook Ladies who appeared in a novel, *An Ogham Wood*, that I wrote some years back. When I visited Wales about ten years ago, I stayed within Snowdonia Park almost the entire time, and I was privileged to meet a Cymric speaker who took me to visit many of its lonely lakes. One could feel the magic in those half-wild places, and oft I stood upon the lakes' edges come the gloaming, longing in my deepest soul to witness the face of a Gwragedd looking back from those dark and pensive waters. And, I suppose, to this day any time I set out on one of Canada's more remote waterways in my canoe, my heart still yearns to glance down and espy the passing form of one of the enchanted ladies of the waters.

◆ ◆ ◆

The son of a farmer on Drws Coed farm was one foggy day looking after his father's sheep, when crossing a marshy meadow he beheld a little lady behind some rising ground. She had yellow hair, blue eyes, and rosy cheeks. He approached her, and asked permission to converse; whereupon she smiled sweetly and said to him, "Idol of my hopes, you have come at last!" They there and then began to "keep company," and met each other daily here and there along the farm meadows. His intentions were honourable; he desired her to marry him. He was sometimes absent for days together, no one knew where, and his friends whispered about that he had been witched. Around the Turf Lake (Llyn y Dywarchen) was a grove of trees, and under one of these one day the fairy promised to be his. The consent of her father was now necessary. One moonlit night an appointment was made to meet in this wood. The father and daughter did not appear till the moon had disappeared behind the hill. Then they both came. The fairy father immediately gave his consent to the marriage, on one condition: namely, that her future husband should never hit her with iron. "If ever thou dost touch her flesh with iron she shall be no more thine, but she shall return to her own." They were married—a good-looking pair. Large sums of money were brought by her, the night before the wedding, to Drws Coed. The shepherd lad became wealthy, had several handsome children, and they were very happy. After some years, they were one day out riding, when her horse sank in a deep mire, and by the assistance of her husband, in her hurry to remount, she was struck on her knee by the stirrup of the saddle. Immediately voices were heard singing on the brow of the hill, and she disappeared, leaving all her children behind. She and her mother devised a plan by which she could see her beloved, but she was not allowed to walk the earth with man, so they floated a large turf on the lake, and on this turf she stood for hours at a time holding converse with her husband. This continued until his death.

—Wirt Sikes
British Goblins

Wood Witchery

Cooking Up Potions

Potions are just herb or fungus-based beverages that possess some beneficial nature. They are none too difficult to make. You just need the liquid essences of herbs and fungi. Herbal essences can be produced with a simple
piece of equipment: an alembic.

An alembic is a simple device used to extract the essential oils from
herbs. It is just a cone that fits over a pot with a spout going off to one
side. With a simple alembic and a bowl to catch the output, a heat
source and a wet cloth, one has the essentials for potion making.

Let's say you want to make a potion of anise, which has many magical, medicinal, and practical uses. You could simply dry the herb and
infuse it into a tea. But if you want to concentrate its potency, you'll need
to refine it into an essential oil. To do this, you need only the alembic. Fill
the lower half of the alembic (the pot) with water and heat it to a boil.
Once boiling, pack it with your anise. I do mean pack it. Make it as full as
you can without making it so full the anise is likely to burn from contact

with the pot. Set the alembic over the pot. Wet a cloth with cool water and place it over the alembic, and place a bowl under the spout.

As the water boils, steam will rise carrying the essential oils of the anise. The wet cloth will "sweat," which carries away heat inside the alembic and that causes condensation that will trickle down the spout. The volatile oils condense at a higher temperature than the water vapor, so they will drip into the bowl while the steam disperses.

Check the pot every few minutes and as the anise boils down, or the water evaporates, add more. You can keep packing the pot with the herb as long as it doesn't get so full the anise burns. Also, dip the rag in cool water every few minutes and re-set it over the alembic to help the condensation process.

An alembic is a simple one-step still dating back to ancient alchemists, but it became a common appliance of medieval households. (Photo courtesy of Demmarest Haney.)

When you have completed the batch, you will have concentrated anise essence, which you must bottle and seal. The essence is highly concentrated; a lot of herb only makes a little oil; so have on hand small vials fit to hold a few ounces each. Reduce exposure to oxygen by bottling as soon as you have enough to fill a vial. Try to fill each vial because oxygen denatures volatile herb oils so you want to minimize exposure to air.

That same process is used to make essential oils from other herbs. These can then be added in small amounts to teas for health or the simple pleasure of drinking, or they can be blended with incense, or mixed with lard to make salves, or mixed in other ways to make potions, or even used in cooking.

An alternate method of extracting essences is to make tinctures. This is even simpler than the alembic method though the result is highly alcoholic. To make a tincture, you will need a potent hard liquor. At the homestead, we occasionally distill a bit of rum or brandy for this purpose, but you can simply buy a bit of rum, whisky, gin, or vodka. Any hard liquor or potable alcohol will do, as long as it is at least 80 proof (40 percent alcohol).

To make the tincture, merely place the herb of choice in a jar. If the herb is dry, fill the jar halfway. If it is fresh, crush it and fill the jar all the way. You don't have to completely mash fresh herbs, just crush them so the surface of the plant is broken all over. Now fill the jar with the hard liquor. Put the mix someplace shady and cool and leave it for a month and a half. The alcohol will draw out the herb's alcohol solubles. After six weeks, strain the mix through a cheesecloth. Just pour the mix into the cloth over a bowl, wad it into a ball and squeeze it with your hand to wring out as much of the essence as possible. Then store the extracted essence in airtight jars or vials. Try to fill the containers completely in order to minimize the tincture's exposure to oxygen, and be sure to store it in a cool place out of direct sunlight.

Woods Lore

Growing Sacred Souls

Not long ago a teen told me one of the most horrific things I have ever heard. And you have to understand, I have heard a lot of awful things in my life. I am a psychotherapist, which means for a living I peer into the inner mental workings of sex offenders, dangerous criminals, and even politicians!

But a little while back I was speaking to a teen about depression. The more we spoke, the more it became clear his entire life was lived online. He was constantly playing some massive multiplayer online role-playing game, or chatting online, or YouTubing. He had been withdrawing from real life bit by bit, becoming disinterested in school, sports, friends, recreation. His life was centered on that computer screen.

Soon I began to put two and two together. The kid wasn't withdrawing because he was depressed, he was depressed because he was withdrawing. You see, depression may seem like something one feels, but in truth the feeling is just a symptom. Most times, depression is something one does, and it is done by cutting oneself off from friends and loved ones, as well as activities that give one's life context, connection, and joy. This youth was being sucked into the virtual friendships and worlds of his computer, and as he left real life behind, depression was the predictable result.

We tend to think of counseling as a process of talking, but often the best counseling is a matter of getting clients to change their behaviors and do what is good for them. I needed to get him away from that monitor and into his life again. I started giving him goals that involved getting out and participating in the world in small ways that were intended to be fun. And each week he'd come back and report he still felt depressed but he hadn't worked on his goals, either. At the time, I thought he just wasn't into the activities his small town had to offer, so one day I suggested he come up to our homestead where we could spend the afternoon with the horses or canoeing. What teen doesn't like horses and boats? And then he said that terrible thing I will never forget. He asked why would he want to go out and do anything when real life was boring compared to all the action going on in his computer world.

Is that startling? The simple truth is that I and many other mental health experts have encountered youth like this. More and more in recent years. And who hasn't seen a cartoon featuring a kid sitting in front of a PlayStation while a gorgeous day beckons beyond the window? We live in an era, for the first time in history, when the majority of young people will grow up within the concrete and steel confines of an urban area and electronic devices will constitute the primary media of their work, education, and recreation. The majority of their life experiences will be compressed down to a synthetic reality. And that is as good as robbing them of the opportunity to grow into whole, happy, healthy persons.

More and more research is showing that if children don't get out into the real world, the natural world, consequences are dire and long term. Strong bones and muscles, solid immune systems, coordination, and overall vigor are dependent on venturing into the varied, unpredictable challenges of the outdoors. Crossing brooks, climbing trees, chasing fireflies in meadows ... youth require experiences like these for full physiological and neurological development. They need them for mental development, as well. Creative thinking is seeded in working out small problems like how to build a tree house, and in experiences like pondering the complex sound of rain falling in the woods. Developing the skill of focusing attention is dependent upon learning the patience required for activities such as fishing or bird watching. In short, we are creatures of Nature and we need Nature in order to fully be who we are.

But ultimately the very survival of Earth is reliant on getting youth out the door, otherwise they will never learn Nature's worth on a soul-deep level. The previous generation was the first in which roughly half of youth were raised in urban areas, and it is now the adults who run the world's industry and governments, and never in history have civilizations turned so willing and blind an eye to the environmental costs of their actions. Japanese corporations hunt endangered whales. The Chinese, Russians, and Americans squabble over who gets to drill the Arctic after the ice caps are destroyed by global warming. South Americans burn down the Amazon—the breathing lungs of the planet—to raise cheap beef, even knowing the thin topsoil will shortly erode away without the jungle to hold it. Such things go on at rates unprecedented in history, and those who do these things refuse to even consider the consequences. They see this irreplaceable world as a mere resource, and in their minds creating wealth right now is all that really matters. But how can people who are raised apart from Nature ever come to value it? What will happen now as a new generation yet more alienated comes into its own?

The truth is inescapable: we cannot live healthy in mind or body without Nature. And Earth needs our children to know her if they are to live well with her. There really is no other option.

It becomes incumbent upon every parent, every teacher, every mentor who wants to see a kinder, greener world to lay the seeds of love for Earth in the next generation. This cannot be accomplished by raising children apart from the natural world. Nor can it be learned through any electronic media: not a televised documentary utilizing the best educational models, nor yet by way of the finest virtual reality games and teaching tools. Such things only play to our rational concepts of knowledge, and to two of our senses: sight and hearing. But we are physical-spiritual beings and, contrary to myth, we have sixteen senses, not five. Youth can only fully develop an appreciation of Earth if they immerse their whole beings in Nature. Nothing else is enough.

If their use cannot be moderated, throw away the cellphones, tablets, and game consoles. Provide youth fun, challenging, and rewarding activities that bring them in contact with Nature. Bring them to farms in spring where they can watch the birth of new calves and lambs. Draw them into gardening and let them experience the joy of nurturing a seed to fullness and the satisfaction of deriving food from it. Encourage them to splash in brooks and let them know it's okay to come home with muddy clothes and scraped knees. Go out with them and lie on blankets on clear summer nights and count shooting stars. Roast marshmallows by a campfire and tell ghost stories til everyone is scared silly. Honor Nature with them, whether it's by the simple act of putting a faerie cottage in the woods, looking after a hurt animal or learning the practices of an Earth-based path. In short, give them abundant opportunities to engage soul and body in the world beyond the door. Let them learn who they are in relation to that world. Let them reap good memories in the doing. So doing, they will grow to know Earth as more than just a resource. They will know her as a Mother, and they will understand why they should love her and do their own part to protect her.

AUGUST'S JOURNEY

Malign

The grandmother lived out in the wood, half a league from
the village, and just as Little Red-Cap entered the wood,
a wolf met her.
Red-Cap did not know what a wicked creature he was, and
was not at all afraid of him.

—Jakob & Wilhelm Grimm
Little Red Cap
Children's & Household Tales

I was nineteen when I met the wolf. I had sold all I owned, took the little
money that had gotten me and bought an old car with a little life left in
it, a decent shotgun, and a good axe, and I had gone north out of a deep
longing to experience true wilderness. I had been on the road for over a
week, having started in the bayous of Louisiana where I grew up and had

traveled across the arid Southwest, up north to the great high desert and then through the rainy and green Pacific Northwest. I had little money, which meant little means to stop and rest anywhere along the way, so apart from sleeping in the car at a rest stop now and then, I made good time. I had no idea exactly where I was going or what I was going to do when I got to that vast northern wilderness, but I knew it held my future. I hadn't met my wife, Daphne, in those days, and looking back it seems a lifetime ago.

When I hit British Columbia I began to feel like I had found the kind of wild I sought, something truly lost and vast. And the further north I went, the more I liked what I saw. I began to take my time, meandering rather than hurrying. I would cover a few hundred miles in a day and when I grew tired, I would stop and pitch camp off one little back road or another, living on trout and icy meltwater, taking time to hike here and there and learn bit by bit this new kind of country. I had grown up in wild country, but I didn't know if the skills I had developed in that steamy, half-tropical setting would transfer to the north. One thing I could tell as I went ever further into the deep bush, this was hard and serious country. A mistake could kill a man. I needed to be sure of every step.

Not long before I reached the far side of the Yukon Territory, I had stopped outside a tiny village called Destruction Bay, a place of rock and ice and unforgiving crags, its only saving beauty an enormous subarctic lake. I had spent the night camping a few miles beyond the village and the next day had bathed in the frigid lake . . . if you can call stripping off your shirt and hurriedly pouring cupfuls of water not much short of turning to ice over your head bathing. But it sure woke me up, and it was good to get the grime of travel off. After, a fire of driftwood and a hot cup of tea and breakfast of sausages helped me warm up. I dressed, checked the map, and figured I might be at the Alaskan border the next day. Where I'd go from there, only time would tell. For now, I needed to get gas and be about my way. So I stopped at the village's only gas station. It seemed every gas station in Canada at that time was full-serve, and while the attendant filled my tank I stretched my legs, knowing I had a long day of sitting and driving ahead.

Do faerie tales really show us a big, bad wolf, or do they reveal a more disturbing truth within ourselves? (Photo courtesy of Rachel Lauren.)

And that was when I first saw the wolf. He was just sitting at the edge of the tiny dirt and gravel clearing watching me. He caught my attention immediately, for I knew it was no dog. I'd tracked coyotes in the bayous and the Mojave, and I knew the lanky build of a wild canid the moment I laid eyes on him. More than that, I recognized the spirit that lay behind those eyes. I could feel it—that thing about a wolf that is a measure savage and a measure noble, and altogether beyond the kenning of most folk now in the world.

"You have a beautiful animal," I told the attendant as he topped off the tank. I figured it was his.

"That wolf ain't nobody's," he said in a gravelly voice, hardly sparing it a glance. "Some woman from Ontario got it from a trapper as a pup. She half tamed it, then abandoned it. Heard tell she went back to Ontario." Then he looked straight at me and said, "Why don't you keep it?"

I regarded him quizzically. "Um ... it doesn't belong to me."

"Ain't nobody's. It's half wild. But if you don't keep it, someone round here's gonna shoot it, that's for sure."

I looked back at the wolf. I hardly had a spare dime to my name and no family who I could turn to. I sure as hell couldn't afford a pet. But I couldn't let it be shot either.

And that was how the wolf and I came to be together as I passed through the Yukon. But it was a long time til we became friends.

◆ ◆ ◆

Two months later it was early summer in the far north and the air had finally become warm. Or at least what I, being fresh from the Deep South, considered warm. The Alaskans I had met were out in shorts and tank tops any time the temperature rose above freezing and the sun came out. It would be a while til my southern blood acclimated that much. But I felt warm these early June days, and that was a sense I had not known in a long time. I was glad for it. I had found my way to the deep interior and was bit by bit making a life for myself, and one of the first things I was learning was that staying warm was partly a matter of skill and partly a matter of attitude.

With no money and no family and being a complete stranger, making a new life for myself in the subarctic wilderness wasn't easy. I did it all by my own two hands, learning as I went. I had set up a semi-permanent camp near a spring-fed lake. The spring was tiny but it had been dammed by beavers over generations into a vast body of freshwater over a third of a mile broad. The beavers had actually built these dams in three tiers and they stood like great walls, each holding back its own level of the crystal-clear water. I had to make everything I needed, and I didn't have much to work with, so I had to shape wood with only an axe and my bowie knife. I wasn't ready to make a log cabin yet, but I had to acquire the skills. By next summer I planned to perhaps buy a mining claim, head deeper into the bush and build a small cabin. I had to learn how to live with the northern wildlife. In the bayous,

I had learned to constantly sweep the ground in front of me with my eyes, then the ground around me as I checked for snakes every few feet. Here there were different beasts that could be dangerous, but especially grizzlies and moose, and I had to learn to avoid them and not become the object of their attention. And I had to learn new ways to hunt, fish, and forage. It was two hundred miles to the nearest town. There was a village about ten miles away, if you can call a couple hundred souls a village, but everything in the village was expensive. A loaf of bread could cost a quarter of a day's wage. To get by, I had to find my own food, supplementing it with bread I baked flat over the fire and pots of rice.

The wolf had proven little trouble to feed. He was happy to content himself with the skin and offal of the enormous lake trout I caught. Hares were at the height of their population cycle that year and I literally could not go a hundred yards without stumbling into them, and he ate a fair few of them, too, mostly the scraps from my hunting but occasionally taking one himself. I tried to get enough for him, too, when I hunted, but I was poor in those days. Very poor. Even the shotgun shells I needed to get dinner were a dire expense, so out of necessity I became very good with the shotgun, learning to pick my shots when two or even three hares happened to pass one another. That way one shell could take several and the wolf and I could both eat with a little to spare. I had also learned to make a number of traps. I learned to make deadfalls and kill-snares to get hares and porcupines without the expense of shotgun shells, and I learned to make fish traps of twigs the thickness of my middle finger planted strategically into the lake's edge in such a way that fish could swim in but not back out.

The wolf, who I'd named Max, and I had been uneasy companions. We got along, but Max wanted to be the alpha. He rarely did quite what I directed him to. Like all wolves, he wasn't noisy. I don't think I ever heard him bark. But he came and went as he pleased. A couple times he tried snarling at me over meat roasting over the fire, but I think he was surprised when I snarled back and stood up to meet his challenge. But I had grown up in the bayous and lived among wild animals most of my life. I knew that with predators you never back down. It's asking for trouble. I wouldn't quite say we had become friends, but after a couple months together we had reached an easy truce and mostly he would accompany me throughout my days' activities though now and then he would vanish into the tundra for days at a time. I always figured that one day he would wander off to go live like a wild wolf and I would not see him again. I realized I would miss him. He was the closest thing I ever had to a brother. But I did not tie him off. He was a free being. If he wanted to stay, he could. If he chose to go, I would wish him well.

Then one day he came home limping. I had been by the fire, sharpening my bowie, when I saw him. And then I noticed the blood. He had gotten into a scrap with some critter or other, and it was a mess. I went to the tiny trailer, all of ten feet long, that I had picked up in Fairbanks for $500, and rummaged through my first-aid stores for iodine and bandages and a needle and gut. I had never stitched a wound before, but I'd studied field first aid in college and figured it should be straightforward enough, assuming the wolf didn't try to kill me when I stuck a needle into its sore leg. But he seemed to know I meant to help as I sat beside him. He laid down and let me do what had to be done. There was a gash but as I cleaned the blood away I realized it was not as long or deep as I had thought. It needed no stitches. I cleaned it and then dried it. When the hair was dry, I rubbed on some disinfectant cream and wrapped it tightly with gauze. But I couldn't let him wander til it was healed. Otherwise the wound was likely to re-open. So I also dug some rope out of the trailer and fashioned a collar then tied him off by a ten-foot lead to a nearby white spruce. He wouldn't be happy about that. In the end, he might hate me for it. And most likely he'd just gnaw off the bandage and I'd have to reset it over and over. But regardless he'd have to stay like that for a few days til the wound had mended.

So I petted him and spoke calmly to him and gave him a whole hare that had been roasting on one of the spits over the fire. I had had a cast iron skillet under that hare to catch the drippings and I poured the drippings into a stew I also had simmering beside the fire. It was made with carrots, potatoes, and rice, the last of the supplies I had picked up from my trip to the village a week ago. Ever conscious of my dwindling money reserves, I at least knew I had a means to make ends meet soon. In the village a man was building a tiny hotel for tourists out of recycled buildings, and he had offered to hire me to help him do it. That job started in a couple weeks. For now, we'd just stretch what little we had. So I sat there beside him, the fire crackling, and stroked his tan and black fur. It barely got dark anymore in this land of midnight summer sun, but when I figured it was late enough I went to bed in the trailer.

Some hours later I was startled awake by a dreadful cry. My eyes sprung open and I thought, *What is that dog crying about?* Then through my sleep-addled mind came the thought, *Wolves don't cry like that.* But I heard the cry again, a horrible canine wail. Not the kind of thing you hear from a creature born to the wilds and determined to be the alpha leader. I rolled off the little couch and looked through the trailer's window. There was Max, still tied to his tree but he had pulled the rope back as hard and far as it could go. He was pulling so hard that the tree, as thick as my wrist, was leaning partly over. And ten feet away from him and not two paces away from the trailer door was a large grizzly, one of the blonde kind of the deep interior. It was just standing there, regarding the wolf, perhaps wondering why it had not run and figuring that whatever the reason, he'd take advantage of his good fortune and make an easy meal of the canine.

I thought, *No bear's going to eat my dog on my watch!* (Did I mention my mind was sleep-addled? I figure it was maybe 3:00 a.m.) I kept my shotgun, the one valuable possession I owned, hanging beside the bed. It held five shells in the tubular magazine. The first two were fine shot with a low powder charge—perfect for hunting hares. The second three were 000 buckshot magnum loads, last-ditch defences against large, dangerous animals. I say last-ditch because I had learned from the bushmen that at close quarters the odds of dropping a huge animal like a charging moose or an attacking grizzly with an ordinary rifle or shotgun were slim. No matter. What had to be done had to be done. Working the pump, I jacked out the two rabbit shells. I glanced to the little shelf over the couch where I had more ammunition and thought I should fill the magazine. I might need every shot. But I heard the wolf cry out again. I had learned that grizzlies can sever a man's head or take an arm clean off with a single swipe. It could kill Max, an eighth the griz's size, with one blow. There was no time. I turned to the door, made sure the safety was off, and jumped out, shirtless, barefoot, into the chill of an Alaska morning, shouting a battle cry at the top of my lungs as my feet hit the ground and leveling the shotgun with the bear no more than an arm's length beyond the barrel.

(I did mention my brain was still sleep-addled, right?)

You ever seen a griz look surprised? At close range, by which I mean close enough to lean forward and kiss it? I have! And I swear I don't think the bear had any idea I was in that trailer by the way it swung its head toward me when I burst out that door, roaring at the top of my lungs. It wasn't a *You're next!* kind of look it gave me. It was a *Where the hell did you come from?* kind of look.

And that surprise probably saved my life, for the griz did the last thing in the world I had expected. It turned tail and bolted. I blinked, unable to believe it. I had figured one of us was going to be taking the rainbow bridge to Valhalla in the next few moments. Then I thought, *No bear is gonna try to eat my dog and get away with it!* And I launched after the griz, running down a trail beside the wild lake still shouting that battle cry.

(I did mention it was wayyy predawn and I was sleep-addled, right?)

A bear moves fast. Very fast. Like car fast. But I could follow it easily enough. The earth was soft and there were tracks and the tracking skills I had learned in the bayous were transferring quickly to the northern bush. But I can't brag. Trying to track a grizzly's fresh tracks over soft ground, well, it's like tracking a man who wears size 20 sneakers over wet concrete. There's no missing it. Then I saw the tracks veer right off the trail and heard brush breaking. I turned right and started running through a thicket down toward the lake's edge. There was a sudden movement ahead and I fired a shell. But the movement was a magpie launching skyward. Ahead was the lake and I heard a huge splash. I broke through the thicket and saw the bear had actually dove into the lake and was swimming away.

Still driven by sleep-crazed thought, I ran down the bank and charged into the water, too. It was only as high as my waist here but it was icy. And it was as I was trying to scramble through the thick reedy growth that the cold water finally cleared the fog out of my brain enough that I thought, *What in hell am I chasing this grizzly for??? If I catch it, what am I going to do with it!*

And so I stopped and watched it swim to the other side of the lake, make its way up the opposing bank, and scramble south in the direction of the high country.

◆ ◆ ◆

Max and I became inseparable as of that day. I don't know. Maybe he was just grateful I'd saved his life. Or perhaps he just figured if that guy with the Cajun drawl was crazy enough to go *mano-a-mano* with a grizzly then it was settled who was going to be the alpha. Whatever, Max and I were inseparable as of that day. We became more than man and wolf, we became a family. He was all I had. I was all he had. And we worked well in the wilderness together. We'd hunt hares together and I could always tell they were nearby by watching him. That keen wolf nose of his could pick up their telltales before I could and he'd lead me to them. He'd come with me on rounds to the snares and deadfalls I'd set up for meat, and when we got back to camp there was no more growling at the fire over food. At night he insisted on sleeping in the tiny trailer, lying contentedly at the foot of the couch. That sounds nicer than it was. That trailer was so tiny that with a big wolf inside, there was almost no room to breathe let alone move. But it was okay. We had grown comfortable with one another.

My job in the village was going well. It didn't pay much, but it was enough to keep us in food and allow me to squirrel away a little money for next year when I planned to buy a few extremely remote acres, go deeper into the bush, and build a cabin. But in order to make that plan come true, we still had to fend for ourselves as much as possible so as to squeeze together every cent possible over the summer. And so when I wasn't working, we hunted and fished, and I learned how to make the skins of hares into rawhide and begin to fashion other things we'd need, such as glue from hide and snowshoes from bent wood and leather strips. Everything we could do for ourselves would get us a step further to our own cabin in the bush, our own place to really call home.

So it was that one day we were heading up a trail to look for wild mushrooms. I had discovered this trail a month ago. It lay west, near the springhead that was the primary water source of the lake. While much of the surrounding country was high blueberry heaths and tundra with scattered taiga forest of diminutive spruce, this trail led to a sheltered little valley of great old birches and cottonwoods. Sphagnum moss grew over the ground so thick that walking over the trail felt like walking on a carpet of deep shag, and the green was so intense it was surreal. The forest was old and large and dense, a rare kind of wood in this part of the wilderness. When I first came back this way, I had succumbed to curiosity and wandered off the trail into that forest. It was so dark beneath those thick boughs that even in the middle of day it was almost like night, but the darkness held a subdued emerald hue. It was a glorious effect I would ever after come to think of as *green shadow* and associate with all the woodlands of the world I would later come to know and love. I don't know what I expected to find in that fey dark wood, but I had this feeling that once, long ago, men had been here before. Perhaps I might stumble upon an old cabin, something long abandoned but that could perhaps be restored. It could become our shelter for the winter. I didn't find a cabin, though. What I found was perhaps less useful but also interesting—an old still. Not a little thing either. I'd been fascinated by brewing since I was fifteen, and I figured by the size of this thing that it could handle maybe fifty gallons of mash at a time. It was old and decrepit, though. Did it date back to prohibition days? Had there been prohibition in Alaska, a mere territory at the time? But aside from possibly the archeological curiosity of the crumbling still, there was nothing of use back there, except the mushrooms. Boletes loved the cool, moist green shadow of this deep wood and they grew abundantly in the dense old forest. And they tasted good and dried well, providing a valuable foodstuff for the long, hard winter ahead. So we came here often to gather mushrooms, and the beauty of this woodland made it one of my favourite of the many demanding jobs of bush living.

As usual, I had my shotgun slung over a shoulder and a large messenger bag at my side to hold the mushrooms. I carried a canteen and bowie also, but we were only a few miles from base camp so I had no other gear. On the way I had spotted and shot two hares that would make food for the next couple days and they were tucked into the messenger bag. I wanted to head down to the spring where I could clean and wash them, then leave them to store in the icy water while we backtracked into the woods to harvest in the cool shade. The day was hot, but in Alaska the ground has permanent frost everywhere just under the surface. The moment the land isn't exposed to direct sunlight, it turns chill, so the deep-shadowed forest was always unusually cool. We had hiked a mile through the wood, following the narrow breadth of a trail over the spongy sphagnum moss. The dense trees rose high and black on both sides, the shade so deep it was like perpetual night beneath those boughs. As we went, I took note of the mushrooms we passed. They were everywhere.

I did not know nearly as much about mushrooms then as I do now. I knew shaggymanes and boletes and that was about it. But boletes and their cousins, leccinums (like a furry-stalked bolete), are among the safest of mushrooms to harvest. Unmistakable with their pored undersides, none are deadly. A few can give you a bad stomachache and flu-like symptoms, but you can sort those out by simply bruising them and cutting them open. If they will make you ill, they will turn blue, sometimes over the span of hours but sometimes in seconds. Among their cousins, leccinums, it was also wise to avoid those with orange caps. But they were abundant and we could harvest sackfuls of edible mushrooms in a matter of hours. I'd take them back to camp, cut them to see which should be used, toss the bad and lay out the rest which would dry almost overnight in the amazingly dry air of a clear interior Alaska summer day.

I had just espied a particularly large specimen that I had never seen the like of before and had knelt to one knee to examine it when we heard a rustle in the forest off to the right. I glanced that way but assumed it was one of the unusual and extraordinarily beautiful sable foxes unique to the north and fairly common around here. I waited a long moment but there was no other sound. Max was sniffing the air but we were upwind of whatever it was. "Just some little critter, my friend," I said to the wolf as I drew the bowie and cut the mushroom neatly at the base of the stem. Its top felt slightly sticky as if it had been glazed in honey, like that most prized of boletes, the cep. If this mushroom was what I thought it was, it would make a wonderful meal. I dropped it into my messenger bag for tonight's dinner. I rose and we walked on.

A hundred yards later we heard it again, the *crack-crunch* of something moving in those darkest of sylvan shadows. But this time what we heard was not merely the soft padding of movement over sphagnum. The noise had been of substantial underbrush crackling as it was forced aside. Whatever it was, it was big. But then it stopped and the forest grew very quiet.

The breeze died away; the air became still.

I smelled it then, rising above the green, fresh scent of growing foliage—the scent of carrion. A predator scent. And suddenly Max dropped his head, hackles rising, and emitted a low snarl from deep in his throat. And we heard another *crunch-crack-crunch* in the forest, this time closer. Max bared his fangs, snarled louder, ears laid flat in the way that is canine language for fear and fight to the death. Whatever it was, it was dangerous, and it was coming for us.

Boletes and their close cousins, leccinums, form an essential part of bush forage for many northern peoples. They are abundant in boreal country, large and easily identified. (Photo courtesy of Tammie Lee.)

Some people run at such moments. I knew from a lifetime's experience that running from predators was to invite an attack. It told them you were weak. It declared you were afraid. It said you were prey. I was not prey. But I also knew there was no way a human could outrun any of the large predators that dwelt in Alaska. And that stench... I realized in that moment that we had stumbled upon some predator's kill site. A big kill, I figured. Maybe a bear had taken a moose calf.

The right way to deal with an aggressive bear is never flee. A steady retreat facing the creature is the way to go about it. In the doing, you show you are strong, also a predator, not afraid but do not wish to fight; that you respect its space and will give it its turf. So I began to back away from the direction of the noise, unslinging the twelve-gauge as I went. The first two shells were always light #4 rabbit shot and I pumped them out, leaving three triple-aught magnum shells—my self-defence loads. I kept five more such loads on a pouch on the shotgun's stock and quickly slid two more into the tubular magazine. Continuing to smoothly back away, we could hear it moving in the shadows now: brush forced aside, twigs snapping. It didn't seem to be coming closer, but it wasn't getting farther away, either. It was pacing us.

This isn't good, I thought. Predators don't pace unless they're up to something. I had the feeling it was looking for the right moment to charge.

Then I caught sight of the creature. Well, sight of its silhouette as it passed in front of a stray sunbeam that fell through the dense green canopy of birch. It was the size of a small bull. And it had the oval shape of a bear with a distinctive hump at its shoulders. It was a large boar grizzly. We had stumbled upon a full-grown boar griz at its kill, so deep in the wilderness it could have no fear of man.

"Dammit!" I cursed, firing a warning shot into the air. The shotgun spoke like thunder and its voice echoed through the forest, sending distant ravens into the air cawing angrily at the disturbance. Such a technique had worked in the past, turning around a charging moose and convincing another bear that had seemed to be considering whether or not to charge that it was best to walk away. But it didn't work this time; the griz charged. There was no buildup, no threatening snarl, no lowering of head or posturing. It just charged. It wasn't a bluff charge. It was much too close already for that. It meant to kill us and eat us there in the green and dark woods if it could.

To hell with that!

I pumped the shotgun, dropped to a knee to steady my aim, drawing my bowie as I did so and laying the back of my left hand, holding the knife, under the pump. There wasn't any time to think about what else to do, or how futile it would be to fight a grizzly with a bowie if the shotgun didn't stop it in its tracks with the next shot—an iffy proposition, for a griz is a huge, powerful animal. If the shot didn't kill it instantly, it would bleed out eventually, but it would have plenty of time to shred me first. There just wasn't time to think about any of that. A grizzly moves fast; unbelievably fast for such a large animal. They can all out run at thirty miles per hour when they get a mind to do so.

I couldn't see anything but its shadow racing at us in the peculiar green-dark of the woods, though. It was a poor target and I had to make the next shot count. There simply would not be time to pump another shell. Just as I was squeezing the trigger, Max bolted at it.

"Max!" I cried out. An instant later I heard sounds of vicious combat, snarling and scrabbling. I could barely see a damned thing, only a huge shadow and a small shadow darting round it. But Max was family to me, the only family I had for thousands of miles. And as I had put my life on the line for him months ago, he was returning the favor for me just now.

I heard a yelp and cried out again, "Max!"

Damn this!

I launched up and ran at the griz, hoping to get a clear enough shot that I could stop the bear from killing the wolf, for brave or not, the wolf would surely lose in the end.

As I got closer, I could see them better—my valiant friend, Max the Wolf, in his alpha glory, doing something the faerie tales never tell you about. The Big Bad Wolf was fighting to the death for his friend. Snarling and snapping, launching this way and that, he antagonized the grizzly, which swung at him with mighty forelegs tipped with claws like four-inch knives. And the hell if I didn't recognize the bear; the very same who'd tried to eat Max back at the beginning of June.

I lined up the shotgun, again dropping to a knee for a steady shot, but the wolf and the bear were all over the place. I couldn't get a good shot without risk of hitting Max. And I was keenly aware Max could not possibly dodge those monstrous claws for long. I had to get closer. Point-blank range, if need be.

I rose, started to race headlong through the semi-dark and promptly tripped over a root concealed by the moss, coming down in a crashing heap. And the moment I fell, I heard crashing again through the heavy brush. I rolled over, bringing up the shotgun, figuring the bear was pressing its advantage and coming for me. But then I realized the crashing was going the other way. The bear had given up, turned tail and ran.

And then I saw Max walking toward me, tongue hanging over his jaw, limping a bit. I rolled onto my side, lifted up and knelt to a knee. I looked him over in the dark shadows, terrified I'd see dark blood fountaining from a nicked artery that would spell his death. But he was unharmed, all but for the limp.

"Crazy wolf!" I said, grabbing him by his shaggy scruff, then pulling him into a hug. And we sat there in the emerald shadow, panting, sitting side by side while the adrenaline passed.

◆ ◆ ◆

That was long ago and Max has long since passed into the Summer Land, or Valhalla, or the Underworld, wherever is the right and proper place for the brave spirits of faithful wolves. Now I and my wife live in the backwoods of Nova Scotia, and when I am not looking after this enormous old homestead, I am invariably off in the woods that have always called to me and felt more like my right and proper home than any place made by human folk. When I go off into those deep, dark woods, I am ostensibly up to something practical. It might be gathering elderberries for late-August winemaking. It might be harvesting mushrooms in preparation for the long winter ahead. But often that's just an excuse to be out there, where I belong, among the creatures I know so well and love so dear. I love to watch the ravens that are abundant in this wood but sadly rare where humans have swallowed up their land. I sit in trees and listen to their calls and clucks of infinite variety, trying to decipher their hidden tongue. I spend my time following the tracks of the mother black bear whom I have gotten to know well enough I tend to think of her as Sister Black Bear these days. She has lived in the woods only a mile from the cottage for years, and every year I go out there and zigzag over her territory til I come upon her tracks and I count the number of cubs she has brought into the world. And every spring and summer I make my way into the woodlands of the coyotes—the closest cousin of wolves in Nova Scotia—and check on the progress of their pack. We have lived in an easy peace for years, those coyotes and I. They do not come onto the small portion of the Hollow that I farm to disturb my livestock. I follow their tracks and see to the well-being of their clan, but I never get too close to their den, respecting their space as they respect mine, and so we live together as good neighbors.

It was one day in September a handful of years ago that I was out and about in the backwoods, just meandering. Often I'll just stick my bowie into my belt or snag my axe and set out all the day, eating and drinking from the land, watching and learning, absorbing Earth's ancient wisdom by taking part in the many tales of her creatures. I had wandered long miles all through the hot late-season day. I'd found a wild gooseberry bush and serviceberry tree and made a meal of handfuls of the little fruits, the former tart, the latter sugary sweet. I had come across an old linden and feasted upon its raw leaves, hacked some kindling with the axe and built a fire by striking the spine of my knife to the jagged edge of a broken rock of quartz and fried some mushrooms on a flat stone. I had meandered down to a brook and meditated by its babbling waters. And I had come across the spoor of many of this forest's creatures: elusive martens, haphazard porcupines, and even the telltales of the beaver, who leave behind the chewed stumps of young fallen trees of which they make their meals. It had been a good day and I'd traipsed here and there from dawn til the last light westered.

Following my nose, I made my way back through the forest til I came upon the Five Sisters, the ancient maples that grew alongside the bank of a pure spring's streamlet. Night fell and a full moon had risen and the darkness was taking on an otherworldly silvery hue. A breeze, perfect and sweet, blew in out of the south, just enough to make the leaves rustle, just enough to sluice away the day's sweat and cool the spirit to pleasant dreams. Ravens clucked for some odd reason. They are usually quiet by night, but they clucked and trilled softly as if engaged in a nocturnal discussion with Sister Moon. Ever fascinated by the language of ravens, I decided to linger in the nightwood, so I climbed the broad trunk of the maple and pulled myself into a crotch where the trunk divided. Then I hauled myself out onto a thick limb that made an easy seat and leaned against the trunk and listened, the sweet late-summer breeze doing its best to lull me into easy dreams. But the clucks and mutterings of the ravens were far too interesting. What were they saying in their hidden tongue? I longed to know the secrets they shared. I always felt as if the knowing was just at the edge of my awareness, if I could just somehow put my mind into their headspace.

So in the tree, beneath a full moon so bright it dimmed the nearby stars, I reclined. The leaves undulated in that mild breeze and beneath their swaying boughs they evoked silver moon-shadow that played like the swimming light on the floor of clear and natural pools. I could not imagine a more perfect moment.

But eventually the ravens' discussion came to an end. I was loath to pull myself from the boughs, but hunger beckoned and handfuls of berries and boletes are highly nutritious but low calorie and not very filling. I decided to hike back the remaining way to the cottage. It was full dark but the moon was more than bright enough to light the way through the wood, and a bit south of me was a dirt path that would make for easy going. So I swung out of the tree and dropped to the ground.

No sooner had I touched the earth than I heard the *yip-yip-yowl* of the coyote pack hot on the hunt. And they were close. No more than a couple hundred yards off and moving fast in my direction. Doubtless they'd been on the prowl and picked up the trail of something and had just launched into full hunt mode. If it was something large like a deer and they felt they had a chance, they would attempt to run it to exhaustion so that tonight the pack could eat well.

The coyotes of Nova Scotia are not like those smallish animals out west where their species originated. Somehow, the east has made them larger. Many have bred with wolves and are forming a new species, what was a generation ago called the *new wolf*, and these days is more commonly know as the coywolf. I've seen them here looking bigger than a husky, almost as big as was Max.

I turned in the direction they were coming from and saw two emerge from the trees, racing across the glade in my general direction. In the moonlight, they appeared only as fleet shadows. I stood my ground, for I have no more apprehension of the Big Bad Wolf, only a feeling of kinship and respect. And the pack sensed my presence there in the ebon shadow of Sister Maple and parted around me like water round a stone. In a moment, the last had run by, howling and yipping, driving whatever it was they were pursuing onward, seeking to wear it down so that eventually they could catch it, kill it, and eat their fill. I did not hold their hunt against them. Many times in the past I had done the same; hunted and killed to fill my belly and feed my family. Many times in the future, I would do the same. To hunt to feed your family, to fight to defend those you love; these are noble things. There is no evil in them.

And so I returned home that night with a story to tell the family, and the years passed and I regularly walked those green woods deep in the pack's territory, careful to respect their space as they respected mine. Until two springs ago when on a hike down to the Rusalka Brook to check the growth of ostrich ferns I came across one of the pack members. A young one, not yet a year, pointlessly killed by a poacher and hung in mockery from a tree.

I had been walking beside a little waterfall and had been lost in the music of tumbling water, pondering what to do next this lovely day.

Then I glance up and there it was, dead and cold, wedged in the crotch of an old birch beside the dirt path where it hung by the neck. I blinked, uncertain at first what I was seeing. My first thought was somehow a coyote had gotten itself wedged in the tree and died. I walked over and inspected it. I found a bullet hole and the scar of a leghold trap. It had been shot with a small caliber rifle, probably a .17 caliber, which has become so popular among so-called "varmint shooters" who kill small animals for the fun of it. It had been left hanging in the tree as if to shame it for the crime of being a wild canine.

I just stood there, unable to understand the hate and ignorance that could lead to such a deed. Never once in my whole life had I seen a coyote or wolf kill for sport. They took only what they needed to feed themselves and their clans. But people call them "wicked," yet it is only humans who kill for sport. Only humans who kill and waste and hang a carcass in a tree for spite's sake. My mind flashed back to memories of Max, the wolf whom I had saved and who in turn saved me. What had that man at the gas station in the tiny village of Destruction Bay said? "But if you don't keep it, someone round here's gonna shoot it, that's for sure."

Why?

Often, anymore, I barely feel human. At least, not if it means accepting such ignorant hate and cruelty. And as I regarded that cold, dead animal, a cold fury began to brood inside me.

But anger by itself is nothing. This person had come onto land that I warded and killed family of a pack that I had nurtured and lived peacefully with for years. I drew my bowie and stabbed it into the birch trunk just over the coyote so that sap could dribble out. It was cleansing and fresh smelling, something to wash away the stench of hate from the little coyote. I sheathed the bowie and let the sap dribble drop by drop over its corpse. Finally I found words. "I am sorry, little brother," I said, my voice raspy and eyes reddening, "but I am going to do something about this."

Whoever shot the coyote was also trapping. I couldn't do anything about it if that someone was off my land and trapping in season, but the season was long done. This was just a poacher. I despise poachers. Even more than I despise sport hunters.

And so I set out into the forest and picked up the poacher's trail. Over the proceeding hours I found several snares, which I cut and confiscated the wire. And I found several more leghold traps, which I also took and brought back to the path. (I should say at this point that I myself have trapped, and I have no ethical problem with it if someone has to eat or needs fur to stay warm. But killing for fun is the action of a sick and bent spirit.) I had no tolerance for it. I hiked home with the leghold traps, got the maul I used to split firewood, and smashed the traps til they were battered wrecks. Then I brought them back to the tree where the coyote had been left and hung them from a branch with a note: "I have flattened your traps. They might be good for paperweights now, so take them if you need paperweights. And don't poach my woods again because wherever you go, I can find you." A week later the traps vanished.

I left the coyote there, though. I thought about burying it, but I left it there as a reminder of human cruelty. To me, it was plain who was really the Big Bad Wolf.

The following year the coyote was desiccated; there was only hide enveloping loosely connected bones. And the year after there was left only bleached bones that had fallen from the tree. At that time, I hiked out that way and found the coyote's jaw and removed its lower fangs. They are sitting in the library of the cottage now and one day, when the time is right, I shall ceremonially fit them onto a silver chain, silver for Sister Moon who watches over the nocturnal pranksters that are coyotes. And I will bear that chain in proud memoriam.

For Wolf is not wicked. Coyote may be a trickster, but he is not evil. When I ventured all those long years ago into the deep dark forest of the far north to find my soul it was the wild canine I first met and who became my brother, who returned love with a burning, loyal courage. Most humans I know would have run at the sight of the great grizzly. It was the Big Bad Wolf who stood against impossible odds for his friend. What does that say?

What I know for certain is this: when it comes to natural beings, humans are rarely good judges of character. When we malign the creatures of the green world, almost without fail it is the darkness within our own hearts we fear, and in ignorance and denial we pretend that darkness is theirs.

In memory of a little coyote brother killed by a poacher, I took these fangs from its lower jaw. I shall honor it as a totem and as an animal ancestor.

Wild Life

Black Bears

A mere generation ago, black bears were rare in North America. Killed out of fear, overhunted, driven out of their habitat to make room for development, they were steadily disappearing from the landscape. But the worst pressure on the black bear was from poaching due to demand in China for their gallbladders. Practitioners of traditional Chinese medicine prescribed bear gallbladders as remedies for various ailments. The active ingredient in a black bear's gallbladder is ursodeoxycholic acid (UDCA). This is actually present in all mammals, but the concentration is a bit higher in bears. Modern pharmacies can now produce it, but many practitioners of traditional medicine continue to prescribe only bear gallbladder. I am a strong believer that peoples are entitled to practice their traditional life ways, including their spiritualities, magics, and medicines, but I also know (not believe, *know*) that right ends when it endangers a species' existence. In Mississippi, for example, black bear numbers were reduced to some sixty animals in the entire state. But aggressive prosecution of bear poachers as well as improved habitat management and work to reduce people's fear of black bears has turned around the decline in their numbers over the last thirty years. Black bear numbers are once again rising.

I have encountered many black bears over my years in wild places. They are universally amazing animals with an amazing range of size and color phases. In the depths of Alaska there is actually a blue variant called a glacier bear. Down in British Columbia there are the legendary spirit bears, ghost-white variants of the black bear. In Asia there is the moon bear, its name derived from the white crescent on its chest. In Louisiana and Mississippi, there is a smallish variant sometimes called a honey bear.

Because black bears eat meat and they can be large (males can reach over five hundred pounds), they suffer persecution by humans due to an unfounded fear. In truth, black bears are solitary, shy animals that shun contact with humans. They feed primarily on berries, wild fruits, and vegetation that they forage throughout the course of the growing season. They do eat meat when they can get it, but most of this is carrion or insects and grubs that they tear out of rotting logs and stumps or dig out of the ground. They are known to dig up the burrows of ground squirrels if opportunity arises, and they will catch fish when they can. They are omnivorous opportunists and will basically eat whatever an area provides. But despite their considerable size and strength, they are not great hunters of large animals. They might go after an injured deer or hunt fawns the first couple days after they are born in spring, but they rarely bother with healthy big game. Reclusive, they typically avoid any creatures they perceive as a challenge. If they encounter a human or another animal they consider possibly dangerous, they will tend to vacate the area or seek safety up in trees (presuming they are still small enough to get up trees).

Black bears virtually vanish during the winter months, retreating to nests among tree roots, or crotches of large trees, or rocky shelters and caves—virtually any dry area sheltered from the elements—where they hibernate through the hard, cold of winter. They can reduce their metabolism greatly, allowing them to go months without the need to eat.

Black bears are shy and cautious, and will generally go to great lengths to avoid danger. (Photo courtesy of Tammie Lee.)

Solitary as wildcats, they prefer to be alone. You are unlikely ever to see even two unrelated black bears together unless they are feeding at a very rich food source like a river full of salmon. In spring and summer you may see a mother with her cubs, and sometimes you might encounter what looks like two or three adults wandering together but these are siblings just entering adulthood and soon to part ways. The black bear's shy, solitary nature runs deep and they will go to great lengths to avoid most other creatures and especially humans. Which is not to say that occasionally one, especially a young and inexperienced bear, might not get it into its head to aggress a human, but it is astronomically rare. The odds are vastly higher you'd drown in the desert than that you'll ever be attacked by a black bear, even if you basted yourself in steak sauce and hiked through a national park.

The black bear is just one more Big Bad Wolf of the wilds that is feared for reasons that have more to do with our own failings than the animal's nature.

Enchanted Forest

An Afternoon with the Bear

Some of the most profound moments of my life have occurred in the company of *big bad* creatures like wolves and black bears. The first large wild animal I ever encountered as a child in the bayous was a black bear digging scraps out of the ashes of me and my friends' extinguished campfire one cool dawn. But there is a day etched upon my memory as one of the most beautiful and profound of my entire life.

I was a grad student of psychotherapy at the time, living in Anchorage for the duration of my education, and I had gone to the Chugach Mountains south of town to hike one Saturday morning. Normally, I preferred wilder country, but today I decided to hike a trail that ascended a mountain and overlooked the beautiful, rugged bay. I arrived at the trailhead and was just donning my daypack when a dozen or so people came running—literally running—down the trail. A couple came panting onto the trailhead and I asked them what was going on. The fellow struggled to catch his breath and finally managed to gasp, "A . . . <pant> . . . a big black <pant> bear is up there on the trail!"

I said, "Yeah, but what's wrong?"

The guy looked at me funny and said again, very slowly, "A big black bear is coming down the trail."

I shrugged, donned the pack and started hiking up the trail. He blurted, "It's going to eat you!"

I told him it wasn't aggressive and he retorted, "How do you know!"

"It didn't eat you, and you were running," I told him and started up the trail.

An hour later I had made it about two miles. The trail was rugged and steep, ascending along the wall of a deep gorge. A beautiful waterfall was at the far end and several hundred feet below a river of sparkling crystal raced down to the sea. Up the incline towered ancient Sitka spruces with trunks so broad I could not wrap my arms around them. Golden sunlight sifted through their needles, dappling the emerald ferns on the forest floor with swimming liquid gold. A mild breeze blew in out of the south, bearing the fragrance of the sea and a warmth that is always treasured in the subarctic. I had spotted the black bear some distance away twenty minutes earlier, slowly ambling down the trail, and I had gone up the incline to stand in the shadow of one of the great trees, leaning against its massive trunk. The ferns growing around me broke up my outline and I was downwind. Dry brown spruce needles comprised the duff of the forest floor. They made a bed that could be walked over soft and quiet. And so I awaited the bear, knowing I would be, for all intents and purposes, invisible to it.

He appeared moments later, still ambling down the trail. A huge male, I estimated its weight at perhaps four hundred pounds. It was in no great rush and paused here and there to sniff at this and that along the trailside or peer out over the gorge. Perhaps it was as taken with the beauty of the setting as was I. I began to move with it, not fifty feet away, concealed by the chest-high ferns but most importantly by the moderate breeze. I was directly downwind of it; it could not possibly catch my scent, though I thought I could smell it, earthy and musky, like a horse that has been sweating. The breeze, steady and gentle, combed the ferns and made the high boughs of the old spruces sough. The rushing of the river a hundred yards below created a sweet susurrus, like the not quite comprehensible whisperings of myriad spirit voices. All that sound gently filled the forest and utterly erased the padding of my feet stepping over the duff.

And so I passed a portion of the afternoon, moving with the great old black, pausing when it did, freezing if it looked up my way so as to vanish among the forest's uncounted broken outlines, walking when it did. I recall so vividly the sweetness of the breeze, the rainbow cast by the lowering sun upon the spray of the waterfall, the sunlight that fell and broke like water over the forest floor. But mostly I recall the bear, quietly strolling, a great, stoic creature taking pleasure in the beauty of the world. A creature not to be taken lightly, but as much to be respected and loved for what it was: the very incarnation of the sheer magnificence of the wild places. That day stands in my mind as possessing all the beauty and wonder of a faerie tale, except on that day, the woodsman and the bear were companions.

To this day I still think of that dozen or so people who came fleeing down that trail. In a way, they did the right thing. They gave the creature its space. But their underlying reason was distorted. They fled because they perceived the great old bear as an aggressor, as if it had blood and death in its heart. And all along it was only another spirit sharing the Earth Mother who, like us, walks the world for a while. And like those hikers, it was only out for a stroll. How tragic that they were unable to look deeper and truer and see the reality underlying that ursine form and there discover a fellow soul. If they had, they might have shared in that day's faerie tale.

Wood Witchery

Meeting Predator Spirits

Long ago I met an old Hopi in the high country just south of the Grand Canyon's rim. We became friends and one day got to talking about the old shamans and the spirits that bestowed them with strong medicine. He told me something I thought at the time was bizarre. He said that when a man met the animal form of his spirit guide, he would know that animal unmistakably... because it would try to kill him. I thought that could not be right because surely an animal linked to a person's spirit guide would only have benevolent intentions.

It wasn't until years later I began to have some inkling of what he was talking about. When studying anthropology in an advanced university course, I read about how aspiring shamans of primitive cultures surviving into the twentieth century would venture into the wilds on a kind of hero's journey to find themselves and their power. Such journeys came with real mortal peril, and however long it took, whatever hardships were endured, the journey would not end until the shaman had a kind of epiphany in which he encountered the spirit world. Later on, I acquired a copy of

Michael Harner's *The Way of the Shaman* and read in it for the first time a detailed account of the profound initiatory experience that may occur on shamanic journeys. It is a frightful event in which the journeyer, while traveling in spirit form, encounters beings or forces that tear him apart. There is not so much pain as fear or humility as the journeyer experiences a profound unmaking, but it is a process in which he is forced to confront his faults: his doubts, frailties, biases, and irrational fears. They are ripped away and after he is rebuilt as a better version of himself. And while Harner's account presents this as a spiritual event, right away I could see the parallels between it and what that old Hopi had told me. There was a time when in a wilder and more perilous world becoming a shaman meant facing real danger.

When I look back on what I have learned of the old magical-spiritual paths through academia and consider my experiences from years in the wilderness where I befriended a wolf and later faced grizzlies as mortal foes, I can only now claim to grasp something of the life changing truth of getting to know predator spirits. Like the Big Bad Wolf, these powerful spirits do truly challenge us with mortal peril, but in the spirit realm there is far-seeing purpose to everything; the spirit guides design such events for the seeker because the danger itself is transformational.

When I lived in the Alaskan bush, there was always a small but very real chance I would be hunted and killed by a bear. And as I was in the heart of grizzly country, living deep in that wilderness taught me a constant keen alertness, and how to see the patterns within patterns that reveal the hidden things in the landscape. I have learned that such alertness and vision are core features of the magical-spiritual mind. I also learned a mutual dependence upon my friend and ally, the wolf I first met in the Yukon Territory. Over the years I would have several more close encounters with bears, and I would come to see Bear not so much as a threat but more like a summer storm: one moment merely a wind and a rain, another a tumultuous tempest. You don't live in fear of summer storms; there is no point, for they come and go as they will and simply are what they are. No. You make peace with them. If you are wise, you learn to live well with them and respect them and give them their place. And when those acutely powerful moments come that you must face the onslaught of the tempest, such moments may define and transform who you are. As it has been observed regarding war, it is a terrible thing, yet it also brings out the noblest in us. Likewise does the tempest. And so you learn to love that which challenges you. It is your forge.

As the world has moved on, so much of the wild lands have been tamed. Their large predators have been systematically extirpated to accommodate irrational human fear. As I consider such lands I feel in them a keen loss. Their lingering half-wild places full of songbirds and hares and reclusive deer are lovely, but they feel to me like sugar candy—cloyingly sweet, wanting complexity, not truly whole. They lack the element of real danger that is essential in a balanced ecology, and they cannot give our spirits what we most need. For the predator is the sharp prick of danger. Its torrent is the defining moment. It's crash is the impetus for transformation. Surviving the predator manifests who we are meant to be. Coming to live well with the predator is the very manifestation of subtle balance and wisdom.

If you follow an Earth-based path, odds are you seek spirit guides. Perhaps you know them as animal familiars, or maybe the folk of your path call them by another name. It does not matter. What matters is that as you seek, do not shun predator spirits. They are complex beings, and they have much to teach, and much to share. They reveal to us the beauty of power in balance, the wisdom of strength that can take what it wants but refrains from avarice. They possess great knowledge. A predator spirit such as Bear or Wolf or Eagle might not be your personal guide, but I have found they are earnest, deep, and willing to share their wisdom if approached with courtesy. Just like their real-world animal counterparts.

After all, we humans are also apex predators, the most capable predator Earth has ever produced. And yet we have facets of kindness and wisdom and a willingness to share what we know. How much more the animal spirits of the Otherworld?

I have no exact technique for encountering predator spirits. You might meet them on a shamanic spirit journey. For all you know, you may encounter them the next time you go for a stroll. I've known people who find themselves adopted by foxes and other predators when they move out to the countryside. Who knows what form, or in what way, they will appear. They come as they will, in their way, like the storm.

What I can tell you is live your life well, practice your path with a whole heart, respect the Earth Mother and live wisely with her creatures, both earthy and spirit. Do this, and when the time is right the predator will come. And the meeting will not be what you expect. It never is. I cannot even guarantee you a favorable outcome. It will be your moment in the forge. Who you discover you are in the crucible of that encounter . . . this is very much your choice.

Woods Lore

_____

Coping with Aggressive Wildlife

If you live in or visit wild places enough, eventually you're going to encounter an aggressive animal. When speaking of such things, people tend to think of the big predators, such as wolves, mountain lions, and bears. But the fact is moose, elk, caribou, even whitetail deer account for most aggressive wildlife encounters. I was even charged once by a beaver. Such encounters are extremely rare, however. Even in the middle of the bush, the odds of such a thing occurring are far less than that of being hit by a car as you walk around town. But it is important to know how to cope with such situations in advance. Different animals have different reasons for becoming aggressive and require different responses. For example, that beaver I mentioned ... the reason it became aggressive was I was standing on a hilltop watching it. The hilltop was grassy and it had rained recently. The grass was very slippery and I lost my footing and found myself sliding on my rear down the hillside as fast as if I was riding a toboggan over greased snow, straight down on top of that beaver. Any animal will become aggressive if it feels threatened and realizes it cannot get away. A beaver is not especially fast on land and when it saw me hurtling down at it, it must have mistaken me for a charging predator. Unable to escape, it did something highly uncharacteristic for its kind: it turned to fight, charging up the hill at me. I seem to recall it hissing like a big cat, but, honestly, that could have just been the sound of my backside sliding over wet grass. But I knew good and well a beaver could fell a large tree with those powerful buck teeth it was brandishing, and I dreaded having it clamp them onto me. I came to a stop with the beaver right about at my ankles and I raised my legs to kick at it, at the same time scrabbling for the bowie I always carried deep in the backcountry, and somehow at the same time trying to scurry back up the hill. I am sure it would have looked comical to a bystander, had there been one in that wild stretch, my arms and legs scuttling but getting me nowhere on that slippery grass. But beavers are not aggressive animals. Perhaps it realized as I tried to scamper back that the whole thing was an accident, or maybe it thought it had scared me. But as soon as it realized I wasn't aggressing, it turned and vanished into a thicket of spruce. Everything came out okay that day, but over the years I've had other close encounters with other aggressive wild animals and it was knowing what to do each time that always made for happy endings where neither I nor the animal were hurt.

First off, it is important to always maintain situational awareness. This means being aware of where you are and what is going on around you at all times. I would hazard a guess that the majority of aggressive wildlife encounters occur because someone was trekking through the backcountry, immersed in thought or perhaps conversing with a friend, and stumbled upon a wild animal. Animals, like people, have a zone of personal space around them, and if you stumble into that zone you risk a fight-or-flight re-action. Even animals we tend to think of as delicate and gentle can suddenly turn and put up a remarkable fight. Just as an example, a whitetail buck in the rut with its antlers is an impressive and dangerous animal, should you provoke a charge by stumbling to close to one. It's rare, but it happens.

Being situationally aware is the first defence, and it is a skill you cultivate by frequently reminding yourself to look around, pay attention with
all the senses, and observe the patterns of the natural world around you.
Learn to watch for breaks in the patterns. You'll spot animals quicker that
way than by looking directly for them, for most are intuitively good hiders. For example, deer tend to blend into tall grass but when they move,
the grass has to make way for them. Watch for grasses that seem to stand
inconsistently with other foliage for hints of where deer are. Use your
nose, an important sense we often overlook. We humans actually have
a fairly decent sense of smell, but we are so vision-sound oriented that
we hardly notice scent anymore. Learn to use that nose. A stench may
indicate a nearby kill site where a predator has cached prey. Or simply
the close proximity of a skunk that might just give you an unwelcomed
spray if you get too close.

No matter how situationally aware you are, if you spend enough time
in backcountry you are eventually going to encounter an animal that for
one reason or another behaves aggressively. If it is a predator, such as a
black bear or coyote, it is first and foremost important to know that you
must NEVER run. That is prey behavior and will provoke an instinctive
chase response from the animal. You are a human; an apex predator. Wild
predators instinctively do not want to tangle with other predators, for they
are well aware that if they are even slightly injured in the confrontation
they might starve to death before they heal well enough to hunt effectively
again. Instead, face the animal, do not show your teeth, do raise your arms
to make yourself look bigger, and back away. Pay attention to how you
move so you do not fall as you back away (which conveys vulnerability). If
you have a weapon to deter attack, such as pepper gas, have it in hand and
the safety removed so you can use it quickly if need be. Plus, having the
weapon ready will give you added confidence that will do more to convey
an air of *I am also a predator so don't mess with me.* You want to communicate
through your actions that you are not afraid and you are dangerous, but
you mean no harm and are ceding the space to the predator.

Some animals, such as grizzlies, may launch a bluff charge to hurry you away. I emphasize again, do not turn and bolt no matter how strong the impulse. Hold your ground and continue to back away while facing the animal. Have a sense of your personal zone of safety, and in the unlikely case the animal crosses that space, you'll have to follow your own internal moral compass regarding what to do. Many outdoors experts advocate dropping and playing dead for a griz. That might work for a griz, but it also might not. A grizzly can hamstring a moose with a single swipe. And they are amazingly fast. I've been charged several times by griz, and when it happened, I fired a warning shot, then prepared to shoot it if it got within my personal zone of safety, about fifty feet. I am glad the warning shot was enough. Mostly what matters with an animal like a grizzly is letting it know you can and will effectively defend yourself but you don't want a confrontation. Again, concede the space, back away, but do not act like prey.

With other predators, dropping and playing dead will incite a deadly attack. Black bears are far less likely to ever be aggressive than a grizzly, but in the extremely unlikely circumstance of an attack, a black bear will not bluff charge. It means business. You will have to defend yourself, so I suggest that in true wild places, always carry a weapon and know how to use it. My personal choice in less dangerous country, like the north woods of Atlantic Canada where I currently reside, is my bowie. It is a big, hefty fifteen-inch knife, and I hope I never have to use it as a weapon, but it is more than sufficient on the off chance it is needed for that role. Pepper gas is another excellent choice as it is nonlethal and effective. Aim for the eyes and nose. Do not spray it into the wind or you'll get yourself, as well. There are also several new nonlethal products around, such as the Bear Banger, a tiny orange tube with a small charge in it that, if triggered, makes a loud blast similar to a gunshot, which can usually turn aggressive predators around.

People tend to think of herbivores as gentle and friendly, but far more people are killed by elk and moose every year than all the wild predators on this continent put together. Herbivores such as deer, elk, and moose have very different minds and must be handled differently. As a rule, they will run unless defending young or mates or they are cornered. Maintaining situational awareness and being sure to give them plenty of space at all times is the most effective thing you can do. But no matter how cautious you are, eventually, if you spend enough time in backcountry, you will stumble upon one and find yourself too close. If you do, just leave. You don't have to run, but clear the area fast. Face it, watch it, but do not look it in the eye or lower your head as either action could be interpreted as aggressive. Generally, that is enough. But at certain times of year such animals may become irrationally aggressive. Bull moose during the rut, for example, may well charge even if you are more than a hundred yards away. I know; it has happened to me more than once. If they charge, you have no hope of outrunning them. Get into a dense thicket of trees if you can, or scramble up a large tree or rock. If there is no such alternative and you have a device like a Bear Banger or carry pepper spray, you'll have to use it and hope it works. Use them quickly, for animals in the deer family are very fast. If using pepper spray, hose it. Dump the whole can in its face unless it turns and goes.

I am quite sure most injuries and deaths resulting from wildlife happen because of what I've come to call the *Snow White Syndrome*: believing the animal will sense how kindly the person's intentions are and so allow the person to approach, perhaps to feed or pet it. In 2013, a woman in Manitoba claimed she was attacked by a wolf when she pulled her car over beside a highway and got out. I was dubious of her account from the beginning and corresponded with Simon Gadbois, PhD, a canine behavior specialist at Dalhousie University, and learned he was just as dubious. Wild wolves are extremely non-aggressive toward people and will go to great lengths to avoid us. Her case was investigated and, sure enough, it turned out she had seen the wolf while driving and stopped her car, got out and approached it with some snacks intending to try to hand feed it. The wolf did bite her, but only a warning bite when she finally got too close, then it ran away. That wolf could have taken her head off, but it only wanted her out of its personal space. Never fall for the *Snow White Syndrome*. Animals cannot read your mind, and it puts you in danger—and if the animal hurts you, the forest service will almost certainly send a tracker out to find and kill it. In such a case, human ignorance becomes a virtual death sentence for the animal.

Finally, if spending the night in wild places, ensure neither you nor your camp smell like food. I remember once Daphne and I hiked out into the Kenai wilderness for a two-week backpacking trip. On our third day of hiking, we noticed the delicious smell of smoked salmon. For several hours as we hiked, we wondered where it came from. Toward the end of the day, we decided to pitch camp beside a gorgeous remote lake and there we came upon a German couple that had been a few hundred yards further up the trail ahead of us all day. For their rations, they had backpacks full of smoked salmon. They reeked of it. And there they were, hiking through country with one of the densest populations of salmon-eating grizzly bears in the world. It was the equivalent of a mouse basting itself in fish sauce and visiting a cat convention. I tried warning them of the peril they were putting themselves in, but they thought it was nonsense. Daphne and I decided to strike camp and moved a couple miles upwind of them. The tragedy of it is, if they had been attacked by a grizzly, it would only be because they invited it, and then the forest service would have hunted down and killed the animal due to their willful stupidity.

Protect yourself and the animals by cooking away from where you'll sleep. Wash utensils thoroughly afterward either in a stream or lake, of if abundant water is not around, scour with sand or grit and bury the residue somewhere a couple hundred yards away from where you'll sleep. Hang your food in a sack from a tree at least a hundred yards away. At night, urinate somewhere near camp. The scent of human keeps most animals away.

Most importantly, learn what kind of animals will be in the wild area you will enter, and if any have the potential to be dangerous, study why that is so and avoid creating the circumstance. That is the best solution. The single best resource on the behavior of North American mammals I know is *Mammal Tracks & Sign* by Mark Elbroch. It is comprehensive and also gives specific info on how to cope with aggression from many of the animals it covers.

In all the years I've lived in wild places, I've only once had to kill an aggressive animal in self-defence—a swamp moccasin that had slithered up behind me and was coiled to strike. I learned in the bayous of Louisiana, where deadly snakes and dangerous alligators were a real risk, to be aware of what was around me at all times. Learning how to convey body language that says *I am also a dangerous predator* has turned away several would-be aggressive bears. But even a big animal like a moose or elk can easily go unseen in the bush. In the far northern bush, I always carried a powerful firearm, and on a couple occasions when I stumbled upon moose and was charged, I was able to turn them around with a single warning shot that broke the silence like thunder. Most folk will never face such circumstances, but knowing how to present a genuine air of confidence in wild places, and how to respond quickly and decisively should the need arise, is the best way to protect both wildlife and the humans who visit their home.

AUTUMN

The Fading
of the Forest

SEPTEMBER'S JOURNEY

In the Kingdom of the Black Bear

The earliest temples of the Gauls were sacred groves, one of
which, near Massilia, is described by Lucan. No bird built in
it, no animal lurked near, the leaves constantly shivered when
no breeze stirred them.
Altars stood in its midst, and the images of the gods were
misshapen trunks of trees.

—J. A. MacCulloch
The Religion of the Ancient Celts

An old forest becomes a mythic place. Even modern folk who resolutely claim they are not superstitious have an intuitive sense of this. Let them deny it all they want, but bring them to an old forest and come sundown the tension builds in their eyes. I've seen it again and again. However alienated from Nature their modern lifestyles have made them, however aloof from the old beliefs they claim to be, deep inside, come nightfall, they know...an old forest is a place where the eldritch touches upon reality and within its living shadows things not of this world, things not quite friendly toward Man—they move, they are present, they watch, ever just out of sight. An old forest is the living abode of faerie tales.

Such thoughts were on my mind as I wandered the path south. Beyond the friendly young trees of the Elfwood that lie near the cottage, past the half-regrown meadows of a vast abandoned homestead, toward the old forest that lay beyond. It was not long past sunup and ever-taller maples rose to either side of the path. The dirt was soft and quiet under my boots, save in some places where my heels caught pebbles that scudded away, clackety-clacking against one another.

I intended to be in the forest only through the day, so I packed light. I had a daypack with two meals, a tarp and some thin but strong rope should I need emergency shelter, a pair of liter bottles of water, and a flint and steel, as well as a light jacket stuffed into the pack. On my belt, I carried a camera and my bowie. I usually take Willowisp, my faithful Australian Shepherd, on such Wildwood wanderings but today, much to his consternation, I had left him behind. I was entering the old forest for several reasons: to seek out late-season mushrooms, to look for groves of wild fruit such as serviceberries and elderberries, and to do some photography. And I also intended to stop at the Shaman Stone later in the day and spend time communing with the spirits. But Willowisp could have come for all of that. He loves the outdoors and is very well trained. But the other reason I was entering the woods in this especially deep region was to do some tracking. Many years of tracking have taught me to read the land like a book. I don't actually need to see an animal to know how it's faring—its life is written upon the medium of Earth as sure as ink on a parchment—and I meant to track down some wildlife today that I generally made a point of leaving alone, and dogs and big wildlife don't mix. They tend to rile one another up. Best-case scenario: the animals take off. Worst-case scenario: the animal goes after the dog and the dog runs to you and everybody ends up unhappy.

So I reached the point on the path where I determined to make my way into the deepest places of the forest, down near the heart of the valley that is the Hollow. From the path I could see up to the west ridge hundreds of feet overhead, and there where the woodlands had been exposed to the harsh northern elements cold winds had long since lashed most trees of their foliage. Down here, well sheltered by the high ridge, the trees were still bedecked in late-summer cloaks of green. I knew if I hiked a couple miles to the slope and started up to the ridge, I would see the land transition from summer to autumn in the space of a few hundred paces.

As the land was still rich with late-season foliage down here, I knew that once in those woodlands navigation would be tricky. At the moment the sky was clear, but if I lost the sun it would be hard to tell what direction I was moving, for the dense forest would prevent me from picking out any landmarks. In the breast pocket of my sweater I carried a small, high-quality compass. I withdrew it and flipped up the cover, shot a bearing straight to the west ridge, dialed it in, then closed the compass.

I started into the forest. It was thick and immediately all directional references save the sun vanished. I had rarely come to this section of the Wildwood before. Here, the trees were old and the air was close and still. A silence hung over the forest, the silence of incipient autumn when songbirds are retreating to lower ground where they will ride out the winter. It was too early in the day for the cries of owls. For the moment, the only sound was that of my own steps as I made my way into the taciturn green depths.

As I went, I could feel that eerie sense of watchful presences. This was an old woodland, full of ancient maples with broad trunks, and more than a few grandmother birches, much bigger than maples ordinarily grow. Scattered spruces and hemlocks broke the patterns of broad leaves with their staunchly green needles. Often I stopped and looked around, having a strong sense of being not alone.

During a bitterly cold evening of the previous winter, Natalia and I had gone out to the little Highland Meadow where our horses often graze to try to catch sight of a comet that was barely visible on the western horizon. It was very near full dark of a moonless, clear night and I went out there first as Natalia had a few chores to finish up at the barn. I hiked to the top of the hillock and took up a vigil near a thick hedge that we have allowed to grow through the middle of the meadow to provide shelter for the horses from the wind. I leaned against a tree and relaxedly regarded the west where the last hints of a sunken sun still lent the horizon a deepening plum glow. A few minutes later I saw her ascend the hillock, but when she reached my position, rather than falling in beside me, she said she had to check on something. I assumed nothing of it, just nodded, and continued to watch the west, scanning the horizon with a pair of binoculars. But I heard her moving up and down the hedge, weaving in and out of the small trees. Finally, whatever she was up to piqued my curiosity enough to draw me away from my hopes of espying the faint comet ostensibly out there somewhere. I called out, "What are you looking for?"

"The troll," she replied in a very matter-of-fact tone.

Okay, I thought. My daughter is looking for a troll on a hillock in the dark on one of the coldest nights of the year while she could be comet watching. At first I thought it was just a game, so I returned to scanning the horizon, but she persisted. I finally called out, "You know, that comet is only supposed to be visible for a few minutes after the sun goes down. You should be nearby in case I manage to spot it, otherwise you might miss it."

Still in that very matter-of-fact tone of voice, she replied, "I don't want to turn my back to the hedge."

Okay, I thought, *that doesn't really sound like game talk.* I faced her direction; I could hear her trudging through the hedge about a dozen yards away just now. "What's this about a troll? Is this some game you're playing with your sister?"

The turkey tail mushroom is a lovely and useful medicinal that helps break down the cellulose of fallen trees.

Natalia said, "Game? No, there are troll lights on the hill. I just wanted to make sure it was safe before we started stargazing." Then she shared with me that now and then over the past several years she had seen odd little lights like tiny lanterns moving through the dark up here on the hill. They didn't scare her, but she had learned to be wary of the hill come dark. That was doubly amazing because this was the place I had seen a fey lantern myself several years before, an event I wrote about in chapter April of my last book, *Seasons of the Sacred Earth*. And to my knowledge Natalia had had no knowledge of that event, nor had she read the book. But the whole family had seen fey lights and other strange things in this forest in the past. We had no doubt otherworldly things lingered in this wood.

Back in the present, as I hiked through the deep late-season forest, I had a very similar sensation: something not quite of this world, not quite friendly or unfriendly, was present in the shadows, always nearby, ever just beyond sight and knowing. Like Natalia's troll . . .

I pressed on.

It took another hour to travel less than a mile. The going was slow because the ground was rough, and also because I am in my heart of hearts a naturalist born. Everything in the woods utterly fascinates me. Every fallen tree presented a trove of things to study: turkey tail mushrooms, unusual insects, shelter for small forest mammals. Standing snags contained numerous hollows created by woodpeckers and squirrels. Often I stopped to revel in the echoing tap-tap-tap of pileated woodpeckers, or froze to observe the sight of gorgeous sapsuckers. But at last I reached the brook which lay at the foot of the western ridge. In some places the brook is deep; in other places shallow; I meant to cross, but I needed to find a narrow area where I could either leap or make use of natural steppingstones, so I skirted the bank til I came to a stand of young spruces growing out of a bed of sphagnum moss so brilliant green it glowed in the sunbeams that tumbled through the forest canopy. Such places are great spots to harvest the unusual Maritime woodland chanterelle mushrooms, which unlike their inland cousins prefer the acid ground of spruce copses, and I stopped to search. I found enough to fill a large bowl I had stowed in the pack, and several hefty bolete mushrooms, as well. Back home, Daphne would slice and dry them, and they would make flavorful additions to our winter meals.

I had just packed away the mushrooms and reshouldered the pack when in this mycological paradise I espied a very special birch. A great and ancient tree, it stood out in the woodland like a matron over her progeny. And where woodland trees often grow slender, up reaching branches to compete for the sun, this one was broad and sweeping. It was as if the neighboring trees fell back to make way for this ancient, wise sylvan being. It still held leaves as green as those of midsummer that gleamed like emeralds in the high sun. And seeing it, I felt as if I had encountered something old and wise and fragile and strong, like an ancestor worn by time, yet made magnificent by it. I knew if there was a tree in this woodland that held a sylvan spirit, it was this one. And it just felt right to stay here and bask in its presence. So, I asked permission of the tree—which could not have known the press of humans, deep in the forest as it was—to spend some time with it. I sat on a stone near its trunk and broke into my rations and there had my lunch in the warmth of noon, sunbeams shimmering and shifting through its high leaves. Lunch was a simple sandwich of cold meat from last night's dinner, a bit of onion from the garden, some of Daphne's homemade goat cheese and flat bread, and a little dried fruit. There, in this ancient sylvan being's stately presence, it felt like a feast among the gods. I felt truly blessed simply to share time with the old tree. Now and then a crumb broke from the bread and, in the tradition of the old Scots, I let those crumbs stay where they fell for the Good Folk. It is greedy, even rude, to take them back. The little spirits could have them, and if they chose to pass, then a passing tree vole was welcomed to the feast.

When I completed the meal, I felt fully sated and rested. Not the rest one gets from merely getting off one's feet, but the rest one experiences only after a long time spent in the creation of art. I felt enriched and invigorated. The ancient birch and I had shared something, something deeper than words, something of the inner depths of spirit and true camaraderie. I rose, touched the tree's trunk and spoke appreciation it for its company. And as I turned to leave, I espied another birch nearby, mature but not ancient. But from my vantage a dozen yards away I could see a large black growth on its side, looking very much like a charred scab, and I knew immediately it was a chaga, the rarest and most treasured of the northern fungi. Having long harvested it, I have a knack for finding it. I know its haunts—the trees and terrains it especially favors. I can spot it a hundred yards away through a dense thicket. Daphne jokes that I have "chagadar." So it was strange that I had sat here for an hour, eaten my lunch, and all that time a large birch holding a substantial growth of chaga—half a dozen pounds at least—was right in front of me at eye level and I had not seen it. It felt as if the ancient birch, like a generous host, was bestowing a guest gift as I prepared to leave.

I rose, bowed my head respectfully to the venerable birch and the one that hosted the chaga, drew my bowie and carefully cut it from the tree's trunk.

So far, it had been a wonderful day in the Wildwood, and the day was yet young. But the real reason I was here lay much deeper in the forest. In the depths of this remote and beautiful region was the coywolf pack I had done my best to look after over the years. Coywolves are coyotes hybridized to wolves. Though only a small percentage of their genetics currently show wolf lineage, they nonetheless pick up many wolfen characteristics: namely larger size and the longer legged, ganglier look of wolves. And they are as clever as their coyote kin. They manage to survive in nearly any environment and evade the depredations of humans. Indeed, I normally avoided going so deep into their territory so as not to alarm them but it was because of the depredations of humans that I wanted to check on the pack. That young coyote I'd found hung in a tree several years ago gave me cause for concern. I'd never figured out who the poacher was though I frequently checked for his tracks and looked for his traps. I'd not seen sign of him since I destroyed his last illegal traps and left them hanging in a tree for him to find. But that didn't mean he might not try deeper in country he didn't think I'd look after. In my opinion, poachers and sport hunters who kill for pleasure are among the lowest forms of life. We humans should be revulsed that members of our species would take pleasure in killing. I had not heard the pack's yipping cries in weeks, and if the poacher had come back, then not only was the stable and peaceful pack in danger, but so were a sow black bear and her two cubs that I also knew ranged the area. Truth was, though I'd been enjoying the day, I feared for them greatly. Especially the bears. Bear gallbladders fetch a high price on the black market.

Now I hunt. I will take a deer or two every year for food and leather and antler. Winter or summer, I may have to trap or shoot hares that get into the gardens or go after the fruit trees. If grouse are in abundance, or geese or ducks, I will take a few for a change in our diet. I make sure to hunt only what is in abundance, what the land can spare. Even if I must kill a weasel getting into my barn to eat the poultry, I never hunt from anger or hate, only out of need. When I take an animal's life, I do not ask its forgiveness. I kneel beside the animal and offer it my respect. I explain that I took it of need and not of want, and I ask that we might meet again in the Summer Lands as friends. Sometimes I will collect its skull and leave it at a sacred place, a shaman tree or stone. This becomes a place of power where spirits can gather and mingle with the green world, and a place a shaman might commune with them. But I have no stomach for those who kill for fun, and whoever this poacher was, he'd gut shot that coyote I'd found in the tree. That's as painful a death as can be managed and wolf and coyote hunters often do it on purpose, in a hateful attempt to wreak some sick vengeance on the animal for being what it is. I mean, you just can't accidentally gut shoot a coyote caught in a trap. This poacher—if he was still around—was one cruel piece of work. I wouldn't have his hate in my forest.

So I gathered my things, cleaned my bowie, and pressed on. I found a place where the brook was shallow and a few widely spread stones could serve as steppingstones. I leapt from one to the next til I crossed the twenty-foot span of sparkling, babbling water. The coyote pack denned up around here. I wasn't sure exactly where as I had never tracked them all the way to their den so as not to spook them. If they suspected humans had found their den, they would take their cubs and move on. They were at peace and safe here; I didn't want to change that. So I began a zigzag search pattern, hiking up to the height of the ridge several hundred feet overhead, then back down to the brook. All I needed to find were fresh spoor to confirm the pack was still doing all right. And I wanted to ensure I found no telltales of a certain poacher's incursions.

The transition between the low ground near the brook and the high ground, only a few hundred feet overhead, was remarkable. In that short climb, the land went from summery to autumnal. The trees had shed their foliage and presented only bare limbs to the sun. Going uphill was work, though, more than the whole hike here.

I made several passes from the brook up to the ridge and back down, moving slowly north as I went. I came across birch bracket and more boletes, but I left them, not wanting to make my pack heavier.

I encountered toothed jelly fungus, a bizarre clear fungus that feels like a damp gummy worm. It is edible but flavorless, and makes a good stock for stews. They are an unusual find, so even despite another half pound added to my pack, I gathered some from the fallen log and left the rest to set new spore for next year. I encountered ancient whittled-down tree stumps, the old work of a tribe of beavers who had long since moved on. But I was not seeing any sign of the coyote pack, and I was growing increasingly anxious for them.

A safe and easily identified polypore, the toothed jelly fungus looks for all the world like a gummy candy version of a mushroom.

Coyotes are largely misunderstood creatures. People fear them greatly, yet since the dawn of European settlement on this continent you could count all the coyote-caused adult human fatalities on one finger (yes, one finger, and I am dubious about those circumstances based on my own research into the incident). Coyotes have earned themselves reputations as pests in farming areas where they are known to pick off sheep and chickens, but if they are not pressured by hunters, coyotes learn to avoid humans and develop stable pack boundaries that circumnavigate human areas. Especially in wild areas such as the Hollow, coyotes go out of their way to avoid humans. I have found coyote tracks a mere twenty feet behind the cottage, traveling a straight route without once deviating toward the cottage or our open lands, which host a number of tasty farm animals. The local pack lives in peace with us and the few other people back here. They have their place and we have ours, and by respecting each others' mutual boundaries, there have never been problems. But when a pack is hunted, its members mourn. Their behavior becomes erratic. They may become aggressive and violate old agreed-upon boundaries. If a pack's senior members are killed, there is no one to teach the young to avoid humans. If a pack's alpha male is killed, the entire pack is disrupted and all activities may shift wildly. I had tried to protect this pack for so long—where were they?

Several more times I ascended the ridge and came back down, continuing that zigzag search pattern as I sought for any sign of their presence. Finally, I had progressed far enough that I heard the Flat Falls. I don't think this place has a real name. I doubt more than a tiny handful of people even know of its existence. It is a place where the brook widens out and descends rapidly, like a mini-rapids. I call it the Flat Falls because it sounds like an immense waterfall, but the sound is an illusion created by the way the slope and enclosing forest captures and amplifies the rushing water's passage. Overall, the Falls only drop thirty or forty feet over a distance of sixty yards. It is not a dramatic fall, but it sounds beautiful. Rain. Babbling brooks. Dew drops on puddles. Sprays and rapids. The myriad sounds of pure inland waters have always brought a deep peace to me, and as I passed the Falls I felt a longing to go down to them.

I worked my way down the ridge, across an ancient logging trail abandoned many decades ago, and further down til at last I reached the Falls. At their heart is a tiny narrow island. It has a sacred feel: a place that is a part of the forest yet cut off from the world. I do not walk there, feeling it is not for me but is something alone for the wights of the wood. But just before the slender little island is a great boulder of a rock, with a naturally flat area on top, which just invites one to come out, sit and let the spirit be carried away by the music of the flowing water. So, you might understand why I call it the Shaman Stone. It is easily reached by way of a couple natural steppingstones protruding a few inches above the crystalline water. I hung my pack from a tree on the bank and skipped over the stones, hopping up onto the Shaman Stone. I needed to. I was deeply uneasy about the whereabouts of my coyote brothers and sisters. And if they had been hurt, what about the black bear sow and her cubs, now half grown. These animals had become precious to me over the years. I felt my own spirit swelling between anxiety and anger. If some spiteful poacher was haunting my woods, I could and would track him down. I was becoming angry enough, I didn't know for sure where that might lead.

I sat upon the Shaman Stone and closed my eyes. I slowed my breathing and felt my heart falling into line. In my mind's eye I could see the rushing waters around me, and suddenly I felt myself moving forward, passing upstream over the waters. I was moving in spirit—the spirit journey had begun.

The Flat Falls are a small falls deep in the forest, just upstream of the Shaman Stone. It is a place of sublime beauty that seems to invite one to sit and ponder.

In the center of the brook is the Shaman Stone, a large, naturally flat-topped stone perfectly sized to sit on and journey as a shaman, the spirit carried away by the sound of the Flat Falls just upstream.

My awareness reached the height of the Flat Falls, and there was a hole in the center of the brook. Another waterfall. A spirit waterfall. And it drew me down, down, down into its depths. At the base of the falls, I found myself in another world, the Underworld, not so unlike this world but every object was pregnant with meaning, somehow more real, somehow less real. I wandered for a time and found Coyote. Not the Coyote prankster of aboriginal legend. But just Coyote—a wild canine spirit. He had no words but I ran with him and soon came to a great bonfire from which sparks rose into the star-strewn night where ancestral shamans of far-gone days danced and drummed. A great forest surrounded the tiny village, and women and men danced around the fire. And somehow all was right in their world. And I knew, somehow deep inside, that all was right in my world, for the Underworld and the green world are profoundly intertwined. And then I knew it was time to leave. I returned to the spirit falls and felt myself travel up and back to my corporeal self.

I opened my eyes and felt redness in them. I felt I had been given a gift from the Ancestors. I felt sure, somehow, everything would be okay. And though it had been a hard day of hiking over rugged ground, up and down the steep slope, I again felt completely rested and energized. Another gift of the powers of this forest. I was ready to continue on. I returned to my pack, removed a bit of Daphne's homemade goat cheese, and skipped back out to the Shaman Stone and left it at the center. Something to smoke would have been better, like a bit of dried pearly everlasting or sumac, but cheese, as well as milk, bread and ale, was always a good way to repay the spirits for their kindness. I returned to the bank, shouldered my pack, and pressed on.

I knew if I continued to head westerly I would encounter the near overgrown remnants of an ancient trail, and that way I went. I picked up the trail in half an hour and turned northerly. It would take me to the decaying, tiny bridge Natalia had long ago dubbed the Troll Bridge. Why it was ever built I don't know, since it seems to lead absolutely nowhere.

The path descended and finally reached a little bowl in the land, a place rainwater gathered. The trees here were small, water-loving species, mostly willows and sumacs, slender and densely pressed, leaning steeply over the path. I wasn't wearing waterproof boots, so I stepped carefully, looking for one little swell of ground after the other to make my way across. I reached the other side of the small, swampy area and had just resumed hiking when I glanced down and froze—seeing what I did washed the worry from me as a wave washes back from the beach. There at my foot was the enormous hind track of the black bear sow. And to either side were the tracks of her cubs. The tracks were sharp and clear, relatively fresh, made within a day or two. The bear family was okay, and I felt a deep tension inside of me release, and it felt like I could breathe for the first time this afternoon. Black bears, like coyotes, are also deeply misunderstood. Shy and reclusive, and largely herbivorous, they represent no real danger to humans, though humans often harass them. But the little family was okay. It was wonderful to see. I found droppings, too, filled with remnants of blueberries. They had been at the high ground, dining well on the lush harvest of wild blueberries. Their movements were sure and confident, which indicated good health. I could have cried, I was so relieved. Instead, I withdrew my camera to take a few photos. I pointed the camera down at the print of one of the bear cubs and realized that another track lay just inches behind it, the cloven hoof and dewclaws of a whitetail deer of truly huge proportions. And it had passed within a short time of the black bear family. It was like I was seeing the cloven hooves of the Green Man overseeing his kith and kin. Call me crazy, if you like, but I know at least one Green Man wanders these woods and looks after its denizens. I've seen him before, and not in the midst of a shamanic trance.

And somehow, seeing this wondrous sight, I knew everything else would be okay. I just knew it, deep inside. The vision the ancestors gave me at the Shaman's Stone was resolving into reality.

I continued on. Crossing the bridge is always a precarious venture. The planks are so rotted they wouldn't hold a child, much less a two-hundred-pound, six-foot man carrying another twenty pounds in gear. The only part of the bridge that is still any good is the north beam, an old rusting steel I-beam that sits on log posts in the stream. But it is hard to see as it is covered over by the rotten boards, and it's only six inches wide. One day soon its supporting posts will collapse, and I'll have to find an alternative way to get over that brook, but for now it is serviceable, but only just, if you're nimble. I made my way across the bridge and started up the path on the other side. Here the ground was suddenly stony and dry, and the remnants of the old trail were much more defined. I often came to this place to camp in early summer and I knew the area well.

I progressed up the trail and soon found coyote tracks. And not just tracks but fresh dung. To a non-tracker, dung is just nasty old manure. To a tracker, it is an important part of the story. Like the bear dung, these droppings told me that several coyotes had been through here, some larger, some smaller. They were eating the odd small mammal, voles and hares most likely, but mainly they were dining, like the black bear family, on the abundant late-season berries. And they told me the coyote group was sticking to its territory, which meant their elders and especially their alpha male and female were okay. And that told me my pack was safe and sound. They still haunted the wood, and the wood guarded them.

The last of my worries gone, I felt I needed a rest. And some food. I'd pushed hard through the day. I took a seat under a shade tree not far away and got into the remainder of the rations I had brought with me—a sandwich of venison and goat cheese, a dessert of fruit leather made from wild apples and chokecherries. I washed it down with cold wild sumac berry tea. Never had so simple a meal tasted so good in my life. All was well in the Wildwood. Its denizens were safe.

The sun was westering, and it gets dark in the Hollow sooner than elsewhere because the ridge blocks the setting sun before it hits the true horizon. It was time to start back to the cottage. But it was an easy walk, not quite a mile and a half away from this location. I rose, shouldered the pack, and left the crust of the sandwich behind and some of the fruit leather for the wood spirits. Then I started up the trail.

Darkness had nearly fully descended by the time I reached the Hollow Brook where it passes not a hundred yards from the cottage. I withdrew a small flashlight from the pack and used it to illuminate the steppingstones and crossed the brook. An ancient stone boundary wall, built in the Scots tradition by homesteaders far back in the early nineteenth century, lay just beyond and I carefully climbed the stones. From here it was just a matter of working my way through the bracken, among young trees of wild cherry, rowan, and apple, and up the slope. From the windows I could see warm light in the immense kitchen and hear the girls laughing about something. Tantalizing aromas emerged, fragrances of frying free-range chicken and garden vegetables. But I paused at the low door near the library, turned back to face south, the direction of the Wildwood. My mind was heavy with thoughts of the day. The forest was safe, its denizens secure. But who was that hateful poacher who had shot one of the coyotes and hung its carcass in a tree in mockery that handful of years ago? I had looked for his return ever since but never found sign of him, and I knew then I'd probably never know. And for that I breathed a sigh of relief. Hopefully, he was long gone, never to return. But today had shown me something I did need to know: I might consider myself the ward of this old forest, but there were other things back there, too, old and wise and not quite of this world. And they were also looking after the denizens of the Wildwood.

I went inside, left my gear below, cleaned and oiled my knife and set it in its place on a shelf, and went up the steps to the kitchen. Daphne offered me a cup of tea and soon dinner was served. And in the darkness beyond the little cottage in the big wood, the denizens of the Wildwood carried on in peace. Yes. It was a good day.

Wild Life

The Dance of Life & Death

One autumn, after a cold, wet, and unsuccessful day of pursuing venison for the homestead, I was heading back to the cottage. It would be full dark before I made it back, but I knew the land well and felt like it would be nice to sleep in a real bed by a hearth after a couple days of hard hunting. I slung my messenger bag over a shoulder, hung my black powder rifle from another shoulder, and began the hike back. It was the very last light of day, that time when the western sky holds the last magenta hue of a long-faded sun while a plethora of silent stars winks into being in the east. I had hiked perhaps two hundred yards when I heard them sweeping out of the forest of ancient maples, red and white spruce, and hemlocks that I call the Old Wood—a pack of coyotes, howling and yipping like the wights of the Wild Hunt itself. And they were moving fast in my direction.

Many people fear coyotes. It is entirely unfounded. A coyote is absolutely not going to attack a grown man or woman who holds position and does not behave like prey. If you've heard stories to the contrary, dismiss them as old wives' tales, for that's all they are. Sure, a coyote is a predator, and if a person runs things might go differently. I emphasize *might*. As a rule, coyotes have an instinctive fear of humans and go to extreme measures to avoid us.

When coyotes behave like this, they are giving chase to something. It was too late in the year for them to be after a vulnerable deer fawn, but they might have encountered an injured deer. More likely, they had located a snowshoe hare and were running it down. But I was roughly a half mile from the forest's edge and heard them moving swiftly along all that terrain. I did not think a hare could lead them on such a long chase and clearly they were getting close to me fast. I stepped against a tall bush. Most of its summer leaves were gone, stripped by the biting autumn air and occasional tempests, but the dense branches would break up my outline and make me near invisible to coyote eyes in failing light.

About fifty yards north was an old rock wall, maybe three feet high, built long and long ago by the old Gaelic settlers to this region, the vast majority of which had long since gone to the cities of Halifax and Boston to seek their fortunes in the urbanizing world. I heard a pitiful bleat and then heard scrambling over the rocks. It was too dark to see anything but flitting shadows, but I knew from the sound a doe had just scrambled over the rock wall. I could hear her bounding through the tall grass, fleeing north. A half mile away she would find an old dirt road and in that open space her long legs might allow her to outrun the pack. Or not. Coyotes aren't as fast but they have unbelievable endurance. Since some of these coyotes had some wolf genes, I suspected they would expertly coordinate their hunts to wear down anything they chased.

She bleated again as she passed me. It was a pitiful sound of fear. And as she passed, I got the impression that she seemed healthy enough. Ordinarily, a pack wouldn't try for a healthy deer, not on this kind of ground. In deep snow, where the deer couldn't run so fast, perhaps. But not across brushy turf, which played to the doe's ability to dart and weave over obstacles, make use of wet areas and find hidey-holes in which to vanish. For the coyotes, a chase across such ground meant the expenditure of a lot of energy with a low chance of a successful hunt. Perhaps the doe was injured, I thought. Or sick. And somehow the coyotes had sensed it. It was possible. They'd be more likely to go after a disadvantaged deer.

The coyotes were gaining on her, and as they did I recalled her pitiful cries, the sound of a hunted creature in terror.

I could put an end to this easily. The coyotes were just coming over the stone wall. All I had to do was step out from the bush where they could see me, raise and fire the fifty-caliber black powder rifle. It would make a loud *boom!*, not the thunderous clap of a modern firearm but enough. More impressively, a black powder rifle spits fire and smoke like an angry dragon. It would put an instant end to the chase and the coyote pack would break and flee into the nightwood.

I could have done it, and part of me wanted to, for I felt for the deer. I've been afraid in the past, too, and known firsthand what it was like to be hunted.

But I didn't. I stood there against the bush and let the pack pass, and I doubt they ever knew I was there. They have keen senses. If they hadn't been focused on the hunt, they would probably have realized I was there, but they ran past, and I let them go unhindered.

I had just stumbled into the ancient dance of life and death that has occurred since before humans walked Earth. The dance is old and whatever the lyrics, the refrain is always the same: *The prey is magnificent but grows too plentiful, and the hunter must hunt or the land shall fail.*

However lovely the deer, however much I may feel for her, it is not my place to interfere in the wisdom of Nature's ways. Deer can double their population every three years if their numbers are not checked. And so Nature has devised an elegant solution that creates diversity and space for many creatures. Deer can live from the varied bounty of the land, feeding on plants and mushrooms that would poison anything but a ruminant. But to keep their numbers in check, predators must hunt them.

Thus from the deer's own abundance, the predators also grow strong. And this mutual dance of life and death makes space for foliage to flourish and many other creatures to also have a chance to become abundant.

This is the way of things. The prey is not good; the hunter is not evil. They are what they are and have, at least, the wisdom to fit Nature's grand plan for them (which is sadly more than we humans oft can claim). And it is not the place of any man to step between Nature's wisdom.

So hunted and hunters passed in the night and once they were beyond me, I stepped away from the bush and continued on my way to Twa Corbies Cottage. Down in the Hollow our root cellar was full of the produce of the gardens and the wild forage of the lands, but also of chickens we had butchered and hares that had ventured into the gardens. Who was I to judge? We, as humans living close to the land, do our best to follow Nature's design for us, just as brother and sister coyote.

And that is how it must be.

That is the dance.

Enchanted Forest

Coyote Guides the Way of Life & Death

As is well known, Coyote is something of a trickster figure in North American mythology, but his benevolence and wisdom are seldom recognized. In this old tale from the near extinct lore of the Caddo Nation, we see a facet of Coyote's wisdom. The clever trickster and predator reveals his desire for equity and a good life in the next world for all the beings who must participate in the dance.

♦ ♦ ♦

The people had many councils from time to time. The errand man went all round to call the people to these councils. At one council Coyote arose and said: "First, we must change our rule about death, because all are not being treated alike. Now when some die they come back to their people, and then others die and never see their people again. I propose to make another rule, so that we may all be treated alike after death. This is the rule that I wish to propose: When anyone dies, let him be dead forever, and let no living person ever see him again. Our Great-Father-Above made a place there where every one of us may go after death. Now when any one dies he shall go from the living forever, but we shall still keep up the fire for six days." All the people were well pleased with Coyote's rule, and so from that time on, even to the present day, the same rule is kept, and when anybody dies he is gone forever, never to return again. The people are taken to the sky when they die and become the stars that we see at night.

—George Amos Dorsey
Traditions of the Caddo

Wood Witchery

Making the Spirit Journey

Many folk who follow paths of Earth-based spirituality have ways of communing with the wild spirits. What is a spell if not an agreement between mortal and numinous? And what are gardens of magical herbs if not ways of interacting with the powers of Plant and Earth? Druid folk enter forests and meditate among trees in order to find the wisdom of their patient, green souls. Followers of aboriginal paths collect natural totems to help them relate to the sacred enchantment of the natural world. The shaman, by tradition, enters the wild place in body, and finds there a sacred place of power and enters through that place into the world beyond this world to commune with the mythic wild spirits that underpin the here and now. And while I cannot speak as an expert on many of the techniques of the other paths, I know the path of the shaman well. I have trod its ways since before I even knew what it was called. And going upon the spirit journey, the most fundamental act of shamanry, is a thing I can teach you. And now seems the right time. You have trekked with me a long way through the wildwood, and learned much of its lore and ways; how to forage some wild foods, how to find your way, of the hearts of wild predators and the deeds of feral spirits. Yes, now it is time to teach you how to undergo the spirit journey.

I am a psychotherapist, and among many other things I learned during all those long years of education, I learned to meditate and to hypnotize. The spirit journey bears similarities to both. It is a meditative state in which you clear your mind so that you can focus your Self on the seemingly unnatural task of exiting your physical body. It is like hypnotism in that you relax and become open, except rather than listening to the voice of a hypnotist, the shaman follows his own direction.

And yet the spirit journey is an experience unto itself. It is healing and enlightening, a means to the wisdom that can only derive of insight into the deeper layers of reality. The consciousness, in some way, exits the here and now. It drifts outward down into the Underworld or perhaps upward to those realms above, there to meet the beings of that alternate reality and learn from them. And as that other reality is somehow linked to the here and now, a skilled shaman can learn to influence our world in subtle but significant ways by taking action in the Otherworld.

Once in Alaska, a Yupik villager told me of a hard winter when the people were hungry but their hunters could not find the caribou. So their shaman set out upon the spirit journey. In the Underworld, he went this way and that, soaring over mountains and tundra plains til he found a great herd sequestered in a fertile valley. The caribou were about to move on, so he told them to stay a while. Because Nature in the Underworld is intertwined with our world, there was also a caribou herd at such a place in this reality and they too stayed in place as the shaman had instructed. Then he returned to his body and told the hunters where the great herd was. It was far off and the hunters were afraid the caribou would surely have moved on by the time they arrived, but they went as their shaman said and indeed found the caribou there, milling about as if waiting. They harvested some and the people were fed and the land was the better for the caribous' numbers were too high. In such a way can the shaman alter events in the here and now through otherworldly interactions.

Learning to make the spirit journey is not difficult if you have even a modest talent for it. But it is important to understand that making the journey is not the same as mastering the shaman's craft. I know there are persons offering weekend retreats where they show folk how to make the journey and give certificates after certifying they are now shamans. The aboriginals I have known would be, at the least, perplexed. How can one become a shaman by making a spirit journey? It's like saying because a child has learned to walk, now it is a warrior. The spirit journey is open to many, shaman and not, alike. But it is just one technique of a far broader craft.

Likewise, many traditional shamans would be dismayed to hear that many folk of the modern world even want to be shamans. Even among their own people, folk find shamans difficult to understand and eerie. It is often a solitary path. The shaman's path is one to be sought only after much consideration, deep commitment, and perhaps only after one realizes the numinous powers have cast one in that direction.

Be that as it may, making the spirit journey is remarkably rewarding and leads to wonderful insights. I have learned that journeys conducted at natural places of power happen almost effortlessly. It is as if the enchantment of such places reaches out and pulls you into its flow. Such a place is the Shaman Stone in the forest near our homestead. When I journey there, I find my spirit-self pulled, literally pulled, into the Otherworld, invariably drawn upstream, up the waterfall, then down an otherworldly waterfall to the Underworld of animal spirits, mythical folk, and my own guide, Black Bear.

You can undertake the journey anywhere, though I do strongly recommend it be done in a solitary, sequestered natural place, and places of power are best. The directions below will introduce you to the rest of the technique.

1. Go to your place. At a minimum, it should be a secluded place where Nature presides. You may journey from there at any time, but journeys conducted during the morning or evening twilight seem most potent. Journeys conducted on sacred days, more so still. All you need bring with you is a media player (like an MP3 player) with a recording of shamanic drumming. (If you have no such recording, you can download one of my own from my website at: http://www.cliffseruntine.wordpress.com. Look under the heading: Cauldron of Enchantment for Shamanic Drumming.) It would be more traditional to have an assistant to provide live drumming, and if you are so privileged, bring that person.

2. Go an hour before dawn or before dusk to the site and prepare yourself by sitting quietly and letting the thoughts flow out of your mind and the tension ease out of your body. You may eat or drink something if you like. I often find it sets me in the right frame of mind to have a cup of tea and share a bit of bread with the birds. Find what works for you. Be still and let your mind and body soak in the healing rightness of Nature.

3. At the first hint of the gloaming (first hint of light before dawn or when the sun goes beneath the horizon in the evening), assume a comfortable position and begin to descend into a meditative state by focusing your mind upon the sounds of Nature around you. If wherever you are is perfectly quiet, focus on the rhythmic sound of your breath moving in and out. Aim to keep your mind clear but accept that now and then a mundane thought will pass through. It's okay.

Your brain is a thinking machine—it wants to think.
It will try to think of anything when you try to clear it.
The moment you recognize you're having a thought,
just let it go. Let it drift away like a spark from the
campfire drifts into the night.

4. When you feel you have attained a steady, clear state,
begin to listen to the drumming. Let yourself immerse
in the rhythm of the drums. As you listen, it will seem
as if the drums draw forth an awareness of a passage
before you, down into the Underworld where the
animal spirits and fey spirits dwell. It might be a pool,
a ladder, a cave or any of a number of other means.
You may feel that you have to take that path down,
or it may seem as if the rhythm of the drums itself
carries you down. Either way, take that way into the
Underworld. (Conversely, you may perceive a path
leading up to the Upperworld. If so, and you wish
to go that way, follow it. Some say it leads to the
realms of the gods.)

5. From here, your path becomes your own and I
cannot guide you. You will have to find your own
way. Let your spirit roam. In that dreamtime place
of the Underworld, you will meet spirits in many
forms, often as great trees or animals or fey beings.
Some will not care for you; some will be indifferent.
Respect them all but there is no need to fear them.
Others will be friendly and even willing to teach you.
Pay attention to them. Sometimes they speak in words,
but often they communicate like animals through what
they do. In time you will learn to communicate in their
way, and if you persist, in time you will encounter one

who in some way or another will come to stand out as your guide.

6. When you are ready to return to the here and now, merely return to that place of entry and follow it back and out, and in the doing your spirit self returns to your physical self.

Woods Lore

Tracking—Speaking the Language of Animals

Tracking is a skill I became fascinated with as a child growing up in the bayous. I still remember the very day I caught the passion. I was early in my single digits. My mother was showing me around a forest and there were old Indian burial mounds all around. We were walking beside one looking for arrowheads (which were not so hard to find then) and I noticed a depression in the ground. I pointed at it and asked if the Indians had made that funny mark in the ground. (I was about six then and having heard all kinds of wonderful stories about the aboriginal folk without yet having met any, in my mind they were like wise forest spirits that left incomprehensible marvels in the woods like mounds and arrowheads.) My mother looked at it and smiled and said, "No, *mon cher*, that's a deer's footprint." It seemed like a magic power to me, to be able to look at marks on the ground and know from those strange chevrons what creatures shared the wood. It was like suddenly learning there was a language that had no words, but was in fact much more pure and true than words. It was there in that moment that my passion for tracking was born.

I cannot teach you to become a tracker in the next few pages. What I can do is offer you an introduction to how it's done. If you want to take the skill further, visit my website for further articles, search your area for local courses, and I cannot speak highly enough about this book as a wonderful learning resource: *Mammal Tracks & Sign* by Mark Elbroch. It is a bit pricey at close to $70, but you will simply not find a more comprehensive resource anywhere. It will walk you through the basics of how to track, what to look for, how to interpret the spoor you encounter, and how to make plaster casts. It also explains specific behaviors of every mammal species in North America.

This is the track of a large male whitetail deer I found late in the spring of 2013. Knowledge of tracking allowed me to estimate the deer's size, determine its gender, age, and territory, long before I ever actually saw it. And long before I harvested our venison, I selected this deer as one the forest could spare due to its age.

The first step in learning to track is learning to recognize the spoor of what lives in your area. As with foraging, I suggest you begin with one animal, something that interests you and is fairly common in your area. I'll illustrate with the whitetail deer, as it has become ubiquitous around much of North America.

The track in the image above is that of a large whitetail deer buck. I found it sometime in late spring. The track was made in hard-packed, gravelly soil, but just after the last rain about two weeks back. It was not made prior to the rain or it would have partially washed out and lost definition. But since the ground had turned so hard as it dried, I could not estimate the track's age any closer than just after that rain.

Still, the breadth and length of the track told me this print was made by an enormous buck. The depth of the track affirmed my heavy weight estimation—at least three hundred pounds. Deer are territorial animals, and a male will typically hold about one square mile in this lush kind of country. But they make long, narrow territories, so that territory might be a quarter mile wide but four miles long, give or take. This was an older deer, and as deer are very abundant around here, I decided to take this one come the hunt, so I set about learning its territory. I crisscrossed the land within a quarter mile of this track and discovered an extensive network of deer trails. Deer create trails all through their territory and move along them. That way, if they are attacked by a predator, they always have a nearby well-established escape route. Well-used deer trails appear in the forest as worn paths, like human footpaths but narrower. In tall grass, they appear as narrow paths where the grass parts.

Following the trails and watching for reappearances of the buck's large tracks, I was able to determine its territory with a great degree of accuracy. It lived between the Elfwood and the Old Wood, feeding in the old clear cuts between. Such land provided water, cover, and abundant food. It was a deer paradise.

Spoor consists of much more than tracks and trails, though. It may include droppings, rubbings, signs of food and material gathering, and bed down sites.

Droppings are very useful—they indicate size, health, and diet of the animal. A deer eating ordinary mid- to late-summer browse leaves nearly black pelletized droppings. A deer on tender, lush spring graze, or who has found a lush spring and feeds near it, will leave a moist mass that clumps together.

Male deer also rub their antlers on shrubs and small trees. This is usually sighted on the trunks as narrow vertical patches, one to two feet long, where the bark has been worn away. This is done in part to scrape the velvet off once the antlers are mature, but as the rut (mating season) approaches, it is also to deposit scent from glands near the eye onto the tree. Does can detect this scent from afar. Males also create scrapes on the ground where they brush away forest duff to make a relatively bare patch and deposit scent from the legs and urine. Often you might spot a cloven hoof print in these patches.

Learning to spot such spoor is an art best learned through practice. As you practice, pay attention to every kind of sign: tracks, trails, nests, signs of feeding, defecation, breeding grounds, playing grounds, where water is, where hidey-holes and escape routes are … everything. To track is to develop the ability to perceive the patterns of the land and the marks of its hidden language. You begin to see everything more clearly, and any spoor will come to stand out as a break in the pattern, presenting new patterns of its own. In time, such things will stand out to your eyes as readily as a moon in the night. Keep plugging away at it and you will develop the ability to read the spoor language of wildlife as readily as you read these words.

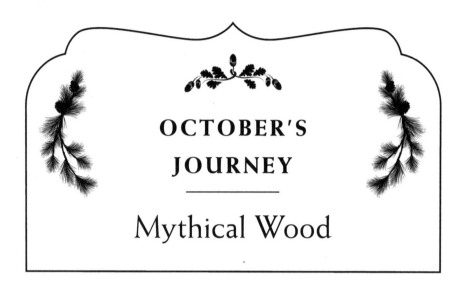

OCTOBER'S
JOURNEY

Mythical Wood

In the wilds were goblins and old gods of every sort, and children who wandered too far from home might find themselves lost in faerie tales.

—Cliff Seruntine
Seasons of the Sacred Earth

There is an ancient balance of give and take that sees to the health of the land. It is old beyond the counting of moons, old as the ebb and flow of life upon this, our sacred Earth. The hare eats the flower and feeds the lynx. The songbird eats the grass seed but spreads some in the doing. The hummingbird draws nectar from the blossom but shares its pollen. Even on our little homestead, we perceive in each season the unbreakable truth of this balance. The goats, pigs, and horses share the meadows with various poultry, each deriving life from the foliage, each restoring nutrients to the soil and turning it as it wanders about, which makes the earth friable and sets wild seed. Without the livestock, the meadows would soon wither and without the meadows the livestock would do likewise. And the animals provide the manure that becomes the compost in our many gardens, and it is because of this compost they yield so richly. The balance between the creatures that share the land is all-encompassing, ancient and wise. Though it is also fragile. If any element goes out of balance, the entire ecosystem will totter. So each spring we plant no more than the land can keep strong, and each autumn we cull the old livestock. We ensure everything remains vigorous by ensuring the land is not tapped for more than it can bear.

Nature, if left to her own devices, will see the balance is sound. If deer numbers go too high, their predators increase and curb their growth. If this did not happen, deer would in a mere decade increase to such a point they would eat meadow and forest bare, extinguish many rare species of plants, and ultimately die themselves of wasting starvation. So it is with all the creatures that share Earth, from hare to moose, vole to eagle. Nature keeps her balance by assuring there are predators to check the herbivores, and herbivores to tend the soil.

But humans, for their various misguided reasons, have long been at war with predators. So many a wild land nowadays lacks the balance it needs to remain healthy, even a semi-remote forest like ours. Once there were wolves here, but no more. The short-faced bear is extinct. The grizzly has been driven far north. Of predators of large animals, there is now only the coyote and its close cousin, the coywolf, and black bears. There are smaller predators in plenty, such as wolverines and lynx, but few that would serve to balance the numbers of larger animals such as whitetail deer.

With a dearth of predators, I try to pay especial attention to the balance of wildlife throughout the forest surrounding the homestead. If grouse numbers grow high, in autumn and winter I will make it a point to take a few. If hares are overabundant, as they are just now, I will hunt them regularly. It provides variety for the pot and useful hide, fur, and feathers. But we take only what Nature has in surplus. And in that way we aim to live in harmony with the ancient balance.

In the last few years, whitetail deer have increased greatly throughout the wildwood. Winter, their primary adversary, has been gentle for several seasons and in such conditions the lush meadows and forests, so rugged and inaccessible, allow their numbers to soar. So for the last several years I have made it a point to track down and harvest one or two each autumn. A couple good-sized bucks provide exceedingly nutritious meat for half the year for a family of four, as well as an abundance of hide and antler for leather, buttons, hilts, and any number of other uses.

This year the deer numbers were at such height that a hunter was allowed two. Provincial biologists figured the average hunter would still be lucky to harvest even a single deer as success rates are about one in four. But decades in the wilderness have allowed me to learn a great deal about locating quarry. As a result, for many years I've been successful on every hunt.

This year, in the course of my ordinary foraging and rambling, I had found tracks of two large deer, one near the Rusalka Brook, and one a couple miles away in our own Eastern Meadow at the foot of the Old Wood. I decided to hunt the Rusalka Brook first, at a place I knew many deer trails came to a confluence.

The problem was the only good cover was nearly a hundred yards from the deer trail, much too far for the traditional bow I tended to prefer. Flintlocks and cap and ball rifles were allowed during the bow season, so that meant I'd have to use my black powder rifle. These weapons are based on the more primitive technology of the muskets of previous centuries. Black powder is an inefficient powder and requires the use of a large, heavy ball or bullet to gain enough power to knock down game. The rounds are not very aerodynamic and they do not build up high velocities, so the range of a black powder rifle is very limited. One hundred fifty yards is about their maximum effectiveness, and that is really pushing it with a maximum powder load and assuming there is no contrary wind. I liked that. Their limited range meant the chance of a shot traveling far downrange and causing un-intended harm was minimal. And given the time-consuming steps it took to load a black powder rifle and render it ready to fire, it was not the kind of thing likely to be chosen for street crimes or accidentally loaded and shot by a child. And I liked black powder rifles for another reason. Living in the woods requires skill and self-sufficiency. If things ever went really bad out in the world, a skilled person can manufacture both shot and powder. All one needs is some lead and a die for the balls, and access to animal manure and urine and some hardwood for the ingredients to make powder. (Let me emphasize: it also takes a whole lot of skill to make black powder. Powder is explosive and the process is dangerous, not to be attempted except by an expert in real need.)

So I set about preparing for the hunt. Two weeks before the season began, I hiked out to the top of a hill that overlooked a game trail and there created a hiding place from local materials. In effect, I cut back into a patch of young white and red spruce, made a little spot to sit, set up a simple shelter overhead to shield me from the frequent cold autumn rains, and laid up brush in such a way as to break the outline of the aper-ture from which I would watch the meadow below. When I was done, the blind was all but invisible, and I tested my work by sitting up there and watching wildlife. Small animals meandered the meadow: grouse, wood-chucks, raccoons, and skunks, completely oblivious to my presence. As long as the wind didn't blow out of the east and betray my scent—which is rare in these parts unless there is a storm, in which case I wouldn't be out hunting anyway—no deer should ever know I was there.

The next couple weeks passed, and around the homestead life car-ried on as usual. It's a busy time as we are prepping for winter. Daphne and the girls harvested wild apples while I cut firewood and occasion-ally ventured into the woods to gather late mushrooms. Between those main chores, the goats were giving us the last of their milk, Daphne was often occupied making cheese, and I was engrossed in mending outbuildings like the chicken coop, which I had to make solid against a mink who liked to raid the poultry flock in winter. Making sure the coop was solid was like telling the mink, "It's easier to look elsewhere for your dinner," and it is one of the many strategies we use to coexist with local life. I also had to ready the fruit trees against predation by rodents and hares, as well as bring in the late-season crops: Jerusalem artichokes, late potatoes, and some cold-loving, slow-growing greens like chard and kohlrabi. It gets so busy at this time of year that every minute from dawn to dusk is precious, and when the sun finally goes down, we collapse in the cottage exhausted.

So when the season finally opened, I was eager and ready. A chance to be still and watch the slow yet sure transition of the land from summer to autumn was a welcomed break, and I set out well before dawn of the first day and made my way through meadow and wood til at last I hiked the winding ways between long abandoned hedges and up the hill to the blind. I slipped into the trees as the sky was first whitening with the dawn and settled comfortably in beneath a roof of woven spruce boughs.

The day passed slow and easy, and through the course of it several does meandered across the trail, but I wasn't after them. I took the time to familiarize myself with the local wildlife. The spruce woods were haunted by various finches who were ever hopping about after the bits and bobs they lived on. Now and then bumblebees would visit the last late-season blossoms still hanging on to summer along the green-sided hillock. A pair of raccoons made their way through at one point, and it was odd to see them up by day. I had to wonder what mischief they were up to. And on a couple occasions I spied several ravens that flew hither and thither, chattering and making a curious spectacle of themselves.

This is a nearly finished example of one of many hunting blinds I have cobbled together over the years. Fallen logs form the far wall, and live trees form the corners of the near wall. A tangle of earth and roots from a windfallen old tree form the front wall. I lashed a line around the back and side walls, hung some old sackcloth from it to create shadow, and leaned spruce and alder boughs on it to break up the blind's outline. More alder boughs were laid over the roof to conceal it and keep it from noisily flapping in the wind. When it was all done, the blind blended into the land so well it was virtually invisible.

But of all the forest's denizens, most noteworthy were a mated pair of bald eagles and their single offspring that would come by now and then and perch at the tops of the three tallest maples to regally survey the meadow, watching for hares, voles, and other prey. I had known these eagles many years. They currently had a nest not far away and I had watched them raise families since we'd first come to live in the Hollow. Their current offspring was an adolescent about four or five years old, and just starting to get a little white in its head. They don't

develop the white feathers for which they are named "bald" until ma-
turity, and I knew that while it was still attached to its parents, it was
none too long til it would fly away for good to make its own way in
the world. Often that young eagle would go off and hunt on its own
but it was still attached enough to its parents that after a while it would
return and join them, always perching between them on the middle of
the three great maples. The parents—so familiar and comfortable with
his presence—would not even glance between them as it alighted in its
usual place. And there the three would sit at the pinnacles of the trees,
a comfortable silence between them, as they soaked up the sun and
surveyed their demesne.

And so a quiet week passed like this. I was in no rush to complete
the hunt. I loved these late-season days with their summery light and
chill evenings, and the wood slowly transforming to autumnal hues as if
caught in the slow flow of the great river of time. It was the hypnogogic
moment of the land as it slowly descended into winter dreamtime, and
from the cover of my blind I became part of the shifting patterns of an
unspoiled primal rhythm.

Raven is a prankster!

This thing you must never forget. Raven is clever. Raven watches.
Raven never misses an opportunity. And though coyote may be stronger,
eagle faster, and owl master of the nightwood, none can outwit the raven.

After a week or so at my site, I had that feeling I always get just before a hunt comes to a conclusion. I was seeing more does going about,
and that would draw the curiosity of bucks with new antlers catching
the first hot blood of the rut. Soon I would make the first kill of the
season, but raven is a prankster and apparently he had plans of his own.

I arrived at my blind before dawn, as always, and made myself comfortable, indulging in some hot tea from a thermos and a breakfast of scrambled farm eggs and goat cheese wrapped up in flat bread, courtesy of my
beloved Daphne. The sun rose and the day grew into the deep blue of

another perfect autumn sky. Halfway to the sun's zenith, I saw the mated eagle pair glide over the treetops like king and queen of the meadow and alight on the ancient maples, as was their wont. Settled, they perched and surveyed the land. All seemed normal and right in the wood.

Did I mention raven is a prankster?

In a moment when the mated eagle pair was each looking in opposite directions, one of the local ravens flew up behind them. It had to have studied the habits of the eagle family because it followed the exact same course their offspring always did, coursing just over the ground up to the top of the middle tree, alighting between them as confidently as the adolescent eagle. And as the eagle queen and king proudly looked out over opposite directions of the meadow, the raven assumed a similar pose as their son, standing tall, head high, slowly surveying the expansive meadow in a most regal, even eagle-like fashion.

Eagle is a mighty hunter, but no creature of the wood can outwit the prankish blackbirds of genus *Corvus*. (Photo courtesy of Brooke Oland.)

This went on for a long moment. Maybe a minute; maybe three. I follow time by the sun, mostly, when I am in the bush and couldn't say exactly. And I was so mesmerized by what I saw unfolding that I wouldn't have taken my eyes from the sight to glance at a timepiece, even if I'd had one on me.

So the eagles surveyed their meadow realm and so did the raven between them. Then the eagle on the left, which I believe was the male because it was smaller (female balds are about 25 percent larger than their counterparts) happened to glance between. For a moment frozen in time, it just looked at the raven, and I swear for all the world it was like it was trying to figure out: *What's wrong with this picture?* Who knows what exactly went through its noble eagle brain in that mixed-up instant. I suspect it was something along the lines of: *Oh, dear god! An evil sorceress has turned our beautiful eaglet into an ugly raven! Now we have to find a princess to kiss it!* Whatever was going through its head, it suddenly unleashed a mighty cry of alarm. I don't mean the majestic screech one might overhear as an eagle soars aloft. I mean a horrified equivalent of: *What the hell???* And its wife turned and saw the raven and echoed the cry.

The raven, one of Nature's most intelligent creatures, had his own thoughts on the matter. It vociferated its own cry: *CAW! CAW!* And that meaning was clear: HA! HA! And it promptly fell out of the tree and spread its wings. The angry eagles did the same, out for some payback.

I thought I was seeing the prankster's last moments in this world as it dove steeply into the gap of a hill and disappeared from sight with the two eagles hot on its tail, but a moment later it erupted from the gap, flapping hard and having built up tremendous speed, but the two eagles emerged just behind it, gaining fast. But then the raven dipped its wings and, as if putting on brakes, it steered so sharply around that compared to the eagles it was like it had just turned a 180 in place. I recalled that eagles are powerful hunters, and stately and graceful in their flight, but they are often driven off from their hunts by crows and even mere songbirds. They are fast and powerful, but that isn't everything. They simply cannot outmaneuver smaller, nimbler birds.

Off flew Raven into the west, over the forest, still emitting its raucous *CAW! CAW!* version of *Ha! Ha!* And the eagles broke off and flew north, not even bothering to give further chase. I suspect they felt rather foolish and did not want to hang around the meadow among all their subjects who might have seen them taken down a peg. That was the last I saw of them that day.

In olden faerie tales, heroes and heroines encounter a whole hidden natural world. A maiden skips through the forest and songbirds sing more sweetly for her joy. Young men share secrets with wise old trees. Wizards seek wisdom in whispering stones. And animals talk, sometimes with people, often among themselves. The modern person looks upon these old tales with a tolerant though condescending eye, knowing they are the mere fantasies of simple folk, told to amuse themselves in the ignorance of the long-ago times. The modern person is cosmopolitan and learned and certainly does not hold the simple ideas of those long-ago folk against them. They could not have known better. They had no access to the enlightenment of contemporary reason. But the modern person, assured by the confines of the apartment, the ponderous predictability of the office, the concreteness of taxes and business and bills, and the insight of science, knows better than to believe mere animals talk and jest, love and lose, and live out deep lives of their own. The heroes and heroines of those faerie tales who found wondrous intelligence in trees and rocks and animals . . . they were just the constructs of simple, flawed thinking.

The modern person knows nothing.

In the green there is room for mystery and enchantment, and there are moments when the amazing can and will happen. And the world beyond the door is deeper and more wondrous than most in the strange, current concrete world can reckon.

Not long after, I got my first deer of the season. A single shot with the muzzleloader, a bright flash of fire and brief cloudlet of smoke, and the deer fell quick and clean. I paused to thank the Green Man and the Cailleach for the gift of meat from one of their herd, and said the prayer I always do to send the animal's spirit with goodwill into the Otherworld. Then, because I had to pack the meat out of this remote location, I gutted, skinned, and boned the kill on the spot and a couple hours later began the long, arduous process of packing it back to the cottage where I completed the butchering, then left it to Daphne to pickle in a brine as preparation for later smoking. And while she did, I went down to the basement to our humble little library where is kept a few thousand tomes. Collected over a lifetime, a huge portion of those volumes have to do with natural science. I pulled up everything I could find on ravens.

I could find no documented incidents of ravens playing pranks on eagles in the usual reference materials: birdwatchers' field guides and books on animal behavior, but in *Mammal Tracks & Sign* by Mark Elbroch, one of my favorite tomes on the art and science of tracking, the author did note that ravens had been spotted playing such pranks on wolves. They would walk near wolves, taunting them, and when the wolves had enough and leapt at them, the ravens would launch into the air, squawking gleefully. And upon reading that, I knew I had just witnessed the same kind of thing. But in the absence of wolves, the raven had opted to tease a pair of eagles. And much the way a human boy might feel compelled to play at the edge of a precipice or tease an ornery bull, the raven had opted to tease the dangerous bigwigs of the animal world, for eagles, like wolves, are apex predators.

I closed the book and leaned back into the comfort of the little couch in the library and smiled. Our aboriginal ancestors had known long before I or Elbroch or any modern rational mind that ravens are pranksters. My little library's shelves were also lined with countless books on myth and magic, as well as a substantial collection of old faerie tales from around the world. Those tomes of ancient, eldritch lore were full of awareness that the denizens of the forest live deep, secret lives unknown to us ever-so-wise modern folk. The denizens of the wildwood are our kin, and sometimes, if we are quiet and watchful, we might even fall into their faerie tales.

Wild Life

Raven—the Winged Prankster

Did you know that ravens have a language? An honest-to-goodness spoken language. Wildlife biologists and animal behaviorists have long suspected this for the simple reason that ravens make and repeat more noises than any other animal, save humans. And there is a certain rhyme and reason to their vocalizations, evident but just a hair beyond our grasp. I knew a naturalist back in Alaska who told me that his team had learned that ravens could count to eight. This happened when they built a blind to observe raven behavior but then noticed the ravens were wary of the blind when an observer was in it. No matter how long the observer was in the blind, the ravens never forgot he or she was there. To thwart the ravens, they began going to the blind in groups. They'd all pile in, then all but one would leave. Still the ravens would behave warily around the blind until the last person gave up and left. It was not until nine persons went simultaneously to the blind and eight left that the ravens would shed their wary behavior. Thus, it was confirmed that ravens can count to eight.

I have always been utterly fascinated by ravens. My main interest is mammals, especially large ungulates and predators of the north, but of all the denizens of the bird kingdom, ravens amaze me for their sheer intelligence and personality. And I have little doubt, based on personal experience, that ravens not only have language, but in fact languages. Years ago in Alaska after dozens of hours of observing them, I began to notice they tended to make certain calls before banking or entering an area. I began to imitate those calls and soon learned I could cause passing ravens to bank and distant ravens to approach on the wing. But here on the coast of eastern Canada, thousands of miles away, the same calls do not work. That indicates to me the calls I used out west have no meaning here. To this day, I have not been able to figure out how to call eastern ravens over or tell them to bank. When I make such calls, they merely eye me curiously but carry on with their business.

In 2012, John Marzluff, PhD, a professor of wildlife science at the University of Washington, wrote that he and other observers had noted some very definite raven words. A cluck means a predator is in the area. (I have noticed ravens doing this as they have passed over me if I am hunting. But if I have merely been foraging, or just out canoeing or riding my horse, they make no such clucks. That tells me they have a sense of intent.) Ravens also trill if they intend to fight a rival raven for a better portion of a meal. They also trill to indicate surrender if they are losing that fight.

In my last book, *Seasons of the Sacred Earth,* I wrote of an encounter I had with a raven not long after we acquired Twa Corbies Hollow. I had been walking down a dirt path not too far from the cottage when a passing raven dropped something it had been carrying in its claws. Perhaps it was some bit of something for its nest. Perhaps it was a morsel of food. As soon as the raven dropped it, it alighted in a nearby tree and watched for me to pass on so it could retrieve the item. But I was dead curious to know what the item was, so I approached it. I hadn't meant to steal it, but the raven sure assumed I did. When I got a few feet from the object, it launched skyward, flapping its wings in powerful, angry thrusts so that I could hear the *whoosh, whoosh, whoosh* of its ascent. And then it raced away to the northwest, not just cawing but bellowing: *Haaa! Haaa! Haaa!* I heard it doing this til it vanished over the forest over a mile away. It was furious!

At the time I had interpreted those cries as the equivalent of being called a thief or some other invective. Well, it was an invective, sure enough, and I later learned that Marzluff had managed to interpret *Haaa.* It means "meat." Now I know when that raven flew off, it was calling me "meat." I think it was using the term in the same sense as when a human refers to a vile person as carrion, or says, *You're dead meat!*

Ravens, and their close kin crows, have long been misunderstood, I think primarily simply because of their intelligence which can seem uncanny to the point of being eerie. The raven was a companion of Norse gods, and a pair (Huginn and Muninn) represents thought and memory. Ravens are thought to be ill omens and familiars of dark witches further south in Europe, and a bit west among the Gaels they are closely associated with the Morrighan, the dark Gaelic goddess of death, battle, and nightmares. In this day, ravens are commonly associated in popular fiction with the macabre and the sinister side of the preternatural. Humans are so spooked by them that, sadly, in many American states and Canadian provinces, sport hunters make a point of shooting them. Which is a pity. I've never known them to do any real harm and as with all the denizens of Nature, they enrich the world with their very being.

But the wise aboriginal folk saw in Raven's keen intelligence an avatar of the benign creator god. Some even believe their brothers are sometimes reincarnated as ravens and consider it terrible luck to bring harm to a raven.

For my part, I think Coyote and Raven are rascals who mean no real harm; they just enjoy a little mischief now and then. The rest of the time, they clean carrion from the land, balance prey populations, and wander with their tribes, making their way in a broad green world full of wonders and challenges ... same as we.

Enchanted Forest

How the Raven Helped Men

I love this old faerie tale, culled from the folklore of the northwestern aboriginal peoples and collected by Florence Holbrook over a century ago.
Unfortunately, Ms. Holbrook does not specify the tribe from which this
tale derives. But it has the air of many of the myths that circulate about the
Raven creator from as far south as Pacific Washington to the Haida of the
Alaskan panhandle. In this tale, we see Raven as kind and clever and a bit of
the trickster, too. And at the end of it, perhaps a little light will be shed on
why to this day one might still see ravens playing pranks on Cousin Eagle.

◆ ◆ ◆

The raven and the eagle were cousins, and they were almost always friendly,
but whenever they talked together about men, they quarreled.

"Men are lazy," declared the eagle. "There is no use in trying to help
them. The more one does for them, the less they do for themselves."

"You fly so high," said the raven, "that you cannot see how hard men work. I think that we birds, who know so much more than they, ought to help them."

"They do not work," cried the eagle. "What have they to do, I should like to know? They walk about on the ground, and their food grows close by their nests. If they had to fly through the air as we do, and get their food wherever they could, they might talk about working hard."

"That is just why we ought to help them," replied the raven. "They cannot mount up into the air as we do. They cannot see anything very well unless it is near them, and if they had to run and catch their food, they would surely die of hunger. They are poor, weak creatures, and there is not a hummingbird that does not know many things that they never heard of."

"You are a poor, weak bird, if you think you can teach men. When they feel hunger, they will eat, and they do not know how to do anything else. Just look at them! They ought to be going to sleep, and they do not know enough to do even that."

"How can they know that it is night, when they have no sun and no moon to tell them when it is day and when it is night?"

"They would not go to sleep even if they had two moons," said the eagle; "and you are no true cousin of mine if you do not let them alone."

So the two birds quarreled. Almost every time they met, they quarreled about men, and at last, whenever the eagle began to mount into the air, the raven went near the earth.

Now the eagle had a pretty daughter. She and the raven were good friends, and they never quarreled about men. One day the pretty daughter said, "Cousin Raven, are you too weak to fly as high as you used to do?"

"I never was less weak," declared the raven.

"Almost every day you keep on the ground. Can you not mount into the air?"

"Of course I can," answered the raven.

"There are some strange things in my father's lodge," said the pretty daughter, "and I do not know what they are. They are not good to eat, and I do not see what else they are good for. Will you come and see them?"

"I will go wherever you ask me," declared the raven.

The eagle's lodge was far up on the top of a high mountain, but the two birds were soon there, and the pretty daughter showed the raven the strange things. He knew what they were, and he said to himself, "Men shall have them, and by and by they will be no less wise than the birds." Then he asked, "Has your father a magic cloak?"

"Yes," answered the pretty daughter.

"May I put it on?"

"Yes, surely."

When the raven had once put on the magic cloak, he seized the strange things and put them under it. Then he called, "I will come again soon, my pretty little cousin, and tell you all about the people on the earth."

The things under his cloak were strange indeed, for one was the sun, and one was the moon. There were hundreds of bright stars, and there were brooks and rivers and waterfalls. Best of all, there was the precious gift of fire. The raven put the sun high up in the heavens, and fastened the moon and stars in their places. He let the brooks run down the sides of the mountains, and he hid the fire away in the rocks.

After a while men found all these precious gifts. They knew when it was night and when it was day, and they learned how to use fire. They cannot mount into the air like the eagle, but in some things they are almost as wise as the birds.

—Florence Holbrook
The Book of Nature Myths

Wood Witchery

Natural Power Objects

Years ago, when we first came to Maritime Canada and were learning our way about the woodlands that were so alike and yet so different from the boreal forests of the far north, I had been out hiking alone one day. Miles from the little farm cottage we were then renting, I wandered through a stand of truly ancient maples and hemlocks. Still used to Alaskan wilderness, where one could not navigate by the sun, I was using an old trick of northern peoples and following a brook that here skipped over stones and there babbled in placid depths. Ahead I could see it swung right then made a broad turn left so that it nearly doubled back on itself, and I decided to travel directly between the two points to save time. It was easy going. The trees were tall and deep forest shade gave no place for brush to obstruct the way. I was idly ambling through waist-high ferns when I glance ahead. There was a break in the canopy of the tall trees, just enough to admit a single slanted sunbeam, and it fell in a spray of gold over a tiny patch of especially tall ferns. And at the heart of that spear of light a bald eagle feather lay upon the fronds like a sword in a stone.

I knew in that moment it was a power object, and I was meant to find it. I walked over, lifted it, and held it up in the gold light. It was pristine, a long, dark feather capped in white, left like a gift from the Earth Mother.

Sometimes we encounter such gifts in the outdoors, and they could be anything. My experience is we rarely ever expect to encounter them, we rarely have in mind we need such a thing when we find it, and yet when we stumble across them, we know...

The collecting of power objects has been a common practice of Earth-based spiritual practitioners throughout the world since time immemorial. From the ancient druids who walk the wood no more to the aboriginal shamans of the remote north who persist despite the press of modern life, people with spirits aligned with the natural world have been able to sense those special power objects when they appear. It could be a feather. Or it could be a smooth stone at a brook's bottom. It could be the canines of an old coyote skull, or the dry rattling seedpod of wild lupine. One can never know exactly til one stumbles upon it.

And such objects have differing destinies. Sometimes they are not meant to be kept. They are simply revealed to remind you there is magic in the land. Sometimes they are meant to be gathered and later given away, perhaps left in another wild place to reinvigorate the land's spirit, perhaps gifted to a friend in need of a moment's encouragement. I have found many power objects over the years and yet I have few. They always seem to find their way to other people or other places. With power objects, the finder must be sensitive to the spirits, careful to keep such things only as long as it is right, and give them away joyfully when the time comes. Otherwise such things lose their enchantment, becoming mere objects of avarice instead of true power.

What is this power? It too varies greatly, and only the finder can discern it. I find it in shiny, smooth pebbles of brook-polished feldspar and quartz, which seem to aid shamanic meditation. But not always. I find raven feathers that help me speak to spirits, but not always. That eagle feather I found long ago made me feel the wild lands of Maritime Canada welcomed us when we were new here. But I have since found other eagle feathers that do not even impress me as objects of power. The virtues of power objects are highly individual and contextual. They may vary with the inherent characteristics of the item, or the innate talents of the finder, or the purpose of the numinous powers themselves.

The collecting of power objects over the years becomes something akin to writing a journal. The power objects tell where one was, what was in the heart, and what was special to the spirits at any given moment. And it is the most personal of journals. No one else can ever read it, for only the collector knows its hidden meaning. Thus it is that some such objects become very personal. Like certain spirit guides, they are never spoken of, never revealed. Like a beloved friend or spouse, their company is perhaps their greatest gift.

Woods Lore

Camping Comfortably

Nothing puts the soul in touch with Nature so thoroughly as spending a night in its company. But nothing makes for a less pleasant experience than pitching a poorly executed camp. Set your camp up well and you'll wake full of joy, feeling at one with the living Earth beneath you. Do it poorly and you will spend a night in what seems like endless misery, dank and cold, as you count down minutes that feel like hours til the sun rises. Many times I've gone out into the forest with no intention to spend the night but ended up just enjoying myself too much to go home. Equipped with only a knife and hatchet, I fashioned a lean-to of spruce boughs, a bed of slender logs to get me up and level off the cold, wet ground, made do with a coat for a blanket, and built a good fire to warm the lean-to. Dinner on such occasions might consist of mushrooms I plucked from a tree, and breakfast would be fish I caught with a quickly knocked-up stick trap, making all and all a very pleasant experience of "roughing it." With sufficient skill, you need little more than a knife and a coat to survive for extended periods in the backcountry. However, that's pretty advanced stuff and not necessary for most people. It is far easier and usually more comfortable to learn how to pitch a tent for a fine old night in the wildwood. And a tent will give you additional protection from biting flies and crawling insects, a big plus most anywhere.

When setting up a tent, imagine you are building layers over, under and around yourself. Your goal is to insulate yourself from the dampness and heat sapping nature of the ground, and the vicissitudes of the air. Your tent needs to be soundly set to hold up to weather and keep out rain should it fall

I suggest investing in a good tent. You don't have to break the bank, but you'll be in for a miserable night if you settle for a cheapy off some department store clearance shelf and foul weather brews. Good tents are made of tough fabric, often heavy-grade ripstop nylon with a tight grain to hold up to the elements. They have a heavy treatment for water resistance. And on the bottom they are made of very heavy-duty tarp-like material to resist water even if it pools around the tent. All that heavy-duty material forms reliable wind and rain barriers. Good tents also have tough, fine-mesh bug screen doors, so if you live in areas rife with black-flies and mosquitoes, a tent will allow you a peaceful, bite-free night. Also—and this is often overlooked—ensure the zippers are very heavy-duty. Strangely, many makers of otherwise excellent tents skimp on the zippers, even though it is one of the most important things. Good zippers will function reliably for years. Cheap zippers will warp under the strain of wind and make it impossible to seal the entry, and you can be sure this will happen at the worst time, i.e., in the middle of a gale when the wind is blowing out of the direction of the tent door.

A good one- to three-person tent is likely to cost $300 to $500, and if you use it much, it'll prove worth every penny. And taken care of, a good tent lasts and lasts. I still have a nice Eureka tent I bought in Alaska some twenty years ago, and it's still going strong (shown before the lake in July's Journey). Tents, oddly, go out of fashion like clothes, and every year makers present catalogues with the latest models. A savvy shopper can get a superb "out of fashion" tent for half or less the regular retail price. You'll do even better if you buy at the end of the camping season, too, when retailers want to clear out last year's inventory. (The tent I just mentioned retailed at nearly three times what I paid for it, but I bought last-year's model in autumn after the camping season and saved a small wad of cash.)

If you are going to backpack to your campsite, a small one- or two-person tent is ideal. It will add as much as ten pounds to your load but be worth its weight in gold unless you know how to knock up quick shelters from local materials. If you are packing with a group, it is more efficient for everyone to share a larger tent (for three or four), with one person carrying the tent while others carry that person's gear.

Also, you should purchase at least one tarp, preferably two. One tarp should be about six inches greater on all sides than the floor dimensions of your tent. Always take it with you. You can buy custom cut tarps, but it's cheaper and just as effective to buy an ordinary tarp and cut it to shape. The second should be several feet broader. We'll go into its purpose a bit later.

You'll also want a good sleeping pad. These days, high-tech, expensive, self-inflating foam pads are popular. I don't see the point of them. They may rip and wear out quickly and are an unnecessary expense. A wool blanket to put under you is just as effective, as is a foam sleeping pad that costs only a few dollars and packs in less space.

To keep you warm through the night, the traditional solution is to wrap up in a heavy wool blanket. Wool is always good. Naturally water repellent and highly insulative, it is reliable and space efficient. A warmer option that takes less space and is of lower weight is a good sleeping bag. Modern sleeping bags are small and light, and can insulate you well into subzero temperatures. The best insulator is still goose down, though it is worthless if it gets wet. I prefer something that is resilient to moisture. Being prepared for the worst is good policy in backcountry. I prefer the old, simple wool blanket though I have several very good-quality sleeping bags for summer, winter, and full arctic conditions. But I didn't pay much for any of them. Sleeping bag designs, like tents, come and go with ephemeral fashion and you can save a bundle by buying last-year's model at the end of the camping season.

When you make your camp, it is important to be aware of the terrain. I've seen people pitch awesomely made guide-quality tents in open areas unshielded from the wind, and those people were shocked to find their $1,000 tents flattened the next morning by a storm. How could they have been surprised? I mean, if a full on storm can tear apart a house, it can sure make short work of even the best tent. Take care to pitch your tent in an area with as much shelter as possible from the wind.

Also, pitch your tent on high ground. Ideal are little flat knolls, even if only a foot or two above the surrounding ground. This will keep water from pooling into your tent if it rains. It's actually fun to be stuck in a tent come a rainy day. I love the sound of rain on a tent roof and an excuse to recline on the sleeping bag all day reading at my leisure. But it's the opposite of fun if the floor of your tent has turned into a wading pool.

When you pitch your tent, clear the ground of sticks, sharp stones, and any other objects that could penetrate the floor or make the site uncomfortable. Place the fitted tarp down first, then pitch the tent on top. This will also give you an added barrier against ground moisture. Many tents come with flies (fitted covers that go over the frame) to help the tent repel water. If it looks like the weather will turn, put the fly on. At least keep it handy if you don't want to put it on. If the weather turns in the night, you'll need to get it on fast because even a little dampness in the sleeping area makes for a long night.

This is a four-person, guide-quality tent of classic design. Daphne and I recently bought it so we could enjoy a roomier, more comfortable base camp, for when we're going to be out foraging for a couple days. It's heavy but I'll usually just pack it and she'll carry my gear, or I might run it to the site with our other gear by horse or tractor, leave it, and we'll hike there on foot later. Though compact when packed, this tent is nearly tall enough to stand up in, and quite wide, with porches to keep muddy gear out of the living area yet also out of the rain. As it was threatening to rain when we set it up, we pitched the rain fly, which will keep it dry even in the worst weather. Notice how the tent is pitched on flat, sloped ground beside a hillock in the trees. The trees and hillock form windbreaks and the slope will keep water from pooling under the tent.

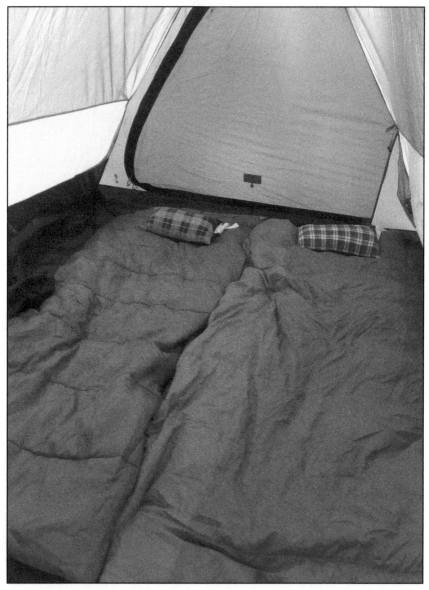

The inside of our guide tent is roomy, with more than ample space for two sleeping pads, two sleeping bags, and all our gear. It is a warm, dry little haven on a rainy day.

Okay, that second tarp: bring it with you if weight is not a big concern or if the weather looks threatening enough to make the extra weight worth the carry. And think of it as an extra roof. If it threatens a downpour and you're in a wooded area, you can situate the tarp over your tent by tying it from nearby trees to form a primary roof that will divert most of the rainwater, keeping your camp extra dry and snug. Remember, your tent is your sanctuary against the elements. You need to protect it til the weather breaks. If it and your gear get soaked and you're someplace remote, you're in for a rough patch. So make sure you situate your tent somewhere you can pitch the roof tarp in case it's needed.

If it doesn't threaten a downpour, you can tie off the roof tarp nearby to serve as a dew and sun shelter. There you can do your cooking and hang out during the day.

A comfortable camp is not difficult to fashion. It just takes a little forethought and a little investment in time and gear. Do it well so that a night spent in the wildwood can be an enriching experience.

NOVEMBER'S
JOURNEY

The Lord of the Meadow

What is life?
It is the flash of a firefly in the night.
It is the breath of a buffalo in the wintertime.
It is the little shadow which runs across the grass
    and loses itself in the sunset.

—Crowfoot, Blackfoot warrior
and Chief of the Siksika First Nation
1830–1890

Summer this year had been long and mild, with a perfect interplay of sunny days and gentle showers. Such fine weather had carried right into autumn, making for enduring lush conditions. For many would-be deer hunters, this makes things difficult. With warmer days, the deer are less inclined to begin the rut, and with abundant food and water everywhere, it is hard to anticipate where they will be. Folk had to go look for them, but in country such as you find in east Canada, thick with woods and brush, it is nearly impossible to sneak about the woods. One's movement will always be given away by the crunch of a leaf or the snapping of a twig or chatter of the watchdog of the forest, the red squirrel, who considers it his sworn duty to announce the presence of everything that passes his midden, be it a meandering black bear, grouse or man. For many a hunter, success would be difficult.

But the skill of tracking I had honed over many years in wild country made the situation different for me. I already knew the territory of the enormous buck I intended to take. And though I hadn't actually seen him in the flesh yet, I knew all his haunts, his routes, and roughly when he was where. Applying that skill, I'd already taken one deer early in the primitive-weapon season, and that left me invaluable weeks to attend to other essentials of backwoods living: gathering firewood, harvesting late-season crops and wild elderberries, tending the horses' hooves. But we needed the venison. We lived by it. But I could do the farm work without angst, for I knew exactly where to find my next buck when the second season came.

This year I had decided to take the second deer with a rifle. For reasons I've mentioned earlier, I normally shunned modern firearms, which is not to say that I do not understand them. In Alaska, where caribou must often be taken at great range—hundreds of yards—I learned to compensate for wind, elevation, and long distance using the elevation and windage dials on professional caliber scopes. I was fully competent to hit a deer-sized target out to five hundred yards. Normally, I would prefer to hunt with primitive weapons that just felt more honest, but with the heavy workload of the homestead this year, I had reconciled the fact that I had to harvest the second deer quickly so I could get back to essential tasks of prepping barn and cottage for what I felt in my bones would be a long, hard winter.

The track of a truly enormous whitetail buck, showing dewclaws above and hoof impressions below. Its hooves were as long as my palm is broad.

My shadow self overlays one of the great deer's bed down sites.

The enormous buck I had selected lived at the edge of the Old Wood and shared its territory with a large number of does. And a number of lesser bucks frequently crossed its range, as well. Some were barely more than yearlings; others were large and mature. But none even came close to the massive whitetail whose tracks I had stumbled across back in September. I figured it to weigh at least three hundred pounds. When I mentioned the deer to a friend, he said, "You'll get a huge rack from that one!" But just because a deer is huge doesn't mean it will sport a huge pair of antlers. I didn't know. I hadn't yet seen the deer in the flesh, only its spoor. But it also didn't matter. I never hunted for trophies and had little interest in how the antlers looked. A deer that large would provide nearly half a year's meat for us. Between it and the first deer, and our homegrown, free-ranged poultry and geese—we would be secure in food for another year.

Over the next few weeks I continued to track the great buck in my spare time because deer's wandering habits change with the year. It never slept in the same place two nights running, but lately it preferred to sleep among thickets of fallen trees in the open, mainly on the west side of the East Glade. And it tended to wander the east and north sides of its territory, staying at the edge of the forest. It bedded down among the tree shadows around midday to chew its cud. I could find no signs of squabbles with the other bucks that increasingly crossed its territory, and I chalked that up to the fact food had been so abundant over the last several years. Sometimes, in my tracking forays, I come across little battlegrounds where bucks had congregated to duel for the does who attend and watch. But I found little of that in its territory, either. This buck was so large no uppity young'uns would dare challenge it seriously. I also learned many other creatures shared the area, including a fair-sized black bear which had obviously come to feast on the wild blueberries, raspberries and wood ants that were everywhere in the East Glade.

Without doubt, this deer was very clever. Old enough to be very experienced, I suspected the deer knew it was being tracked. Its age alone told me it was well versed at avoiding bears, coyotes, and humans. Had I not seen it yet because it also knew to avoid me?

I became evermore fascinated with it, going to the East Meadow and the Old Wood at every opportunity, looking into every nook and cranny for any little trace of the old buck's spoor. When one tracks an animal in this way, the tracker absorbs the story of its life. One is no longer merely tracking quarry but coming to know—truly know—another living thing. In *The Old Man and the Sea*, Hemingway wrote: "'Fish...I love you and respect you very much. But I will kill you dead before this day ends." I had come to feel more and more this way about this deer. It was a great old deer, respectable and noble. I learned its habits and preferences. And I very much wanted to see it every day all the more. Yet I also had to kill it; it is the way of Nature. Predator falls upon prey; prey becomes the life of the predator; and one day the circle goes round and the Huntsman comes for us all. But as Hemingway's old man came to realize he loved the fish he knew he must catch, so I knew I had come to love this old, clever buck.

There was a place in the heart of the East Glade that was a confluence of many deer trails. It seemed that at some point nearly every doe and buck in the region passed there, and I became sure that when the leaves of the fading trees had all finally fallen, and the rut had finally begun in earnest, this is where the bucks would gather to duel. And so my older daughter, Arielle, and I hiked out there one day a couple hours before noon, when we were least likely to disturb the deer, and set up a trail camera. That very afternoon, we started getting the first images of does and young bucks visiting the site, stopping to graze, wandering about, as if coming to see if the action had begun yet.

A few days later I hiked out there to exchange the camera's memory card and examined the photos back at the cottage. There was an enormous amount of deer activity. Still, there was no sign of the great deer I'd been tracking. After months I'd spotted many of the other deer that lived round abouts, and in just the last few days the camera had caught images of many more, but the great one remained ever beyond sight. If not for fresh spoor, which I regularly came across, I might have begun to perceive it as a mythical figure, like Sasquatch, with just enough reality to it to leave a trace of itself now and then.

It wasn't until the camera had been set up for nearly a month that I finally caught my first glimpse of him. By this time, the younger bucks were growing incautious and venturing into the open to offer the first tentative clashes, but this was more like practice for the later rut duels. The days had at last become sharply cold and the nights were bitter. The hardwoods scraped only bare bones against the sky. One sunset the camera caught images of several does visiting the site just at sundown. They scent-marked the area, letting the bucks know they had come to watch the jousts and see who would win the right to court them. And I knew the time of the rut had finally come. And in the very next image, he appeared, unmistakable from the very first. Head held high, he stepped into the gathering place, carrying himself like the Lord of the Meadow. And I knew for certain then that yes, I loved him as a brother. And just as certain, I knew I was soon to kill him. And I also knew in that moment how I must bring this hunt to its conclusion. The Lord of the Meadow was far too clever merely to be sneaked up on; I would have to bring him to me.

It was nearly November when my camera took that first photo of the great deer. Over the next couple weeks, I became busy with other things that could not wait and had to set aside the hunt. There had been a hard frost and that meant certain things had to be harvested now, among them several bushels of Jerusalem artichokes, some of which had to be stored for next year's planting, and more of the wild apples as they fell from the trees. Daphne renders many into apple butter and jelly, and they can easily be packed in wood chips and stored in the cool root cellar beneath the cottage. As well, a huge old apple tree had toppled one night in a strong wind and I needed to cut it while the wood was still green. Few woods make as pleasant tasting a smoke as apple, and this wood would later be soaked so it would smoulder, and burned in the smokehouse when it came time to salt and smoke cheeses and meats.

It was a clear, cold day when I at last could turn my attention back to the hunt. The rut site was in the heart of the East Meadow. I was sure he'd come from the cover of the Old Wood, taking advantage of the scrub and young spruce for cover to conceal himself. The best place I could position myself was behind an old rock wall at the edge of a broad swath of young woods to the north. It was a remnant of an old Scots homestead abandoned in the nineteenth century. The prevailing wind was usually out of the east so it would carry my scent away from the deer's incredibly sharp nose. And the crisscrossing shadows of the tangled boughs would entirely break up my outline. I would be effectively invisible to the deer. The downside was it was two hundred yards from the rut site. But after harvesting so many distant caribou on the open tundra, I did not consider it a meaningful problem.

Even so, my quarry was clever and I took additional measures. I had found a spot where deer had urinated the day before and had rubbed some of the dirt onto my coat. I stuck small boughs of spruce into my gear belt and hat brim, not so much to break up my outline further, but to conceal my scent. To become invisible to wildlife, you must become part of the land. Humans are visuo-centric and tend to think in terms only of what can be seen. But a woodsman must think like animals who see with their noses even more than their eyes. If you are to pass unseen among the animal kingdom, you must eliminate your scent as well as your image.

I did not set out to the site early that day, for deer are most active at dawn, noon, and dusk. I didn't want to interrupt their daybreak activities and so give myself away. To sneak up on the great, canny deer, I had to give him no reason to suspect my presence, even if he was driven by the hot blood of the rut. So I set out at 9:00 a.m., after their morning browsing, while they were resting and chewing their cud. I carried my bolt action rifle, six rounds, and a daypack with two meals, water and tea, a small spade and hatchet, my bowie, a book on MP3, and my heaviest arctic gear, including boots rated to -100 F. I'm sure the reader is thinking the other stuff makes sense but why the extreme weather gear when it was only late autumn with the days not yet below freezing? To that I will ask: Have you ever lain an entire day on the ground behind a pile of stones in the shadows of trees so dense the rays of the sun never touch the Earth? Such places have a slow, creeping cold. It doesn't bite you all at once, and for a long while, in fact, seems barely there at all. But it settles in all the same as the blood becomes still, as it must when one is motionless for the long hours required of the hunt. Earth and stone and shadow are remarkably effective at drawing the heat out of a body, and it can soon feel as cold as glacier ice if one isn't prepared.

It was a perfect day. The sky was clear with the odd marshmallow cloud and a clean light breeze bearing the first hint of coming winter blew in out of the east. The land had metamorphosed into a place of brown hues of fallen leaves, the dark grays and blacks of desiccated wood, contrasted with eternal evergreens and bright-red wild cranberries clinging to dry canes.

About noon, the first deer appeared in the meadow, just twenty yards from me. They were a pair of does that were so tightly bonded I assumed they must be sisters. Smallish, I was sure this would be their first breeding year. They moved like twinned particles, the one doing exactly as the other did, pausing frequently to browse upon the sedges and tall grasses that grew oddly lush along the stone wall. (I suspected the stones held heat and kept the ground warm, thus allowing for this small area of late-season green.) Naturally cautious and attentive, as are all deer, one was always looking around while the other fed. I smiled and watched them pass. They were a beautiful sight and I wished them well. They went to the gathering place, two hundred yards up the stone wall from me, browsed for a while, scent-marked, then drifted east in the direction of the tall and forbidding Old Woods.

Within an hour another pair of does appeared, more loosely attached and their size difference marking them as at least a couple years apart. And not far off from them came a small spike buck, a yearling male sporting two antlers of a single tine each. They appeared out of the woods at the far side of the meadow and I watched them through my binoculars. They stepped gingerly around fallen logs, using them cleverly for cover, pausing frequently to browse. The late-season foliage was not especially nutritious—they had to eat a lot to keep their weight up for the long hunger of winter. But they also made their way to the gathering place. As had the does earlier, these hung about a few minutes, browsed a bit and scent marked, then moved on. The spike buck never quite joined them but made sure to trail them.

I chuckled quietly, for I knew what he was up to. He was cautiously courting one of those does, following her from a small distance, hoping to be the buck present in that instant when her estrus was finally at its height and she was willing to breed. He had little chance, though. Eventually, one of the many more mature bucks around here would pick up her scent and drive him off. Unless luck favored him, he was unlikely to have a breeding opportunity for a year or two, after he put on enough size to drive off competing bucks.

And as the afternoon wore on, other wildlife put in an appearance. A pair of grouse flew into a birch just to my left, right overhead, and stayed in the tree a couple hours, quietly clucking among themselves and preening.

A redtailed hawk that had lived and hunted here for years ghosted high over the meadow and at one point, I saw it tuck back its wings and rocket toward the Earth. It disappeared behind a slope, but it did not rise again for a long time, so I knew it had gotten its meal.

A murder of clever ravens flew by and one turned back and circled directly over me, just above the tops of the trees, cluck-cluck-clicking raven words that must have meant: *Something's amiss here.* Then it started to fly off, came back yet again and flew more circles, not fifty feet over me. I knew the grouse had not seen me, and they hadn't been a mere ten feet away. How had the raven known? I was afraid its attention would give me away, just as circling buzzards alert one that something is dead or dying beneath them. In a measured voice, I said, "I'm here." I rolled on my back and waved at the raven. It squawked, apparently satisfied it had proven itself correct, and flew off in the direction of its kin.

The day was growing late by now, and it was time to do what had to be done to draw out the great deer. I had brought a pair of antlers with me. I'd found them in the woods several years ago and had saved them for purposes like this. They were large and a pain to carry, but very useful come the rut. I needed to make the old buck believe some young upstarts were in his territory, raring to dispute who got to court the does. I took the antlers and "rattled" them. It's an old huntsman's technique of lightly tapping a pair of antlers together to emulate a pair of bucks clashing as they fight for does. It was only the very beginning of the rut, but that made it the right time to turn to this technique.

Clashing bucks don't hammer at one another endlessly. They aren't aiming to hurt one another. Sometimes they may injure one another by accident, but mostly the clashes are just rituals—ways of testing one another's worthiness to breed. To rattle correctly, one lightly clatters the antlers together just few times, just for a moment, then sets them aside a good twenty minutes or so. This is sometimes called "rattling up a buck." Young ones and does will come to see who's sparring. Old ones will come to drive off the interlopers. And even though it isn't very loud, the sound carries. I knew in time the great one would hear. He would come . . .

Not long before sundown I had the privilege of seeing a fisher. It appeared just ten yards from me, leaping out of the grasses right up to the top of the rock wall, which was about a yard high and thrice that thick. It looked about, then scuttled down the other side. To my surprise, it went right to a well-trodden deer trail and veered north, following the trail. I was not sure what it was after, and I assumed it might not even be hunting because it moved pretty fast. It was a powerful hunter and nothing was likely to attempt to prey on it, not even the area's lynx or bobcats or coyotes, and it must have been aware of that. It moved like it owned the place.

Time passed and the sun descended the last few degrees to the horizon. I rattled the antlers for what I figured would be the last time today. He would either come now or I would give it up til tomorrow. I was just shifting a little to stretch and reveling in the fact that I was warm despite the deepening cold because I had taken the precaution of bringing such ridiculously heavy clothing. And then I glanced toward the gathering area, and there he stood, the great one, at the far side of it. I was amazed at his skill in movement. He hugged the topography of the land, staying just below the ridge, which made him invisible to anything north, and he stuck to the thickets of young scrub, which played to his natural camouflage and broke up his outline. The sun was just touching the horizon beyond the trees and the meadow was growing dark. I glassed him with my binoculars, which have broad lenses that provide a powerful light-amplifying effect, and confirmed it was the very deer I had identified as my quarry months ago. He stood tall and proud, unmistakable with his bold antlers and hefty build, and he looked around, doubtless trying to spot the upstart bucks my rattling antlers had imitated.

I breathed a deep sigh. So, it all came down to this moment. Over the last two months I had learned this deer's ways, his territory, his nature. I slipped a few inches to the side where my rifle lay upon my daypack, which would serve as a rest to ensure a steady long-distance shot. I had earlier stuffed the pack with a blanket, not for me, but to cushion the rifle, thereby dampening any natural tremor that the body can introduce into a precision instrument. Even though the old deer was two hundred yards off, I knew it had extremely sensitive ears, and I carefully slid the bolt action's two-stage safety off with constant pressure so as to mute even the slightest sound of a *click*. I knew anything . . . *anything* . . . out of the ordinary would make this deer bolt.

I settled the Weatherby's stock firmly but lightly against my right shoulder, sighted in on the two-hundred-yard crosshair, and compensated a couple inches right for the stiff easterly breeze.

And I said the prayer I always pronounce when I am about to take an animal's life:

*I am sorry to kill you, brother. I do so of need and not of want, that your
kind and mine may flourish. Mine through the gift of your meat and hide
and antler. Yours by thinning your numbers so your kin may live well
upon the land. May we meet one day in greener glens as friends and brothers.*

And then I squeezed the trigger. A .308 is not very loud as rifles go, nor does it offer much kick despite its impressive power. There was only a sharp clap, a light shove on my shoulder, and a second later the great one fell.

He fell.

The deed was done. We would eat well this winter. But I felt, as I do at the end of every hunt, a deep sadness, too. It is the way of Nature that brothers prey upon brothers. Hemingway understood this and also wrote: "It is good that we do not have to try to kill the sun or the moon or the stars. It is enough to live on the sea and kill our true brothers." In my case, I live with the forest, and sometimes while there kill my brothers. But it is never without a certain sense of loss. There is respect for the beast, and the recognition of its worth . . . its gift to the world, its beauty and strength. But there is balance, also, and the deer numbers had to be culled

And so I sat behind the small stone wall in the shadows of many trees, the air growing evermore biting with the falling night, bearing the clean fragrance of evergreen and mint of birch, and I felt sadness and mirth mingle. The great one fell; we would eat well. The deer numbers were a bit smaller, but the meadow now had no lord.

◆ ◆ ◆

That evening and the next day were very busy. The great buck was enormous, more so than I had even thought. Normally, I would either shoulder a deer and carry it out of the woods or, as I had with the one from the previous month, partially render it on the spot and pack out the meat, leaving behind a good third of the weight in bones and offal. That simply wasn't going to work here. There was so much meat to contend with. Not to mention useful bone and hide and antler. Even rendered there would be several hundred pounds to deal with. So after gutting the deer and bleeding it to keep it fresh, I had to get an axe and walk the trails to remove as much detritus as I could. These are old trails, barely good enough to be considered footpaths in many places, and it was not easy prepping the ground for the next essential step.

At dawn I drove my small tractor up into the meadow, a risky process that took hours. The buck had fallen on the steep side of a hillock and the tractor had to be parked at the top. Then I had to haul the deer up that steep face. It was only twenty yards but at a 30-degree angle, and moving it took every last ounce of my strength exerted over half an hour. But I finally managed to get the deer up and into the tractor's cargo bucket. Then there was a long, slow drive out of the meadow. Daphne was with me and walked in front of the tractor, occasionally clearing out the odd small log that seemed to creep back over the trail and form a hazard. But after several arduous hours, we finally managed to get tractor and deer across the meadow and down to the dirt path that cuts through the south side of the homestead and took that all the way back to the cottage.

Butchering is a family ritual, filled with togetherness. The carcass is hung from one of the mid-sized poplars near the cottage and rendered joint by joint. Everything usable finds a place. Large bones go for soup and later to feed the dog. Small bones might be burned if we have a use for the minerals and ash, or they could be put in the Elfwood for the wildlife. The antlers might become knife hilts or used for buttons or other art. We usually tan the hide. Every scrap of meat is rendered. I do the cutting and

Daphne packs it away as I work, either to one of the deep freezers or to the house for pickling in salt or brine, then later to the smokehouse. Where it only took me a couple hours to render the last deer, this enormous buck took three times that and by the end of the task we were all exhausted. We celebrated the harvest and hunt with a cookout: potato salad, fresh venison steaks with wild cherry sauce, grilled onions, apple pie—all from the bounty of the homestead, the good gifts of living traditionally and close to Earth. At the end of the meal, we even took the time to play croquet in the yard. The girls asked about Frisbee, but I was drained by that point, and ready to simply collapse and sleep a good twelve hours.

But the next day there were things I needed to do back up at the hunting site. I had left some gear sequestered behind the stone wall, and my camera was still out at the deer's gathering place. And I had a bit of the buck's fur with me, that I saved for a special purpose. So a couple hours past dawn I hiked out to the site. It took about forty-five minutes to get there from the cottage. I paused at the hunting site to put my gear into my messenger bag, then I hiked on up to the rut site. It was a couple hours til noon. I had timed it so in order to be in and out with a minimum of interference to the deer.

The day was clear, blue and perfect, and the mild northerly breeze promised winter soon. I dropped to a knee, dipping a hand into my pocket, and withdrew the old deer's fur which I had shaved from its hide with my bowie. I said: "I was sorry to kill you, brother, for I knew you to be magnificent and worthy. May you walk the green glens of the Otherworld and find your joy in endless springs and golden sunbeams. May the Green Man, horned lord of the wood, keep you safe, and may the Lady Cailleach count you among her sacred herd. I honor your strength and courage."

I tossed the fur into the breeze and watched the brown bits float away. I nodded. The deer had been a noble beast. It had lived a good, long life for a deer, and it had met a clean, quick end. It was as good as any mortal creature could ask for. Still, the meadow felt emptier for the loss. There was no more a great one to walk the grassy ways and eldritch shadows of the Old Wood.

A new Lord of the Meadow takes his rightful place at first light at the gathering place of the rut. (Photo courtesy of Tammie Lee.)

One last thing to do ...

I rose, retrieved the trail camera. Then I began a slow, pensive hike back home.

The day passed and I attended to the innumerable other chores of woods living. Good work, but demanding work. At the end of the day, as the sun set, I came inside. The cottage was warm, and it felt good knowing that heat was the work of my own hands, from gathering firewood of windfallen trees and thus contributing to the sustainability of the forest. The kitchen was fragrant with Daphne's fine cooking. I went upstairs to the study and sat down, removed the trail camera's memory card and inserted it into my computer. I didn't know what I expected to see. More wildlife, doubtless. I had gotten some amazing shots of deer, eagles, ravens, and other wildlife from the camera at that location. But the image that appeared was a wonder, such a wonder it brought redness to my eyes, and a tear fell down my cheek. For the circle was complete and the meadow had its great one again. In the image before me, a new Lord of the Meadow had taken his rightful place in the East Glade.

If you are not a huntsman, I expect you might not understand, but those of us who live traditionally and follow the ways of Nature honor and love the very things we also must pursue. It is with deepest respect we take them, deepest sorrow we see them fall, and deepest joy we see the land renewed.

The Lord of the Meadow! Long may he walk it.

Wild Life

The Ingenuity of the Wild Tribes

People nowadays are often surprised to learn animals can be as clever as humans. I think it reveals a skewed anthropocentric kind of thinking. Whether we believe we are the product of random evolution or the design of a sublime power, we like to perceive ourselves as the pinnacle of Nature. When we see other animals applying reason and cleverness, it challenges that notion. It threatens us. Could that be why some persons hate and kill those animals that are clearly the cleverest and most like us—like coyotes, wolves, and ravens? But what if, rather, our entire understanding of intelligence is inside out and that leads us to misjudge our own intelligence as compared to the creatures of the natural world?

As a clinician, I have given many intelligence tests. I use them to detect peculiarities in a person's thinking and determine goals for treatment. But people often want to know what their IQ is after a test. I tell them and tell them it is a number without meaning. Whether your IQ is a low 70 or a high 130, IQ has never been successfully linked to happiness or true success. This is because intelligence tests are very limited; they can only measure those things the test designers thought were pertinent. If the designer thought mathematical reasoning and visual-spatial comprehension and vocabulary size were the most important dimensions of intelligence, that is all the test will measure. And it would tell you nothing about a person's moral compass, personal sense of purpose, concepts of happiness, ability to relate to friends and spouse—areas vital to living a full life.

Ponder intelligence and the tree. A psychologist once stated a tree has an IQ of about three. It is true a tree can tell nothing of how to add 2 + 2, nor can it read a book. But find the human who can find peace anywhere in the good Earth and with slow, deliberate patience turn sunlight and the elements into food. Find the human who knows how to stand outdoors through summer storm and winter gale and greet the next spring the stronger for it. Find a person who, by dint of his very existence, purifies both air and water. A tree is effortlessly brilliant at things we cannot begin to fathom how to do. Indeed, for all our ability to comprehend mathematics and language and science, we might be one of the least intelligent of organisms because we persist in living in ways that harm ourselves and slowly kill this Earth that is our one and only home.

When we begin to see intelligence more holistically, as an organism's ability to live well in its role in Nature, we quickly come to realize most creatures are brilliant, each in its own way.

This spring I was out hiking the East Meadow searching out early season wild forage and encountered this woodpecker's amazing home (shown in the photo below). I did not see the bird but I knew this was the dwelling of a pileated woodpecker by the squared entrance. Look where the entry was built: directly beneath an old fungal growth called birch bracket, almost as hard as the host tree's wood, that served as a porch. The photo does not do the image justice, but the porch was large enough to shield the entry from the incursion of wind and snow. The woodpecker was ingenious to situate its home in such a way.

The characteristic squared entry marks this as a woodpecker home, but the porch of birch bracket is remarkable ingenuity.

◆ ◆ ◆

Later in spring I had been hiking through the Rusalka Wood west of the cottage. We were on our way down to the brook to harvest the abundant spring growth of ostrich ferns when I spotted this red squirrel. He was just finishing a dried mushroom. Squirrels actually know how to dry foods, just like we do. Often they will suspend mushrooms in the crotches of trees or perch them on logs til they are bone dry. Then the mushrooms are relocated to their caches to get them through the long winter and early spring.

This red squirrel was leisurely finishing off a tasty dried mushroom and presented an image too beautiful not to capture.

◆ ◆ ◆

Most recently we had a remarkable visitor at the homestead, a Canada goose who was a grifter. She would pretend to be one of our little flock of domestic geese, thus getting fed and housed with them. The morning the goose first appeared, my wife, Daphne, came running back to the cottage to tell me there was a wild goose walking around the barnyard. That in itself wasn't exactly remarkable. Sometimes geese pass through on their way to wetlands north or south, and as our land has several ponds, they often stop and stay a few hours down by the water. But she said, "No! It's with our geese. It's walking around with them and acting just like them, drinking at the waterer and eating at the feeder. I think something's wrong with it."

And so I darted back with Daphne to the barn to see what was the matter. And there she was. (I call it a she, but I don't actually know what gender it was. Wild geese are very difficult to sex.) And sure enough, she wasn't out by the ponds or standing aloof from the other geese, waiting for a chance at some of their grain. She was right in among them, waddling about with a certain arrogant sovereign air that is common to domestic geese who perceive themselves the lords and ladies of the farmyard. And she was acting just like one of our geese, scuttling the ducks about as if overseeing them, showing annoyance with the laying hens. She let us get almost close enough to touch her, just as our own geese do.

At first I was sure there was something wrong with her. Maybe she was injured and settled on our barnyard as a safe place for food and shelter. But then why socialize with our domestic geese? None of the passing wild geese had ever even shown a hint of desire to have anything to do with them. But this peculiar goose stayed out with them all afternoon, eating and drinking and wandering the meadows with them. As the sun went down, the geese retreated to their roost in the barn and the wild one went right in with them, making herself right at home.

The next morning we woke to find she had left at the break of day, and I have since given much thought to what that strange goosey visit was all about. It is true that Canada geese are more numerous now, and in urban areas they often visit the ponds of city parks where they get used to people who toss them crumbs. But in the countryside, where many people hunt them, they tend to be far more cautious. It was a couple days until it finally occurred to me: this goose figured if she fit herself right into our flock of farm geese no one would be the wiser, and then there would be a meal ticket and snug place to sleep in it for her. I laughed when I realized what she'd been up to. I have no idea where that goose has moved on to, but I wish her well and sincerely hope to see her again.

If you read the old faerie tales, not the watered-down, sugary-sweet Mother Goose renditions, but the real old tales, you will discover the wild-life that share Earth with us were perceived by the folk of old to be very clever and wise—peoples in their own right. They had goals and dreams and virtues and vices, much as we do. In many of the myths of the aboriginal folk of North America, animals were even seen as wiser than human-kind. Raven, for example, is attributed with having given people the sun and moon so they could know when it was time to wake, work and sleep, and he gave humans fire so they could keep warm and cook. From myth to fact, the wild tribes possess a keen and marvellous intelligence. It is not to be confused with our kind of intelligence. We are adept at the use of words and dabbling in abstract concepts. But animals have minds that allow them to fit into the natural world in ways that are nothing short of prodigious.

A pair of our white domestic geese allow the strange wild goose interloper to wander with them, though their cautious sidewise glances and unusually quiet demeanors portrayed clearly they didn't know what to make of the peculiar business.

Enchanted Forest

The Old Lady of Winter

As winter's touch becomes keen and icy winds strip the last branches bare of leaves, it seems time to consider a most special and complex lady, as associated with Nature and winter as the Green Man is with Nature and summer. She is the Cailleach Bheara (CAH*lok VAER*rah), a creatrix being who must surely come out of most ancient legend. Old lore speaks of her remembering the Ice Age and indeed relates her directly to the great continental sheet glaciers which a few millennia ago carved out of the north both valleys and mountains while flattening plains. Though her myth derives out of the old Celtic lands, it was, strangely enough, that I first heard whispers of her existence in the far reaches of the American Northwest when some Yupik folk once told me of the Old Lady who haunted the icy lands and threatened to take disobedient children. But it was difficult to learn more of this myth from them. It was only after getting to know them a long time that they shared their faerie faith with me at all. But of the Old Lady, as they called her, they would say very little.

Thousands of miles to the east in the Scots highlands echoes of her memory still linger. There the Old Lady is a complex mythological entity. She embodies at once fear and love. Aging with the year, in spring she can be a young maiden, in summer a ripe and lovely woman, in autumn a matron and come winter, she is a hag. At all times she is a protectrix of wildlife, with an especial fondness for antlered beasts, but also loved by foxes, swine, sheep, and it seems all wild creatures. She shepherds the wildlife and keeps them safe from avaricious huntsmen. And if at the homestead I must hunt to fill the larder, I ask permission of and offer thanks to both the Green Man and the Cailleach for the goodness of the wild game.

Below is a piece of her tale, a tiny piece only, telling a bit of her relationship to winter and the wild creatures who love her.

◆ ◆ ◆

The only tool that Beira (an alternate spelling of *Bheara*) used was a magic hammer. When she struck it lightly on the ground, the soil became as hard as iron; when she struck it heavily on the ground, a valley was formed. After she had built up a mountain, she gave it its special form by splintering the rocks with her hammer. If she had made all the hills of the same shape, she would not have been able to recognize one from another.

After the mountains were all formed, Beira took great delight in wandering between them and over them. She was always followed by wild animals. The foxes barked with delight when they beheld her, wolves howled to greet her, and eagles shrieked with joy in mid-air. Beira had great herds and flocks to which she gave her protection—nimble-footed deer, high-horned cattle, shaggy grey goats, black swine, and sheep that had snow-white fleeces. She charmed her deer against the huntsmen, and when she visited a deer forest she helped them to escape from the hunters. During early winter she milked the hinds on the tops of mountains, but when the winds rose so high that the froth was blown from the milking pails, she drove the hinds down to the valleys. The froth was frozen on the crests of high hills, and lay there snow-white and beautiful. When the winter torrents began to pour down the mountainsides, leaping from ledge to ledge, the people said: "Beira is milking her shaggy goats, and streams of milk are pouring down over high rocks."

—Donald Alexander MacKenzie
Wonder Tales from Scottish Myth & Legend

Wood Witchery

Bone Shrines

I had been sailing a small cutter rigged vessel south of the Alaska coast for several days, heading west of the village of Seward with no particular plan or direction in mind except to smell the sea air, witness the sprawling subarctic glaciers calving into the ocean and touch upon another element of the wilderness. I wished Daphne had been with me, but she had to attend to some things on land, so I traveled with just our two daughters, Arielle and Natalia. I had my sea legs, they did not, and on day four we encountered a stiff headwind blowing twenty-five knots. Such a wind was well within the capacity of the ocean-crossing craft I was soloing, but nothing causes a vessel to heel more than a headwind, and she was angling a good 20 degrees as she rose and dipped her way through eight-foot rollers. Within an hour of hitting those winds, the girls were pallid and vomiting. I decided to find a sheltered place on the coast and put in. Ducking below deck, I checked the charts and saw there was a vast, broad bay a few miles north with a little cove on the west side. I went above, changed course and resheeted the sails. The girls slowly began to shake off the seasickness after changing heading, as it relieved most of the heel from the boat and made it feel as if the waves were only gently rolling under us. Running to a stiff port stern wind, we made seven knots and found ourselves entering the bay in an hour.

It was a magnificent place, surrounded on all sides by vast forest and sky-vaulting mountains. Dolphins leapt through waters blue as only the north can make them. We put into the little cove and discovered we were not alone. A quarter mile south there was a small group of people set up at a semi-permanent camp, and to the west I could see the crumbling remains of an ancient hunting cabin upon a rocky outcrop at the foot of great spruces. The girls were curious about the people and we paddled to shore on a tender to meet them. We learned they were a team of archeologists leading an excavation to study the ancient tribe who used to hunt and fish here seasonally, when the waters were lower. They were very friendly and gave us a tour of the dig. I asked them if the old cabin lying a mile west had anything to do with the site and the question perplexed them. "What cabin?" they asked. How could they have missed it, the girls and I wondered. To us, that little crumbling place virtually cried out for notice. That night we returned to our vessel for a dinner of fresh caught Irish lord, and the next morning breakfasted on tiger prawns I had caught with little traps I threw over the side of the boat before bed. Then we paddled for the farther shore where lay the cabin.

Getting to it meant scrabbling up a hillside that seemed to be made of a pile of enormous boulders. It was a steep ascent, but not so much it was a risk to the girls. As I clambered up one great boulder after another, I began finding skulls. Fox skulls set on stumps. Raven skulls set on leaves of ferns. Moose skulls staring eyeless out from rocky perches over the woods and waters. Marine skulls of salmon, sea trout and rockfish, dolphins and sea lions. Hundreds of skulls—maybe thousands—surrounded the cantilevered, crumbling cabin, all facing out from it in every direction. What kind of place was this? It had the feel of something keenly eerie but strangely neither unfriendly nor macabre. It was just . . . itself.

Hitting a heavy headwind, the boat rolled over waves and heeled steeply and the girls became very seasick. I changed course and we made our way into a vast, wild but sheltered bay, and though the waters instantly calmed it was another couple hours til the girls were back to their spritely selves.

I reached the top of the hillock. As I climbed onto the cabin's tiny crumbling, tilting deck, to my right lay the calm cove and the enormous bay beyond with its panorama of blue water, vaulting mountains spilling glaciers and vast blue-green forest. To my left lay a very different panorama, the open North Pacific sea roiling with white-capped waves and cumulus clouds mounting the welkin. The cabin sat upon the pinnacle of a rocky, wooded hill on a narrow isthmus of land where many worlds met: wild ocean and tame cove and icy high country and sylvan paradise. And all converged at this little cabin where skulls from each of those realms gathered, facing outward in all directions.

The crumbling shaman's cabin was deep in the wilderness, wedged at a joining place of vaulting mountains, low evergreen forest, inland water, and wild sea. It was a meeting place of four worlds. There is a special power where worlds meet, for there the veil between Earth and the Otherworld is thinnest and enchantment flows most freely.

The air around the place felt like electricity lay in it, like that sense you get if you stand on a hilltop as a powerful thunderstorm builds. You can feel the power hanging latent but ready in the atmosphere. This was like that. It was just like that. I felt powers and presences watching. Very great powers. Gods and elemental forces and brooding, swirling ancestor beasts. We had stumbled upon a place of power unlike anything I had ever encountered before. How could the archeologists not have noticed this place? It virtually roared!

I greeted the powers and said we came with good will and would be grateful to understand what was going on here. But neither I nor the girls had any sense of what this place meant. But I think it was in that moment I first found in my heart a story that became a novel I wrote over the next two weeks while on that sailing trip. It was just then inside my soul all at once, and over the next two weeks I poured it out in the form of a novel titled *An Ogham Wood*. Many people have since commented that the novel felt like a true myth that had been waiting for someone to find it and tell it. I found it there, at that cabin which seemed to defy the notice of several scientists and their students a bare mile away.

The girls could sense the power of that place as well as I. To this day they still speak of it in hushed tones of awe.

That cabin does not want to be discovered. It does not even want to be known. I will say no more of it, nor even hint at where it was. But what it was—that question consumed me and a few weeks later when we returned to port and I had a chance to delve into the dusty depths of a favorite used bookstore in Anchorage, I finally learned what it was about while poring through old tomes about primitive hunters and shamans. It was the practice of many ancient peoples to take the skulls and bones of the creatures they hunted and bring them to a power place and there lay them to look over the land. It may have seemed macabre, but it was done in deepest respect for the gift of life the wildlife gave through their meat, hide, and horn, and in time at such places all the power of those animals' spirits mingling and gathering coalesced to form a point of brilliant focus, a sort of nexus to the Otherworld, and there shamans would commune with ancestral animals and other spirits with ease. And ever since then I have kept the practice. The bones or skulls of the deer, grouse, hares, and other creatures of the wild that I occasionally take to fill our larder are brought to a sacred place and there left to themselves, to keep one another company, and sometimes to be visited with and communed with as ancestral spirits. For I did not hunt them out of want or sport, but out of need, as is the way of Nature since long before the dawn of Men, and so there is no enmity between those animals and I. Even if I find natural kills in the bush, the bones of a coyote perhaps, I will deposit them at this sacred place to join the assembly of animal ancestors.

It is not hard to create such a place, but it does require a couple things that I do not believe can be gotten around. Such places must be created in lonely, natural areas that are already places of power. There are many kinds of places of power in varying cultures, such as springheads, the banks of certain rivers and lakes, some bogs, sacred groves, a mountaintop. Sensitive persons often know they are at such a place when they approach it. It feels like a place where enchantment flows and this world meets the other. Ancient monuments sometimes mark such places, such as the standing stones one may find scattered around the British Isles.

When I find the bones of an animal that has passed on in the wildwood, often I will take one of its bones—the skull, preferably—and bring it to mingle with other animal spirits at a sacred gathering place.

Find such a place and take note of it. In your future rambling through wild places, if you find the bones of creatures that have passed away, bring them to this sacred place. Lay them about with respect. Welcome them and invite them to mingle with the spirits already there. Do not bury the bones; that is to forget them. We keep the ancestors close through the tokens of their remembrance. If you hunt only out of need, bringing the skull of the beast to such a place is a sign of great respect. If you bring animal skulls, set them on some kind of raised vantage and face them outward, providing a view of the surroundings and leaving the skulls as sentinels.

Visit as desire dictates but never casually. Such a place is not to be taken lightly. Power will build over a great deal of time. I cannot say how long. But over time the spirits will gather and this site will become a place to know them and undertake powerful spirit journeys and find the great gift of wisdom.

Bring a gift, which is courteous. Good smoke is a fine gift, such as dried berries of sumac to smoulder over charcoal. Or you may simply leave a crust of bread, perhaps a bit of cheese, or spill a swig of ale or wine over the ground. Do this to show respect for the ancestral spirits that will come to dwell there.

Though such a place becomes a site of old bones and whispering ghosts, do not think of it as a graveyard. At least, not a graveyard in the way they are known in much of the Western world. This place becomes more like a shrine to the ancestors. Remnants of their material selves are there, true, but those remnants serve as contact points between the living and the dead, just as a Shinto shrine serves as a place for the living to speak with their ancestral folk. A graveyard is a place to bid farewell. A bone shrine is a meeting place.

Woods Lore

Fire from Stone

For any journeyer in the wildwood, fire is a tool of great importance: a means to cook, to brew warming beverages, to purify water, and to keep warm and safe through the long night. Yet in this urbanized era the art of starting a fire has been almost lost. I had never realized how much this was so until, when visiting a friend who is a retired S.A.S. officer who operates a bushcraft school in Nova Scotia, I was amazed to learn that one of the more common things students asked for was to teach them how to make a campfire. I had grown up with campfires. I had thought of them as simple affairs beginning with layers of dry duff, then tiny twigs, then moderately sized twigs and progressing up to hefty logs. But even much of that basic skill is now lost. Most notably, people now have an utter dependence upon matches or lighters to start fires. Which are fine and good—and I carry them in my gear when in the bush—but what if it rains? What if you take a spill in a brook? A soggy match is as useful as stale bread. No, stale bread is more useful.

But to start a fire you need only iron and something to strike it. I prefer a magnesium rod as it gives extremely hot sparks and will work even if wet. But a stone will do nicely, as long as it has silicon in it. Flint is ideal (mostly found in Europe) and chert (mostly found in North America). Other silicon-rich stones, such as granite, will do in a pinch.

You elicit sparks by striking the iron across the stone. It is best to break the stone and strike along an edge. Steel is alloyed iron and will work just as well as iron, so long as it is carbon steel. Stainless steel is harder and more resistant to wear and will not shed sparks easily (except AUS8, which in my experience works well for this purpose). Some stainless steel is so hard it is almost useless for starting fires. That is why, except in conditions I expect to be very wet, I will always carry a knife of dependable cold carbon steel. Among such a tool's many uses, it is also a dependable component in starting fires.

This is a typical steel and magnesium rod combo. It is good for starting thousands of fires and will work wet or dry. It throws showers of 5,500-degree F sparks with each strike and can easily light any viable tinder.

Set the tinder right below the steel and strike downward so that it is showered with sparks. It took only one strike of the rod and steel to set a spark in this bit of chaga tinder, now smouldering into a coal.

Lastly, you will need a tinder to catch the spark and develop it into a hot coal. It is that coal with which you actually build the fire. There are natural and man-made traditional tinders. One example of a natural tinder would be a dried bit of fungus, such as chaga, which readily catches sparks and makes a clean, long burning, extremely hot coal. Charcloth is a traditional man-made tinder that also works well, and is made by putting a bit of scrap cotton cloth in a can, sealing it so oxygen cannot get in, and building a fire around the can. The heat will toast the cloth, leaving behind a black, charred fabric (hence the name: "char*cloth") that will readily catch a spark and grow it into a coal. If you are using a magnesium rod, which throws intensely hot sparks of some 5,500 degrees F, you can also use toilet paper for a tinder. Just rough it up with your fingers so the fibers can catch the sparks. The super-hot sparks will cause the roughened toilet paper to burst into flame. (I've never been able to light toilet paper with ordinary flint or chert and steel. The sparks just aren't hot or plentiful enough.)

To make fire from the coal, be sure to have fine, dry kindling ready. Dry mushroom shaved thin is a favorite of mine as it tends to light like old newspaper. But pine needles, tiny twigs, and dry, browned grass also work well. Once you have your coal smoking, place it carefully beneath a bit of your finest kindling. Blow on it gently. It will smoke more and more, then begin to flame. Learn to go slowly and smoothly through the steps. Never rush or you're likely to put the little start of a fire out. When you have a little flame happening, slowly place more and larger kindling over it. Be careful not to go too fast or you will suffocate the tiny fire.

Visit my website and look under *Homestead Skills* to see a more detailed presentation of the process: http://cliffseruntine.wordpress.com.

◆ ◆ ◆

If traveling for any length of time outdoors, it helps to carry at least a small stainless steel pot to heat water or cook a little food. You can make do without pots (such as by using the hollow of a stone), but that is more advanced woodscraft. You can cook by placing your pot directly on the fire, and at times that's simplest and best, but it is usually best to place the pot beside the fire. It will catch the heat from the side, which is less efficient, but cooking will go slower, which is better. However you do it, having your pot close to the fire will blacken it with char. If you want to save yourself a bit of cleaning, there is an alternative.

Rinse several small stones of one-quarter to one-half pound in weight and set them on a large stone near the fire and let them get very hot. When they are good and hot (I dab a little water on them and see if they sizzle), use a couple little sticks like tongs to put them right in your pot. Stones hold a lot of heat and will quickly heat any water in the pot and keep it boiling. Add one stone at a time as the pot begins to show signs of cooling. Using this method, you can cook anywhere, e.g., in a hole in the ground lined with birch bark, in a hollow of a boulder, or in a ceramic mug. It is a very versatile outdoor cooking technique.

Conclusion

For they were of the Wild as we were, the Wild to which in our
desolation we turned for a solace and a refuge, that ageless
Wilderness that had ever been and would, somewhere, always be,
long after we had followed our little lost companions and were gone.

—Grey Owl
Pilgrims of the Wild

So wrote Grey Owl, a lone voice at the dawn of the twentieth century,
of the beavers, and by turn all the creatures vanishing as the wilderness
succumbed to the depredations of a voracious human species.

A British man who came to Canada fell in love with the wilderness and
with its aboriginal people. And in that wilderness he sought to live their
lifeway which he had read of as a child and come to love from afar. He befriended the Ojibwa and was eventually adopted into their tribe and given
the name he took to be his true name: Grey Owl, journeyer and hunter. But
when he first began his journey into the wilderness, he did not understand
the soul of the wild. Like the modern folk of his era, for him Nature was
mainly a resource. Oh, he loved it. He reveled in the solitude, in the quiet
waters of lonely lakes, in the vast swaths of boreal woodlands, in the simple
pleasure of venison roasted over a fire on an autumn day or waking to the
first gold traces of dawn light harkened by the melancholy cry of the loon.

But Grey Owl was a trapper and took all he could from the wildwood to make his living.

Until one day . . . one day he tracked down a beaver den where he found a mother with two young kits. Beavers were being hunted to extinction to fill the European hunger for pelts and with few left they were very valuable. And though he knew it was wrong, Grey Owl killed the mother. He placed her in his canoe and began to paddle away, knowing he was leaving the kits behind to perish, for they were yet unable to fend for themselves against the rigors of wild country. They cried and cried, the kits, and he was struck to his heart by how much they sounded like small children. He recalled the aboriginal name for the beaver: *ahmik*. It means *Little Talking Brother*. Suddenly he was struck with a heretofore alien notion: it was wrong to leave the little ones to die, and wrong to wipe out a species for human want.

On a level, Grey Owl had been aware of this. The Ojibwa had taught him as much. The Ojibwa woman, Anahareo, who became his wife, had told him it is the right way of a man—as it is for all creatures—to hunt to feed himself. It was a path in balance to take a creature for fur to clothe oneself against the chill of the north. All creatures take a little from each other as they need. It is part of the great balance. But to take and take out of greed and vanity, as was the new way brought to the Americas by the colonists; to kill and slash and reap all that one could to fulfill an insatiable hole of avarice within the soul . . . no, it was wrong.

Grey Owl had heard it, and he knew balance was the way of the Ojibwa he admired. But it was not until that moment, paddling away on his canoe, hearing the cries of those beaver kits, that the truth pierced him. Some window of perception opened in him then, and he knew Earth was more. Her web of life was far more profound than just a collection of entities, some of which could be amassed for wealth. Her creatures—legged, winged, scaled, and finned—were no mere objects. They were spirits. They were the little people, made flesh to travel through the green world a while. They had lives and joys and sorrows of their own, and no man could be wise while denying it. And so Grey Owl dipped his oar and whirled his canoe about and returned for the kits. He retrieved them, brought them back to his cabin, and there he and Anahareo raised them.

The experience of coming to know and love those little beaver kits was the unmaking of who he was, and the beginning of a shamanic remaking. Not that he was a shaman, but you don't have to be to love the wild, or to let it make of you a wiser, better person. Grey Owl was so moved by his experience raising those beaver kits that he spent the rest of his life writing and speaking of the richness of Nature. He became a bard of the wild places, with a dream of inspiring compassion for the living little brothers and sisters with whom we humans share this sacred Earth.

I suppose, in a way, the same happened to me along my journey into the green world. When I was a child, my mother and sister and I lived in deep poverty back there in that steamy country at the edge of the bayous. We needed what the land could give us, and I spent a goodly portion of my youth getting all I could. But I loved that country, too. Loved it so much I hardly knew we were poor. From my perspective, if I had boots on my feet, a knife on my belt, and a rifle on my back, I had all I needed to get by in the world. I fished and hunted and foraged several days every week to bring us game to supplement my mother's meager earnings. And I had for a time come to see the land's varied life as mere food awaiting harvest. And then came the day of the fox, the little red fox who leapt among countless blossoms and butterflies more colorful than the gleaming hues of a rainbow while sunbeams spilled out of a lucent sky. The little fox who skipped for joy's own sake. And I knew in that instant all I had learned in church and school about the soulless, emotionless lives of wild creatures was wrong. I came there in that moment to *see*, though I was yet a long way from understanding, that the world was far, far deeper than anything I had been taught. That was the day I first caught a hint of the hidden truth at the root of all life: that Earth is alive and there were spirits everywhere, and the creatures of this world are our brothers and sisters in joy and peril. It is odd that the mere sight of a fox at play can teach so much, but a life in the wild has taught me that the deepest lessons are often found in Nature's little faerie tales.

◆ ◆ ◆

So Grey Owl and his wife, Anahareo, tried to care for the kits whose mother he himself had killed. No one knew what to do exactly to raise beavers in those days, so they made do as best they could. They made for them a home out of a spare tin stove and let them wander to the lake to romp and into the stove to rest. And one day, when they were old enough, he set them out into the lake to start their own lives. And often he kept tabs on them with hopes they would build their own lodge, start their own family, and in this place where he could offer them some small measure of protection they might begin to flourish.

One day Grey Owl went to the lake and he watched for them, but they did not come. He became concerned and began a long vigil there in the shade of the tall elms. But though he waited and waited, he never heard the beaver pair clap their broad tails upon the water, nor did he see the telltale of a log drifting with purpose across the lake as an unseen beaver dragged it to its dam. And slowly, reluctantly, he came to realize the pair had not survived. Most likely they had been poached by a trapper. He felt a keen loss beyond words. The beavers were near, so near, extinction. Grey Owl felt the sacredness and spirit of the land was fading as its little animal folk vanished to Man's greed. He wrote:

> *And in the grove of stately elms the little tin stove [in which we raised the kits]*
> *was placed high in a hidden spot with its door open, faced towards the lake.*
> *So that the small wandering spirits that might sometimes be lonely would see,*
> *and remember, and sometimes enter in, as they had done in life when they were*
> *small. And so the stove that knew so many tales might learn another and a last*
> *one, a tale of which the end is lost forever, a story we could never, never know.*

From a pair of beaver kits, Grey Owl came to know the greatest truth right down to its core: there is magic in our sacred Earth. For it is a marvellous realm of Little Animal and Plant Folk and elusive otherworldly spirits. It is a realm of endless mystery and a place of wonder. Grey Owl—who never claimed to be a shaman—had come to know this deepest shaman-truth in his bones. And I feel certain he understood our own lives were only rich when we lived well with it, just as our lives are impoverished when we become distant from the love of Earth, which leads ultimately to the callous abuse of its little creatures and the fading of its lands.

◆ ◆ ◆

In turning these pages you have ventured with me into the wildwoods that I have called home for so many years. You have come to learn the secret paths of black bear families and the hidden language of ravens. You have walked the green-shadowed ways where a forest's summer warmth holds preternaturally long against the sure and coming winter. You felt the bitter-sweetness at the felling of a deer taken with respect, and rejuvenating joy at the rise of a new horned lord of the meadows. You encountered an old cabin long abandoned in the deep wilds where ghosts of ancestor spirits commingle. You experienced the wonder and peril of the wild Inuqun of the far north. What more can I share?

Only this: there is enchantment beyond your door. These pages are but an arrow, pointing out that door and into some far green place. Go and wander there a while. Live well and wise with its spirits, little and big, animal and human, tree and grass, of this world and the other. Love the cool, green shadows of lonely places and do not fear them if they are eerie, only go with courtesy and good intent. This is the Wildwood Way.

Bibliography

Compton, Margaret. *American Indian Fairy Tales.* New York: Dodd, Mead & Company, 1907.

Dorsey, George Amos. *Traditions of the Caddo.* Washington, DC: Carnegie Institution of Washington, 1905.

Elbroch, Mark. *Mammal Tracks & Sign: a Guide to North American Species.* Mechanicsburg, PA: Stackpole Books, 2003.

Froud, Brian, and Alan Lee. *Faeries.* New York, Toronto, London: Bantam Doubleday Dell Publishing Group, 1978.

Goss, Theodora. "Hungarian Fairies," *Endicott Studio,* 2006, http://www.endicott-studio.com/articleslist/hungarian-fairies-by-theodora-goss.html

Grey Owl, *Pilgrims of the Wild.* London: Lovat Dickson Ltd., 1934.

Grimm, Jakob and Wilhelm. *Children's & Household Tales.* Berlin: Realschulbuchhandlung, 1812.

Harner, Michael. *The Way of the Shaman.* San Francisco: Harper One, 1980.

Holbrook, Florence. *The Book of Nature Myths.* Boston: Houghton Mifflin Company, 1902.

Keightley, Thomas. *The Fairy Mythology.* London: H. G. Bohn, 1928.

Kollmuss, Anja, and Julian Agyeman, "Mind the Gap," *Environmental Education Research* 8, no. 3 (2002).

Kuo, Michael. *100 Edible Mushrooms: With Tested Recipes.* Ann Arbor, MI: University of Michigan Press, 2007.

MacKenzie, Donald Alexander. *Wonder Tales from Scottish Myth & Legend.* New York: Frederick A. Stokes & Co., 1917.

MacCulloch, J. A. *The Religion of the Ancient Celts.* Edinburgh: T & T Clark, 1911.

Masson, Elsie. *Folktales of Brittany.* Philadelphia, PA: MacRae Smith Company, 1929.

Mears, Ray. *Essential Bushcraft.* United Kingdom: Hodder & Stoughton, 2003.

Olcott, Francis Jenkins. *The Book of Elves & Fairies.* Boston: Houghton Mifflin Company, 1918.

Ralston, W. R. S. *Songs of the Russian People.* London: Ellis & Green, 1872.

Selhub, Eva, and Alvin Logan. "Your Brain on Nature: Forest Bathing and Reduced Stress." *Mother Earth News*, January 2013.

Seruntine, Cliff. *Seasons of the Sacred Earth.* Woodbury, MN: Llewellyn, 2013.

Sikes, Wirt. *British Goblins.* London: S. Low, Marston, Searle & Rivington, 1880.

Thayer, Samuel. *Nature's Garden: A Guide to Identifying, Harvesting & Preparing Edible Wild Plants*. Bruce, WI: Forager's Harvest Press. 2010.

Thoreau, Henry David. *Walden*. Boston: Ticknor & Fields, 1854.

Yeats, W. B. *The Cat & the Moon, The Wild Swans at Coole*. London: Macmillan, 1919.

To Write the Author

If you wish to contact the author or would like more information about this book, please write to the author in care of Llewellyn Worldwide, and we will forward your request. Both the author and publisher appreciate hearing from you and learning of your enjoyment of this book and how it has helped you. Llewellyn Worldwide cannot guarantee that every letter written to the author can be answered, but all will be forwarded. Please write to:

Cliff Seruntine
℅ Llewellyn Worldwide
2143 Wooddale Drive
Woodbury, MN 55125-2989

Please enclose a self-addressed stamped envelope for reply, or $1.00 to cover costs. If outside the USA, enclose an international postal reply coupon.

GET MORE AT LLEWELLYN.COM

Visit us online to browse hundreds of our books and decks, plus sign up to receive our e-newsletters and exclusive online offers.

- • Free tarot readings • Spell-a-Day • Moon phases
- • Recipes, spells, and tips • Blogs • Encyclopedia
- • Author interviews, articles, and upcoming events

GET SOCIAL WITH LLEWELLYN

 Find us on Facebook

www.Facebook.com/LlewellynBooks

Follow us on

www.Twitter.com/Llewellynbooks

GET BOOKS AT LLEWELLYN

LLEWELLYN ORDERING INFORMATION

Order online: Visit our website at www.llewellyn.com to select your books and place an order on our secure server.

Order by phone:
- • Call toll free within the U.S. at 1-877-NEW-WRLD (1-877-639-9753)
- • Call toll free within Canada at 1-866-NEW-WRLD (1-866-639-9753)
- • We accept VISA, MasterCard, and American Express

Order by mail:
Send the full price of your order (MN residents add 6.875% sales tax) in U.S. funds, plus postage and handling to: Llewellyn Worldwide, 2143 Wooddale Drive, Woodbury, MN 55125-2989

POSTAGE AND HANDLING:

STANDARD: (U.S. & Canada)
(Please allow 12 business days)
$25.00 and under, add $4.00.
$25.01 and over, FREE SHIPPING.

INTERNATIONAL ORDERS (airmail only):
$16.00 for one book, plus $3.00 for each additional book.

Visit us online for more shipping options.
Prices subject to change.

CLIFF SERUNTINE

SEASONS
OF THE
SACRED EARTH

FOLLOWING THE OLD WAYS ON AN ENCHANTED HOMESTEAD

Seasons of the Sacred Earth
Following the Old Ways on an Enchanted Homestead
CLIFF SERUNTINE

Join the Seruntine family on a magical journey of green living at their homestead hollow in the Nova Scotia highlands. Share their magical experiences as the family lives in harmony with the land and respects nature's spirits. Growing and hunting most of their food, Cliff and his family share hands-on practical home skills you can use, too.

With a warm, personal style, *Seasons of the Sacred Earth* chronicles the Seruntine family's adventures following the old ways. They celebrate the Wheel of the Year by leaving apples for the Apple Man, offering faerie plates during Samhain, and spilling goat's milk for the barn bruanighe. In return, the land blesses them with overflowing gardens, delicious ales, and the safety of their farm animals. Through their journey, you'll discover the magical and the mystical are never farther than Earth and Sky.

978-0-7387-3553-5, 336 pp., 6 x 9   **$16.99**

The Healing Power of Trees
Spiritual Journeys Through the Celtic Tree Calendar
SHARLYN HIDALGO

Walk in the footsteps of Druids and tune into the sacred power and ancient wisdom of trees.

From the birch to the willow, Sharlyn Hidalgo introduces all fifteen revered trees of the Celtic Tree Calendar and describes their unique gifts. Go on guided journeys to meet the deities, totems, and guides of each species. Honor each tree with rituals using runes and oghams, symbols and letters of the Celtic Tree Alphabet. Learn from the author's personal stories of revelation. Cultivate a relationship with each of these grand energetic beings, who offer healing, guidance, and higher consciousness.

The Healing Power of Trees is your guide to living the principles of the Celtic tradition—tuning into the rhythms of nature, respecting the land, and fulfilling our role as stewards of our Eart

978-0-7387-1998-6, 288 pp., 6 x 9 $17.95

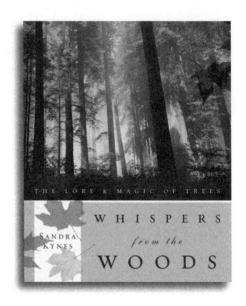

THE LORE & MAGIC OF TREES

WHISPERS
from the
WOODS

SANDRA
KYNES

Whispers from the Woods
The Lore & Magic of Trees
Sandra Kynes

A walk in the woods makes it easy to understand the awe and reverence our ancestors had for trees. When you become reacquainted with the natural world, you gain access to different levels of energy and awareness that, in turn, can bring deeper meaning and spiritual satisfaction to your life.

Trees are a gateway into the world of spirit. By exploring a variety of tree mysteries and traditions, *Whispers from the Woods* offers many ways for you to begin to live in harmony with the earth's sacred rhythm. This guidebook presents the essentials of the Celtic Ogham and tree calendars, then goes on to include instruction in meditation practices, shamanic journeys, feng shui, spellcraft, and ritual. The second half of the book, set up in an easy-to-use field guide format, offers a wealth of information on fifty trees, including their attributes, lore, powers, and seasonal correspondences.

978-0-7387-0781-5, 288 pp., 7½ x 9⅛ $18.99

To order, call 1-877-NEW-WRLD
Prices subject to change without notice
Order at Llewellyn.com 24 hours a day, 7 days a week

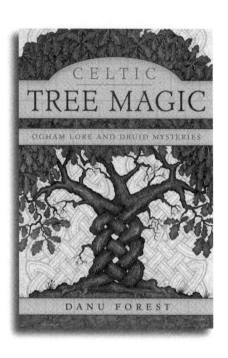

Celtic Tree Magic
Ogham Lore and Druid Mysteries
Danu Forest

Celtic Tree Magic explores both the practical and the magical/spiritual aspects of the trees in the Celtic Tradition, covering the often misunderstood areas of ogham in a way that is clear and accessible while in sufficient depth to satisfy both beginners and those with more experience. This book also provides practical exercises, magical charms, and spells using the ogham; examples from folklore and myth as well as hands-on tips for growing and tending trees together with their spirit guardians; making salves, tinctures, and ointments as well as green crafts and how to fashion certain magical tools from relevant woods.

978-0-7387-4101-7, 312 pp., 6 x 9   **$17.99**

Celtic Tree
Mysteries

Practical Druid Magic & Divination

Steve Blamires

Celtic Tree Mysteries
Practical Druid Magic & Divination
STEPHEN BLAMIRES

Trees are living, developing aspects of the Green World. So too is the magic associated with them. It could be said that they are the only thing that has remained constant since the days of the ancient Irish Druids. Now, *Celtic Tree Mysteries* revives the ancient knowledge and lore of the trees with a practical system of magical ritual and divination.

You will create your own set of Ogham sticks by working on three levels: physically, you will learn to locate and identify each of the 20 trees … magically, you will perform Otherworld journeys and rituals to prepare yourself and your Ogham sticks for use … spiritually, you will align yourself with the forces of the Green World in your area.

You will also learn to open the deeper, hidden meanings contained within the beautiful, ancient Celtic legends, especially the apparently superficial nature poetry, which contains very precise and detailed magical instructions.

978-1-56718-070-1, 304 pp., 6 x 9   **$21.95**